AMERICAN POSTFEMINIST CINEMA

CINEMA

Women, Romance and Contemporary Culture

Michele Schreiber

EDINBURGH
University Press

Traditions in American Cinema
Series Editors Linda Badley and R. Barton Palmer

© Michele Schreiber, 2014

Edinburgh University Press Ltd
The Tun – Holyrood Road
12 (2f) Jackson's Entry
Edinburgh EH8 8PJ
www.euppublishing.com

Typeset in 10/12.5pt Sabon by
Servis Filmsetting Ltd, Stockport, Cheshire,
and printed and bound in Great Britain by
CPI Group (UK) Ltd, Croydon CR0 4YY

A CIP record for this book is available from the British Library

ISBN 978 0 7486 9336 8 (hardback)
ISBN 978 0 7486 9337 5 (webready PDF)

CONTENTS

ACKNOWLEDGMENTS

This book's journey from inception to publication has been a long and sometimes circuitous one, and there are many people to thank. The project began as my doctoral dissertation while I was a student in the Cinema and Media Studies program at the University of California, Los Angeles. Anne Mellor, Steve Mamber and John Caldwell gave me valuable feedback on the manuscript during the dissertation stage. The chair of my committee, Janet Bergstrom, provided both personal and professional support, and was 100 percent behind my idea from the beginning. Vivian Sobchack's ability to cut to the chase over a glass of wine and her tireless advocacy on behalf of her students has been an inspiration to me. Thanks also to the Department of Cinema at San Francisco State University, especially the incomparable Bill Nichols, for helping me get to UCLA in the first place. While revising the book, I received departmental support from the University of Wisconsin, Milwaukee and chair of the Department of Film, Rob Yeo. One of my fellow Conceptual Studies travelers, Vicki Callahan, was a great mentor and imparter of wisdom during my time in Milwaukee and in the years prior to my arrival.

Heartfelt thanks are due to everyone in the Department of Film and Media Studies at Emory University who have helped with this book in ways both big and small. I could not ask for better undergraduate and graduate students to teach or for a more collegial department environment. Amy Aidman, Tanine Allison, Bill Brown, David Pratt, and Daniel Reynolds have been great colleagues whom I always look forward to seeing at faculty meetings. Eddy Von Mueller has provided impromptu therapy sessions and comic relief when needed and Karla Oeler has blessed me with her kindness and constant encouragement. Annie Hall helped me keep things light with Southern anecdotes, her homespun wisdom, and her expertise on all things Emory and Atlanta. The chair of the department of Film and Media Studies, Matthew Bernstein, has been such a tremendous source of support that I do not have enough words to express my gratitude. He has done everything possible to help me excel at my job and finish this manuscript, including reading and commenting on countless drafts. I am extremely grateful to have him as a mentor and he and his wife Natalie Bernstein as friends.

Many thanks are also due to the indefatigable Barton Palmer who has been a great champion of the book and helped me find a home with Edinburgh University Press. To Linda Badley for her support, and to my editor at EUP, Gillian Leslie, who has been an absolute delight to work with. Thanks also to the anonymous readers who provided essential feedback on the project, and to Judy Bozarth for her help in the final stages of manuscript development.

I also need to extend thanks to those whose help has been of a more personal rather than professional nature. The members of my Emory writing group, Monique Allewaert, Dierdra Reber, and Andrea White, provided much-needed cheerleading during some very challenging times. Jennifer Barker's friendship has seen me through multiple phases of our personal and professional lives and I am grateful to be able to rely on her as a sounding board for both. And, special thanks go to my oldest and dearest friends, Kate Devivo, Shelly Hirschtritt, Leora Kaye, and Liz Whatley, for keeping me honest and never letting me forget what I was like when I was thirteen.

My family has been an essential source of encouragement, without whom I would have probably given up this goal long ago. Lisa, David, John and Paul Joire make me laugh and help me keep things in perspective. My parents, Jeanette and Dan Schreiber, have been unconditionally supportive of me since I was nine years old and almost wore out our VCR by watching *Gone With the Wind* and *West Side Story* on repeat. Not only are they wonderful parents but they are great friends and fellow cinephiles who see more movies than I do these days. Their movie fandom inspired this project and their lifelong romance will always be a model against which I compare any cinematic one.

And, finally, the biggest and most heartfelt thanks go to my husband, Brian. He is a wonderful partner in crime and, along with Lila and Norman, my greatest source of joy and laughter. Through the highs and the lows of this journey, he has always had my back and every word of this book is imbued with his generosity and integrity. I dedicate it to him, with love.

ILLUSTRATIONS

INTRODUCTION:
WOMEN, POSTFEMINISM AND ROMANCE

Half a century separates the publication of Betty Friedan's *The Feminine Mystique*, the book commonly credited with igniting the second wave of the women's movement, and Facebook Chief Executive Officer Sheryl Sandberg's 2013 best-seller *Lean In: Women, Work, and the Will to Lead*, which assesses the challenges that American working women continue to face today. Reading the two volumes side by side, one cannot help being struck by the dramatically different cultural landscapes they describe. Socially and professionally, American women have soared to unprecedented heights in this fifty-year period, yet the elevated terrain they occupy today is something of a plateau. In 1963, Friedan identified the 'problem that has no name' experienced by those who 'learned that truly feminine women do not want careers, higher education, political rights – the independence and the opportunities that the old-fashioned feminists fought for.'[1] Five decades later, Sandberg admits that in the United States of 2013, 'women are better off than ever' but that the 'revolution has stalled'; women remain 'hindered by barriers that exist within ourselves' by internalizing 'the negative messages we get throughout our lives.' As a result, in Sandberg's view, American women today 'compromise our career goals for partners and children who may not even exist yet.'[2]

Sandberg's argument is corroborated by a 2012 Pew Research Study that showed that in 2010 women made up almost half – 46.7 percent – of the American labor force. This represents an 8.6 percent increase over 1970 when women comprised only 38.1 percent of the labor force. The same study found a correlation between these changes in women's professional lives with a major shift in their personal experiences, that is, that women married at 'lower rates and later ages than ever before.' Thirty-three percent of 18- to 34-year-old women in 2012 were married, a decrease of 40 percent from 1960's 73 percent of women in this age range. Clearly, American women have made great strides in the public sphere, realizing significant achievements that they seek to balance with their personal lives.

What, then, do we make of the fact that in contemporary popular film, the lives of these women are still represented almost exclusively in the romance genre, which is not only one of the oldest and most classic of female-oriented forms, but a form in which marriage is the desired narrative resolution? Looking at some of the most popular films with female protagonists made in the recent past, including *Working Girl* (Nichols, 1988), *Sleepless in Seattle* (Ephron, 1993), *Bridget Jones's Diary* (Maguire, 2001), and *Bridesmaids* (Feig, 2011) reveals a dramatic gulf. While this 46.7 percent of women in the labor force may be unprecedented, the fictional representation of their lives is anything but. The exciting social and political developments of the past five decades have challenged, provoked and opened up new avenues of thinking about gender expectations, with affairs of the heart as only one aspect of a broad spectrum of issues that are central to women's lives. Yet, romance itself remains the dominant concern of the contemporary woman in American cinematic narratives as she negotiates the complicated interplay between and among private and public, political and personal, and self-identity and group identity.

American Postfeminist Cinema examines these interrelated issues as portrayed in a series of movies made from 1980 to 2012 that I call the postfeminist romance cycle. These films provide compelling evidence that the complex and mixed messages that have permeated American culture since the turn from the feminist rhetoric of the 1960s to the postfeminist rhetoric in the 1980s have found their most potent realization in popular romance films for and about women.[3] These films depict and reflect contemporary women's anxieties, and perhaps more importantly, anxieties about women, in light of these profound changes. This close study makes apparent how the romance film became the safe, dependable and often pleasurable terrain on which these knotty and provocative female-centered issues are negotiated.

This book expands upon the rich body of scholarship on postfeminist media culture by arguing that the romance genre plays an essential role in that culture, and that the cycle's patterns reflect and inform the postfeminist era's most potent anxieties. Case studies delineate how the symbiotic relationship between postfeminist discourses and romance results in these popular films' mediation of the illusory notion that contemporary women's lives can be reduced to either/or options. The most significant of these is the age-old choice between career versus love and family, but such dilemmas also include the choices between sexual expression or abstinence, and self-absorption or community investment, among others. The films represent this conundrum of personal and often political alternatives for women, and, typically in their concluding moments, offer resolutions that, at least on the surface, appear to resolve these quandaries.

I analyze the machinations of these heterosexual romance films not to render them as bad objects or to suggest that there is a fundamental opposition between feminist politics and romantic desire. Rather I argue that it is illuminating to examine how this span of films that targets 'everywoman,' uniformly appropriates a type of narratological and discursive framework as a way of reconciling these two elements of the contemporary female experience, in an attempt to smooth out the bumps and fissures that can arise when they meet.

In fact, pitting serious, explicitly political sentiments against seemingly more pleasurable feelings related to romantic love or consumerism constructs a conflict that is buttressed by the postfeminist cultural landscape. In postfeminist thought, feminism takes on a negative connotation, what Yvonne Tasker and Diane Negra have described as 'an "othering" of feminism.' Feminism is either construed as 'extreme, difficult and unpleasurable' or, in keeping with neoliberalism, is turned into a self-serving, self-absorbed discourse about one's own personal choices that lacks social or political resonance.[4]

Popular media is where postfeminist discourses are most visible and persuasive because they are usually intertwined with an otherwise appealing individual, product or narrative. In this context, 'choice' and 'empowerment' are defined quite differently than in decades past. Diane Negra argues that 'across the range of the female lifecycle, girls and women of every age are now invited to celebrate their empowerment in a culture that sometimes seems dedicated to gratifying their every desire.'[5] Susan J. Douglas concurs, arguing, 'buying stuff – the right stuff, a lot of stuff – emerged as the dominant way to empower ourselves.'[6]

Not surprisingly, in light of this shift that worked 'to commodify feminism via the figure of woman as empowered consumer,'[7] successors to political feminist figureheads such as Betty Friedan or Gloria Steinem are nowhere to be found. Instead one sees consumable fictional characters and contexts that serve as stand-ins for real women. An oft-cited example of this tendency is *TIME* magazine's hotly debated June 1998 cover story, 'Is feminism dead?,' which featured pictures of Susan B. Anthony, Betty Friedan and Gloria Steinem fading into a picture of the television character Ally McBeal.[8] Indeed, during much of the postfeminist era, the media has used fictional characters as a way of talking through women's social and political progress.

The films in the postfeminist romance cycle are perhaps the prototypical examples of how appealing, consumable elements of postfeminist culture can also provide illuminating glimpses into the mechanics of that culture.

Examining postfeminism and romance side-by-side, I argue, is fundamental to truly understanding how both function. Romance, surprising as it may seem, shapes the postfeminist mindset. But even more interestingly, postfeminism is reshaping romance. The postfeminist romance film is always about a woman who has choices, but the most important choice – of a romantic partner – has already been predetermined and made for her by the conventions of the cycle. In spite of this predicable and reliable structure, and the degree to which the mythology of heterosexual romance has worn thin over the last thirty years, the films have remained incredibly popular.[9]

Why has the cycle lasted so long and remained so resilient? As we will see, it is because these films, like other postfeminist media, elicit and reward complex spectator engagement in which pleasure and critique can coexist, and romance can be both seductive and problematic: there can be problems and solutions. When one watches a postfeminist romance film, there is pleasure from observing the changing nature of contemporary women's everyday lives along with the intoxicating allure of the traditional 'happily ever after' resolution. Rather than traverse explicitly political ground that might pit these two kinds of pleasure against each other (as is often the case in postfeminist culture), the postfeminist romance cycle films reframe these debates into a question best summed up by self-help author Lori Gottlieb: 'What does it mean to be empowered and also want happily ever after?'[10]

THE CONVENTIONS OF THE POSTFEMINIST CYCLE

Anyone who has viewed even a few of the postfeminist romance films under discussion in this book is acquainted with what Amanda Ann Klein has called a film cycle's 'slavish repetition' of 'the same images, characters and plots that they enjoyed in previous films.'[11] Postfeminist romance films follow, or at least gesture toward, the reliable, familiar, formulaic plot structure that mythologizes the redemptive qualities of love and heterosexual coupling that has characterized the film genre for decades. However, as much as romance is about 'what happens' in the film, it also exists as a subject for discussion apart from individual films and groups of films, that is, romance informs the ways in which we discuss our own love lives. As David Shumway has argued, discursive analysis is essential to understanding romance so that one can 'emphasize the role that stories and other representations play in shaping experience.' He further says that 'discourses are not doctrines or systems of ideas but rather groups of related narratives in terms of which men and women have projected the "natural" course of their lives.'[12]

Shumway's use of the word 'natural' here is notable because it is exactly the tension surrounding changing cultural conceptions of what is 'normal' for both genders that infuses postfeminist romance films with their own historically situated set of concerns. Romantic love is an oft-desired part of a full and happy life for both heterosexual and LGBT (lesbian, gay, bisexual, and transgender) individuals alike. However, we will see that in the postfeminist period, the language of heterosexual romance is appropriated to speak not just about love, but also to advance normative assurances in an era when traditional conceptions of gender are in a state of upheaval.

Admittedly, this study focuses on only one piece of this much larger landscape, specifically that which deals with straight women and heterosexual romance. There still remains much to be written about the limited representation of non-heteronormative romantic love in American cinema. The exclusion from this study of lesbian and queer romance films such as *Go Fish* (Troche, 1994), *Kissing Jessica Stein* (Herman-Wurmfeld, 2001), and *Imagine Me & You* (Parker, 2005), among others, is not an endorsement of the industry's resistance to offering a wide range of diverse representations of love. On the contrary, the book's focus on the complex operations of the postfeminist cycle highlights the uniformity of the industry's resistance to dealing with anxiety-provoking deviations from heterosexual gender norms. It aspires to contribute to the conversation of how such models might be challenged in the future.

The postfeminist romance cycle is what Amanda Ann Klein would call an intrageneric cycle because it adheres to the traits and tropes of the romance film genre, but 'serves as a cross-section of one specific moment in time, accurately revealing the state of contemporary politics, prevalent social ideologies, aesthetic trends, and popular desires and anxieties.'[13] Its thirty-plus years is significantly longer than the cycles about which Klein speaks, but this longevity results from the persistence of postfeminism's particular combination of politics, ideology, desires and anxieties. Subdividing the contemporary crop of romance films into smaller cycles or subgroups would not provide this kind of revealing glimpse into how the discourses that sustain 'one specific moment in time' can endure for decades. Isolating how romance speaks through postfeminism, and how postfeminism speaks through romance, allows us, as Raphaëlle Moine describes, to '"reconnect" film texts and their contexts' by integrating what he calls structural and textual theories of genre with its functional definitions.[14]

ROMANCE'S NARRATIVE STAGES

As David Bordwell, Kristin Thompson, and Janet Staiger have argued, the romance plot is highly ubiquitous in Hollywood films. The narrative structure and the formal elements engaged to support this structure have become so reliable that they frequently tread on the terrain of cliché.[15] My characterization of romance's 'stages' pertains to the postfeminist romance film, but relies on, and has relevance for, the structure of films released prior to the 1980s.[16] My framework is broad and flexible enough to account for both comedies and dramas – a matter that I will discuss at more length – and for films that experiment with the typical narrative trajectory. Indeed, it is not uncommon for these stages to be presented out of order or even skipped altogether.

For instance, there are many popular films – such as *When Harry Met Sally* (Reiner, 1989), *Something to Talk About* (Hallström, 1995), *High Fidelity* (Frears, 2000), and *Someone Like You* (Goldwyn, 2001) – that feature relationship breakups as the impetus for romance narratives. Some but not all of these employ the well-known 'remarriage' framework as outlined by Stanley Cavell.[17] By contrast, in some texts, like *The Night We Never Met* (Leight, 1993), *Sleepless in Seattle*, and *The Lake House* (Agresti, 2006), the two protagonists never actually meet until the end of the film.

In addition, many contemporary films work within the chaste tradition of classic romance films and feature protagonists who never actually consummate their love for each other, but remain in a state of longing, including *Broadcast News* (Brooks, 1987), *The Age of Innocence* (Scorsese, 1993), and *Lost in Translation* (Coppola, 2003).

By and large, however, romance texts can be expected to follow the following trajectory:

The First Meeting

The two primary characters' first meeting is one of the least consistent of the structural elements of the romance narrative. In fact, the manner of meeting (the 'meet cute' as described in screenwriting manuals) can be one of the primary points of differentiation among romance texts. This stage is of chief importance because the (early or delayed) meeting sets the tone for the rest of the film.

The Courtship

The courtship involves a series of interactions between the two characters that endear them to each other, even if they are not looking for love. This occurs either through in-person exchanges, or through letters, phone calls, or e-mails. Montages, usually set to lively, popular music, are the most frequently used stylistic device used to visually convey the courtship process in the postfeminist romance. The characters share comedic moments, or engage in activities that expose their qualities, talents, and backstories, and which render them 'special' or 'different.'

There is usually a scene or a series of scenes that signal a sort of 'falling in love' moment for one or both of the characters. For instance, in *Pretty Woman* (Marshall, 1990), Edward's (Richard Gere) 'falling in love' moment is evident

Figure 1   Katharine (Kristin Scott Thomas) and Count Laszlo (Ralph Fiennes) in *The English Patient* (Minghella, 1996).

when he uncharacteristically takes a day off from work to engage in equally uncharacteristic activities, such as sitting in a park and having a picnic, and eating dinner in a diner. At the end of this day, Edward's moment is joined with Vivian's (Julia Roberts) when she finally kisses Edward on the mouth (something that she vows she does not do with her clients).

Similarly, in *The English Patient* (Minghella, 1996), when Katharine (Kristen Scott Thomas) accidentally comes across Count Laszlo's (Ralph Fiennes) journal and discovers that it contains repeated amorous references to someone named 'K,' she asks him if she is the K in his book. His expression reveals that she is, and their exchange of glances indicates the shift of their relationship into the romantic realm. Often characters are represented as unaware that they are falling in love, or they resist the feelings; however, even if there are extenuating circumstances that may prevent the two protagonists from ending up together, they will inevitably act on or admit their feelings for one another during this courtship sequence.

The Consummation

The tone with which a film represents the sexual consummation of a romance depends largely on whether it is comedic or dramatic. As I will discuss in Chapter 4, romantic comedies do not usually portray the sexual act in an explicit manner, and if they do, it tends to be rendered comedic in some way. Because most contemporary romance films aim for a PG (Parental Guidance) or a PG-13 rating in order to attract the widest possible audience, the consummation is generally limited to the 'falling in love' moment. If the two protagonists have sex, they are often shown in bed after the fact, with an edit serving to keep most of the sexual act hidden. And, if sex is discussed, it is generally done with comedy that diffuses the associated emotions.

Romantic dramas, on the other hand, tend to be more explicit in their representation of sexuality. In fact, Catherine Preston argues that sex and the display of the female body is the main point of differentiation between what is generally designated as romantic comedy versus romance drama.[18] What is notable about sexuality in romance dramas is that it is often represented most explicitly when the love affair is 'forbidden' in some way, usually in the act of infidelity or rebellion, such as in *Cousins* (Schumacher, 1989), *Legends of the Fall* (Zwick, 1994), *The English Patient*, *The End of the Affair* (Jordan, 1999), *Titanic* (Cameron, 1997), *Unfaithful* (Lyne, 2002), and *The Notebook* (Cassavetes, 2004).

The Problem

After the cathartic consummation of the relationship through sex or the 'falling in love moment,' problems arise. These problems can derive from one of the other plot points of the film, initially unrelated to the romance, but more often than not they are a result of one of the protagonists not being completely honest with him or herself or the other about something. For instance, in *Kissing Jessica Stein*, Jessica is not honest with her family about the fact that she is dating a woman, and thus does not tell her girlfriend Helen about her brother's upcoming wedding.

Often the conflict is caused by one character's unwillingness to overcome his or her own stubbornness to accommodate the relationship, as in *Keeping the Faith* (Norton, 2000), when Jake (Ben Stiller) will not commit to a relationship with Anna (Jenna Elfman) because she is not Jewish, or in *Something's Gotta Give* (Meyers, 2003), when Harry (Jack Nicholson) is unwilling to give up his womanizing ways. Often miscommunications arise between the two protagonists, or one or the other is merely scared to commit to the relationship. The two characters part, convinced that the relationship is at an insurmountable impasse. Montage sequences are frequently employed at this stage of the narrative to depict one or more of the characters mourning the loss of the relationship. Their daily routine is seen to have lost its luster. This – what we might call post-breakup – montage regularly reveals the passage of time through visual cues, such as seasons changing and holidays being celebrated.

Notting Hill's (Michell, 1999) digitally composed sequence, set to Bill Withers's 'Ain't No Sunshine' that shows William (Hugh Grant) mourning the loss of his relationship with Anna (Julia Roberts), is a classic example of this type of montage. The sequence shows William walking through his Notting

Figure 2   William (Hugh Grant) in *Notting Hill* (Michell, 1999).

Hill neighborhood, first during the summer, then through the rainy fall, then the snowy winter, and then back into the summer, in one long continuous, digitally manipulated shot. In addition to differing weather patterns, the course of time is clear from William's use of his coat. He begins with it slung over his shoulder, then he puts it on while shivering in the winter, and then he removes it again in the spring. Time is also clear from the progression of his sister's relationship with her boyfriend. At the beginning they appear blissfully in love, and toward the end they are fighting and presumably in the midst of a breakup. We understand that the length of time chronicled is around a year, based on both the seasons and the prominent placement of a woman in the mise-en-scène: she begins the sequence pregnant, and ends it with a baby in her arms. The montage successfully and succinctly conveys mood, narrative information, and a fairly precise idea of how much time has passed since William and Anna's breakup.

The Resolution

In order for a problem or problems to be resolved, one character must either admit to being wrong, and/or be willing to change whatever it was that brought on the problem in the first place. Thus, love functions as a transformative agent, causing one or both of the central characters to become better versions of him or herself, or themselves, than they were at the film's outset. The transformation serves as both the impetus and the reward for a character's willingness to progress beyond the emotional place in which he or she began the narrative. This resolution stage commonly comes by way of a dramatic scene in which one of the leads (usually the one with the problem) has a revelatory moment in which he or she realizes the other character's importance to his

Figure 3   Zack (Richard Gere) and Paula (Debra Winger) in *An Officer and a Gentleman* (Hackford, 1982).

or her life. This typically is followed by a rapidly edited sequence in which the character with the problem runs, or employs some form of rapid transportation, to tell the other of the revelation. The problem character's efforts to get to the destination are usually crosscut with scenes of the object of affection's activity at the same moment, that sees the latter entirely oblivious to the dramatic denouement that awaits. Sometimes he or she is on the verge of making a decision or taking an action that will betray the romance, raising tension and suspense about whether the problem character will get there 'in time.'

This type of sequence has its origins in pre-1980s classic romances such as *The Apartment* (Wilder, 1960) and *Manhattan* (Allen, 1979). Some of the best-known postfeminist romance cycle examples include Zack carrying Paula out of her blue-collar factory in *An Officer and a Gentleman* (Hackford, 1982), Harry's run at the stroke of midnight on New Year's Eve in *When Harry Met Sally*, Jerry's run through the airport and 'you complete me' interruption of a women's group therapy session in *Jerry Maguire* (Crowe, 1996), a scooter ride through a gay pride parade in *The Wedding Planner* (Shankman, 2001), and a rapid drive down New York City streets in *Friends with Kids* (Westfeldt, 2011).

The End

The happy ending is a mainstay of the romance narrative structure, and its promise of long-term happiness is what drives romance's continued cultural currency. The happy ending generally sees one or both of the protagonists admitting love and having learned an important lesson from the problem stage, along with acknowledgment that forming a long-term partnership will bring them the happiness and fulfillment they seek.

For heterosexual partnerships, the narrative either implies or visually demonstrates that marriage is the next step. But not all romance narratives end happily. One of the most common exceptions to the happy ending stage is death as the primary factor that prevents the formation of a couple. Harkening back to the classic melodramas and women's films such as *Dark Victory* (Goulding, 1939), *Letter from an Unknown Woman* (Ophuls, 1948), and *Love Story* (Hiller, 1970), death is the ultimate source of pathos, and one of the few obstacles that cannot be overcome. Contemporary films such as *Titanic, Sweet November* (O'Connor, 2001), *Autumn in New York* (Chen, 2000), *Ghost* (Zucker, 1990), *Moulin Rouge* (Luhrmann, 2001), and *P.S. I Love You* (LaGravenese, 2007) present death as the ultimate transformer, teaching the character who lives about the importance of love. These films suggest that romance has the capacity to withstand or overcome death, continuing in spirit beyond the grave.

Variations on the happy ending structure in the romance film have been the subject of some discussion by film scholars. For instance, Celestino Deleyto has argued that some contemporary romance films' alternative endings suggest that 'heterosexual love appears to be challenged, and occasionally replaced, by friendship.'[19] He cites the film *My Best Friend's Wedding* (Hogan, 1997), in particular, as questioning the redemptive possibilities of heterosexual romance through its 'unhappy' ending that sees the female protagonist – Julianne (Julia Roberts) – failing to lure her best friend Michael (Dermot Mulroney) away from his fiancé (Cameron Diaz). After watching the two get married, she finds solace in the company of George (Rupert Everett), her gay best friend. The two end the film twirling away happily on the dance floor.

Deleyto raises a compelling point in suggesting that this film's ending contests heterosexual love. However, two qualifications should accompany his case. First, the film does, for all intents and purposes, have a happy ending that reinforces heterosexual coupling; it's just not the central female protagonist who gets the classic happy ending, but her friends instead. She is a perfect example of the quirky, discombobulated postfeminist romance heroine who is pitted against a more conventionally feminine counterpart (a common trope on which I will elaborate more in Chapter 1's case study of *27 Dresses* (Fletcher, 2008)). She does not win in this narrative, but given her resemblance to so many other female protagonists, we as viewers have confidence that she will win the love of another man sometime in the future. The fact that she is played by Julia Roberts only further confirms this belief.

This presumption leads to what I consider as Deleyto's second oversight, which is that we should take the ending of *My Best Friend's Wedding* at face value within the confines of the text. Even if we were to accept that Julianne has chosen a friendship with George over heterosexual love (a problematic assumption in itself since Julianne does not choose this position, but is forced into it when Michael rejects her), the film's allegiance to all other romantic comedy conventions broadens its message and instantiates a discourse beyond the text. The ending is not an ending for her but a beginning. Julianne has come to recognize throughout the course of the narrative that she values romantic love, and it is assumed that she will seek a more willing heterosexual love match in the future.

My counterargument is not meant to dispute Deleyto's assertion that contemporary films can offer an alternative approach to romance structures, but merely to suggest that films like these have implications beyond the confines of their plot structures, and that they should also be read through this supplemental lens. Julianne's pairing with George does not posit a real alternative to the romance narrative any more than do individual episodes of the wildly popular postfeminist television show *Sex and the City* (1998–2004), which exhibit and reinforce the staying power of Carrie, Miranda, Charlotte and Samantha's friendships in the absence of fulfilling romantic relationships.

Certainly, in reality, many women live perfectly happy and successful lives without a man and in the company of close friends; but films like *My Best Friend's Wedding* are so steeped in romance narratological strategies that one should approach the ascription of truly alternative paths with caution. Even films such as *The Break-Up* (Reed, 2006) or *Celeste & Jesse Forever* (Krieger, 2012) that chronicle the dissolution of a long-term relationship between each of their two main characters, suggests that there is a possibility for a romantic future, beyond the ending: a 'to be continued'.

In other words, as Woody Allen aptly surmises following the similarly 'unhappy' ending of *Annie Hall* (Allen, 1977), even when one affair ends, people will keep looking for love because they 'need the eggs.' As Deleyto argues in a more recent work, a film does not necessarily need to have a happy ending in order to be defined as a romance.[20] And David Shumway has contended, 'While relationship stories end both "happily" and "sadly," no ending can ever be assumed to be final. Another breakup or another relationship is always possible, if not likely.'[21] Happy ending or unhappy ending, consummated or unconsummated, popular culture perpetually reinforces the notion that romantic love is integral to a fulfilling life. As Shumway suggests, what a film communicates about love and romance trickles into, and out of, the culture at large.

Romantic Comedy and Romantic Drama

It is already clear that my definition of the postfeminist romance cycle includes both comedic and dramatic films. Admittedly, this is an unorthodox approach, as scholars tend to separate romantic comedies and romantic dramas (usually called melodramas or women's films) into two mutually exclusive genre categories. More contemporary discussions of female-focused and female-targeted films have challenged these boundaries, including Karen Hollinger's discussion of the female friendship film, Suzanne Ferriss and Mallory Young's book on the 'chick flick,' and Diane Negra's work on the neo-liberal bent of postfeminist media.[22] My case studies will further illustrate how instructive and necessary such a comparison can be. Examining trends that cut across previously demarcated genre lines allows us to delineate how romance ebbs and flows in accordance with ideological shifts. Sometimes, as described in Chapter 4's consideration of sexuality, the marked difference between comedies and dramas is integral to the discussion of how discourses of romance differ based on a film's tone. Without considering both types of films concurrently, this contrast would be muted and the richness of romance underestimated.

The ubiquity of the romantic comedy in contemporary culture has made it the default discussion category for film critics. Consequently, 'rom-com', not 'rom-dram', has become common industry and lay-person parlance for any film having a romantic plot, with the consequence of a proliferation of books on the subject. However, even romantic comedy scholars have addressed the blurred boundaries between comedies and dramas.[23] For instance, Tamar Jeffers McDonald has argued that the lines of demarcation between the two forms are unstable: 'while films of the genre [romantic comedy] generally end well and may elicit laughs along the way, I am also aware of the importance of tears to the romantic comedy.'[24] Indeed, 'the mixed emotions these films commonly depict and elicit' that lead to the simultaneous laughter and tears of which McDonald speaks, can just as easily be applied to dramas.[25]

As Peter William Evans and Bruce Babington have conceded, a film's ending can be a tricky barometer for identifying its category. They argue, 'In some films . . . the happy ending is often little more than a precarious arrangement, as likely to be breached as honored. On these occasions romantic comedy seems at times to draw very close to melodrama.'[26] Many of the most seminal romantic comedies do not have a traditional happy ending. For instance, as I noted previously, *Annie Hall* is considered one of the great romantic comedies of all time, but it does not see Alvy and Annie's relationship end happily. The same is true of the more contemporary film *500 Days of Summer* (Webb, 2009). Likewise, dramatic films such as *An Officer and a Gentleman* and *The Notebook* can have happy endings, and numerous other texts defy these happy versus sad parameters. What are labeled dramatic films can have comedic moments, and comedic films can have dramatic scenes. Definitive codification is difficult because both types of films elicit feelings of sentiment, nostalgia, affection and pleasure.

To be sure, there is a great deal to be gained from expanding the parameters of romance. Doing so allows us, as Celestino Deleyto's work has evinced, to acknowledge the 'variety of discourses, approaches and ideologies articulated by the texts.'[27] In *The Secret Life of Romantic Comedy*, Deleyto argues that the romantic comedy genre has been defined too narrowly, excluding otherwise appropriate films from the canon simply because they do not fit scholars' pre-ordained criteria. This type of compartmentalization can 'obscure the importance of the interrelations between the various types of stories.'[28] His aptly titled book points to the crossover between dramatic and comedic elements in films such as *Rear Window* (Hitchcock, 1954), *Crimes and Misdemeanors* (Allen, 1989), and *Before Sunset* (Linklater, 2004). The fact that romance can stray from romantic comedy and find a 'secret life' in unexpected places is a clear sign of its fluidity.

My objective is not to refute the past and it scholarly discussion of genre categories such as romantic comedy or melodrama but only to argue that they are not appropriate for an examination of the postfeminist romance cycle. As Rick Altman has argued, 'genre theorists have generally sought to describe and define what they believe to be already existing genres rather than create their own interpretive categories, however applicable or useful.'[29] In this case, creating an expansive, rather than limiting, framework helps us delineate how romance is structurally stable and cyclical, ebbing and flowing in accordance with historical shifts.

Visual/Cinematic Style in the Postfeminist Romance

The aesthetics of most postfeminist romance cycle films are quite conventional, exemplifying what David Bordwell has called 'intensified continuity,' which merely heightens classical style through various narrative and aesthetic techniques. In fact, one of Bordwell's illustrations of this style – which includes rapid editing, bipolar extremes of lens lengths, reliance on close shots, and wide-ranging camera movements – is *Two Weeks Notice* (Lawrence, 2002), a postfeminist romance film.[30] He discusses how a dialogue scene among the female protagonist, Lucy (Sandra Bullock), the male protagonist, George (Hugh Grant), and June (Alicia Witt), another female love interest, uses rapid editing, close shots, and camera movements to contribute to the developing love triangle where 'the straightforward technique throws all of the weight into the flow of the action.'[31]

Most films in the postfeminist romance cycle, like *Two Weeks Notice*, conform to Bordwell's model, which he characterizes as a 'vanilla-flavored version of intensified continuity' in which form is engaged to support plot.[32] A quintessential example of this heightened yet still safe use of formal conventions is the aforementioned montage sequence from *Notting Hill*. It adapts the montage to convey the passage of time using what we might call an intensified style of digital manipulation, rather than classical editing. In fact, the montage sequence is one of the most oft-used, cliché-ridden devices for conveying story information quickly in romance films. As Bordwell states, 'nothing indicates more clearly the persistence of classical construction than this summary device.'[33] It is most commonly seen in comedic texts, usually in the courtship or problem stage, to convey the passage of time and the progression of feelings, and features one or more pop or rock songs from the film's soundtrack.

Another key formal element of the cycle is what I call a 'mise-en-scène of luxury.' It may be most noticeable in romance-of-manners films that feature period sets and costumes; Jim Collins has characterized this as the 'excessive mise-en-scene' of the adaptation film that sees the 'interplay between narrative and spectacle . . . forming an entire taste culture.'[34] However, it is equally significant in films set in contemporary times, wherein clothes, settings, and particularly the décor of domestic spaces are key to orienting the viewer not just to historical time, but also to class, and the protagonist's relationship to commodity culture. Most of the films I will discuss in the case studies were made with sizable budgets, which results in production design filled with products and décor that sometimes indicate middle class, but usually signify upper-middle-class economic status. Indeed, class plays a largely unspoken but significant role in the postfeminist romance film, as the wealth and upward mobility of the female characters undergird their personal dilemmas, but also enable a pleasurably commodified backdrop for their love affairs.

Certainly, the class dimensions of love are evident in films dating back to the silent period. However, class in the postfeminist romance is rarely discussed. Romance's transformative effects, and its momentum toward a permanent commitment (and quite possibly marriage), suggest its promotion of middle-class values, and as a result, capitalist structures. The high production values and glamorous, well-appointed décor and costumes in many of these films create an attractive environment for product placement, and sell romance, even if it is a failing romance, as an attractive lifestyle.

Contemporary texts such as *Sex and the City*, as well as *The Devil Wears Prada* (Frankel, 2006), *Confessions of a Shopaholic* (Hogan, 2009), and director Nancy Meyers's entire oeuvre (a subject of one of Chapter 5's case studies) are excellent examples that market the link between an attractive, upwardly mobile lifestyle and romance. In these texts, even if our protagonists stumble through their efforts to achieve a sense of satisfaction in their romantic relationships, their lifestyles – filled with designer clothes and accessories, spacious and attractively decorated apartments, and expensive restaurants – remain desirable to viewers. In the postfeminist period, these intersections among commodity culture, female desire, and feminist ideas of choice, function, as Negra has argued, to attach 'considerable importance to the formulation of an expressive personal lifestyle and the ability to select the right commodities to attain it.'[35]

THE HISTORY AND POLITICS OF THE POSTFEMINIST CYCLE

The reliable structure of the romance film and the subtle variations on it outlined thus far have, throughout film history, resonated closely with American historical, cultural, and political developments. For instance, Virginia Wright Wexman has discussed the degree to which film's early history reflected cultural acceptance of shifting conceptions of love. Inspired by John D'Emilio and Estelle Freedman's *Intimate Matters: A History of Sexuality in America*, Wexman tells how movie theatres became the site of romantic coupling (for example, 'making out' in the balcony, which was so popular in the 1950s and '60s), and that 'the movies were ideally positioned to instruct audiences about the changing mores regarding romantic love.'[36] Stanley Cavell has famously argued that screwball comedy films of the 1930s, such as *It Happened One Night* (Capra, 1934), *The Awful Truth* (McCarey, 1937), *Bringing Up Baby* (Hawks, 1938), *The Philadelphia Story* (Cukor, 1940), *His Girl Friday* (Hawks, 1940) and *The Lady Eve* (Sturges, 1941) were 'fairy tales for the Depression.'[37] Thomas Wartenberg and Wexman's work has contributed to our understanding of how the evolution of types of couples in movie romances tells us a great deal not only about performance style and presentation, but more significantly about broader social trends concerning race, class and sexual orientation.[38]

The social, political and industrial changes that occurred from the early 1980s to 2012 contribute to our understanding of the postfeminist romance cycle, like any cycle, as, in Klein's words, a 'mold placed over the zeitgeist, which, when pulled away, reveals the contours, fissures, and complicated patterns of the contemporary moment.'[39] By entwining the romance genre with current-at-the-time socio-political issues, the films of this period maintain a balance between fluctuating conceptions of romantic ideals as well as evolving portrayals of the position of the woman at its center. Thus, over thirty-plus years, the films in the postfeminist American cycle present women's personal and professional gains (per the aforementioned Pew statistics), including the slow and often conflicted cultural embrace of female sexuality and rights.

As we know, both comedic and dramatic pre-1966 romance films were predicated on the suppression of sexuality. These code-era films adopt aesthetic and narrative techniques that suggest but do not explicitly represent the sexual chemistry between the female and male protagonist. Influential romance films, like *Kitty Foyle* (Wood, 1940) and *An Affair to Remember* (McCarey, 1957), feature autonomous women with their own careers and strong convictions. However, the romantic affairs in which they are entangled, with their witty repartee, longing glances, and strategic elliptical edits necessarily require marriage, the only socially acceptable place – narratively speaking – in which these romantic feelings can be fully realized.

The classical era of the romance film began to decline in the late 1950s and early 1960s, seeing its last gasps in a subgenre of films often referred to as 'sex comedies.' Best exemplified by the Doris Day and Rock Hudson trilogy, *Pillow Talk* (Gordon, 1959), *Lover Come Back* (Mann, 1961), and *Send Me No Flowers* (Jewison, 1964), these films reveal the increasing tension between the constraints of the classical romance conventions and the suddenly ubiquitous discussion of women's sexuality, heralded by cultural milestones such as the publication in 1953 of *Playboy Magazine* and the Kinsey report on Female Sexuality, as well as the introduction of the birth control pill in 1960. Tamar Jeffers McDonald suggests that these films 'could in fact be called "Battle of the Sexes comedies" since this more accurately encapsulates their dynamic.'[40]

By the beginning of the transitional period of the 1970s, which saw the restructuring of the big studios and the advent of the Motion Picture Association of America (MPAA) ratings system, Hollywood was actively searching for ways to connect with a younger audience because the classical romance films lacked currency: they no longer matched the mood of the time. There is no better example of this era's attitudes toward romance than the ironic 'happy ending' of *The Graduate* (Nichols), made in 1967, a turning point year for Hollywood. The lead character Benjamin (Dustin Hoffman) makes the seemingly romantic gesture of rescuing Elaine (Katharine Ross), the daughter of his older lover, Mrs Robinson (Anne Bancroft), from her wedding to another man. They successfully escape the disapproving crowd of wedding attendees and catch a passing bus, but their celebratory smiles soon fade into blank stares when they realize that they do not know what they are supposed to do next. They share no loving embraces, no promises of love, but merely sit silently next to each staring off into the distance.

Similarly, the 1970s saw a handful of classically inspired romance films such as *The Way We Were* (Pollack, 1973) and *Love Story* achieve popularity and box-office success but the decade was dominated largely by revisionist romance films, also called 'nervous romances,' and 'radical romantic comedies,' both of which are best described as reflecting a sense of romantic ennui.[41] Either by experimenting with form or questioning the stability and perseverance of the institution of heterosexual marriage, the 1970s romance film reflects many of the social and political movements whose platforms challenged the assumptions at the heart of the genre. Of these movements, second-wave feminism was the most significant. Its precepts subtly, but rarely explicitly, were voiced

Figure 4   Ben (Dustin Hoffman) and Elaine (Katharine Ross) in *The Graduate*
(Nichols, 1967).

through these films' disenchantment with marriage as a desirable conclusion
for both female and male protagonists.

Flora Davis argues that while the feminist movement was frequently blamed
for the rising divorce rate, which increased by 100 percent between 1963 and
1975, it was as likely that the 'second wave was, in part a response to the
insecurity of marriage.'[42] Whether feminism led to divorce or divorce led to
feminism, it is clear that the tone of 1970s' romance films was inextricably tied
to the fact that as of 1975, 'there was one divorce for every two marriages.'[43]
There were not only fewer romance films produced, but the films that were
released, such as *An UnMarried Woman* (Mazursky, 1978), which I discuss in
Chapter 1, reflect a more cynical perspective on the conventions and expectations of the classical romance, and maintain a tenuous connection to feminist
politics.

This landscape began to shift again in the early 1980s, with an increase in
the production of romance films and a marked change in tenor that saw cynicism slowly turn again to lightheartedness, optimism and nostalgia. Catherine
Preston claims that in the 1960s and 1970s, the average number of romance
films per year was in the single digits – seven and five per year, respectively. Yet
by 1984 the numbers began to increase into the double digits, to an average of
twenty per year. By 1991, the average peaked at forty romance films per year.[44]
Steve Neale has called this contemporary cycle film the 'new romance' film
that incorporates 'markedly – and knowingly – "old-fashioned"' attributes.[45]
Mimi White similarly highlights the retrograde tendencies of this new crop of
films, as she discusses their implications for the female protagonists at their
center. Focusing on a group of 1984 films – including *Romancing the Stone*
(Zemeckis), *Thief of Hearts* (Stewart), *and American Dreamer* (Rosenthal) –
that 'reintroduce romance with a vengeance,'[46] she contends,

On the one hand they attempt to construct, address, or fulfill the socially perceived and circumscribed demands of an audience with an increasingly feminist consciousness, as female protagonists are afforded narrative agency within fictions that engage strategies of self-conscious fictionality. At the same time the films can be seen in terms of postfeminist and neoconservative pressures, as the weight of narrative development hinges on and concludes in the formation of a traditionally conceived couple.[47]

The dynamic of ambivalence that is central to White's examples is central to the postfeminist romance cycle. That is, the coexistence of a feminist consciousness by way of a female protagonist who is professionally and personally autonomous (and has narrative agency), and a narrative structure that foreshadows the formation of a heterosexual romantic partnership.

As I will describe in more detail in Chapter 1, the postfeminist romance cycle relies on the structure of stages outlined in a previous section, but this structure has a subtext that reflects the socio-political and cultural position of the woman at its center. The female protagonist's status as a single woman or as a participant in an unfulfilling relationship is seen as a result of some problem from which she suffers. Although it is not socially mandated, heterosexual romantic partnership is presented as a desired complement to this female character's otherwise fulfilling life. However, the choice she makes to be or not to be in a relationship, and the subsequent success or failure of that relationship, are both inextricable with, and often representative of, her perceived failings or quirks. These idiosyncrasies are implicitly, if not explicitly, linked to her social position, and the 'problem' she must overcome.

The postfeminist romance film gestures towards the political precepts of second-wave feminism, and absorbs, without necessarily reinforcing or negating, its ideals. It is frequently self-conscious and self-reflexive, and reveals, through plot structure and characterization, an awareness of romantic cultural tropes as circulated by other past and present media texts. The postfeminist romance film cautiously reconciles past and present narrative conventions and how those conventions align with past and present conceptions of womanhood.

These postfeminist romance films operate in an experiential space between multiple sets of oppositional tendencies, resulting in their deeply ambivalent and often contradictory affect. What is particularly fascinating about postfeminist culture for the purposes of this study is that, as the opening Pew statistics and Sheryl Sandberg's book attest, there are still traces of political feminism's forward momentum toward equality for women woven with a shift backward toward women's embrace of more traditional conceptions of individualized femininity. Angela McRobbie's characterization of postfeminism as a 'double-entanglement' is particularly useful here. For her, this double-entanglement is comprised of 'the co-existence of neo-conservative values in relation to gender, sexuality and family life . . . with processes of liberalization in regard to choice and diversity in domestic, sexual and kinship relations.'[48] Or, as she argues specifically in reference to the film *Bridget Jones's Diary*, postfeminism 'seems to mean gently chiding the feminist past, while also retrieving and reinstating some palatable elements, in this case sexual freedom, the right to drink, smoke, have fun in the city, and be economically independent.'[49]

McRobbie's double-entanglement paradigm has a great deal in common with White's discussion of the return of 'romance with a vengeance,' and both frameworks inform how postfeminism will be characterized throughout this book. The double-entanglement term provides a historical and ideological demarcation, by marking the shift away from the political feminism of the 1970s. Postfeminism also describes a mentality that simultaneously looks backward and forward, both politically and historically. In other words, my spotlight is on how the postfeminist romance cycle films attempt to convey, sometimes successfully, occasionally not, the possibility of the coexistence of ideas and desires that postfeminist culture frequently posits as being at odds. *American Postfeminist Cinema* uses case studies of cinematic 'either/or's to explore the potential of the 'both/and.' In this context, the term postfeminism reveals a struggle and/or conversation, not an impasse.

Unlike scholars like Diane Negra who argue that postfeminist media culture leaves no 'open spaces' for spectator negotiation, with 'conservative norms . . . as the ultimate "best choices" in women's lives,'[50] I argue that despite the conventionality of the postfeminist romance cycle, these films do provide a range of experiences and provoke a range of interpretations, some of which might reflect progressive, politically engaged feminist attitudes and others that celebrate decidedly 'old fashioned' and conservative ideas of femininity. Heterosexual romantic coupling is always the desired resolution of postfeminist romance films and for that reason they might be considered retrograde and, even more extremely, antifeminist. However, to pigeonhole these films and stop the conversation there is to ignore the many complex issues with which they engage, and to assume that women spectators cannot find a variety of pleasures in the same texts that they simultaneously understand to be limited in their representations of women's choices.

In fact, the truly interesting work begins once we recognize the cycle's normativity. Because these films speak to one another and to the same sets of issues, an individual text's full meaning is revealed only when viewed within both the context of the cycle more generally, and the set of false binaries that underlie our case studies. The cycle promotes and elicits an ongoing process of oscillation, narratively and spectatorially, between the past and the present, between the realities of one life and the fictional realities offered by film and other media, between being sexually active and demure, and between being completely independent or occasionally dependent. While particular films and some issues taken up within the cycle are more antagonistic and conservative than others, the process of engaging with them as a group better reveals their ambivalence and sense of indecision. In other words, the postfeminist romance cycle films mirror the balancing act at the heart of the contemporary female experience.

Framing the Book

My case studies are organized according to both how, and in what ways, romance has become interwoven with women's own anxieties, as well as the broader cultural anxieties about women's changing social and political status. By arranging the case studies into clusters of the fallacious 'either/or's, we can gain a broad view of how seemingly different films actually have a great deal in common. This approach also enables some chapters' case studies to consider multiple media at once.

As illustrated by such seminal 1980s feminist works as Tania Modleski's *Loving With a Vengeance* and Janice Radway's *Reading the Romance*, romance has the capacity to flow in and out of multiple media forms, and even to circulate into the language women use to discuss their own relationships.[51] The tendencies of which they speak have proliferated by leaps and bounds over the last thirty years, and there has been a veritable explosion of forms through which romance has extended its reach, including self-help books and new media such as YouTube, blogs and dating sites. In addition, 'reading' or watching romance has itself become a performative act: media consumption is (sometimes) embedded in the texts themselves.

The lines between reality and fiction have never been more blurred, particularly when it comes to the way that women articulate their own relationship to the mythology surrounding both real and fictional romance. However, film remains the most effective and persuasive medium for disseminating ideas about heterosexual romance even in the midst of our romance-saturated media environment. Consequently, when I mention other media texts in the case studies, the emphasis is on the way in which they connect to or establish a discursive relationship with films.

Chapter 1 places the postfeminist romance cycle into historical context by examining in more detail how it both follows and deviates from the traits and tropes of its predecessors, the classical romance film and the 'feminist' romance film. We will better understand how this continuity and deviation operate by tracing how variations on the structural and discursive tendencies outlined earlier operate in the examples of films from different historical periods: *Kitty Foyle*, *An UnMarried Woman* and *27 Dresses*. The chapter demonstrates how the anxiety over women's changing social and political status over the last thirty years creates new problems for the romance narrative to solve in old ways. By delineating, as a starting point, the landscape of the romance film throughout different periods of Hollywood cinema, we acquire a historically nuanced understanding of the postfeminist romance before delving into the case studies that trace the anxieties that permeate the postfeminist romance cycle.

Chapter 2 presents the first of these case studies. It examines how the postfeminist romance film serves an ameliorative function, a bridge, so to speak, that is bolstered by contemporary transmedia and intertextual media landscape. The binary 'either/or' that emerges from this cluster of films and related media texts pits a fantasy-driven sentimentality, often associated with women and driven by fictional or historically retrograde conceits, against a more practical and calculated outlook associated with a masculine, business-oriented present day. We will see how this tension in the films *The Jane Austen Book Club* (Swicord, 2007), *He's Just Not That Into You* (Kwapis, 2009), *You've Got Mail* (Ephron, 1998) and *Must Love Dogs* (Goldberg, 2005) circulates into and/or takes inspiration from Jane Austen novels, chick lit, YouTube videos, self-help books, and Internet dating commercials.

Chapter 3 elaborates on Chapter 2's analysis of sentimentality versus pragmatism, in one particular area: it addresses how the postfeminist romance cycle poses questions about the historicity and temporality of 'true' romance. This chapter's case studies are grouped according to how they work through questions of the relationship between constructions of time and women's subjectivity, and include analyses of *Somewhere in Time* (Szwarc, 1980) versus *Kate and Leopold* (Mangold, 2001); *Me Myself I* (Karmel, 1999) versus *The Family Man* (Ratner, 2000); and an episode of *Sex and the City* entitled 'Ex and the City' and the film *Sleepless in Seattle*.[52] These texts bring to light the political implications of the 'post' in postfeminism and how these historical questions are channeled through the 'gendering' of time. Ultimately, the chapter considers whether the alignment of female characters with a discourse of romance risks placing women in an ahistorical and overly subjective position that minimizes their agency and investment in the objective present.

Chapter 4 continues the previous chapters' examination of the reverberations surrounding the postfeminist romance's preoccupation with the past, but here the past is that of girlhood. Postfeminist culture's fixation on naive girlishness and hyper-sexualized boldness simultaneously results in a paradoxical representation of sexuality and romance. Case studies of comedy films – *When Harry Met Sally*, *Pretty Woman*, and *13 Going on 30* (Winick, 2004) – alongside thrillers – *Fatal Attraction* (Lyne, 1987), *Unfaithful*, and *In the Cut* (Campion, 2003) – make it clear that the postfeminist romance film struggles to maintain a balance between depicting women as demure girls and sexual coquettes. The chapter concludes with a brief consideration of how these contradictory sexual identities find some degree of balance in the more recent films

No Strings Attached (Reitman, 2011) and *Friends with Benefits* (Gluck, 2011), and in the television program *Girls* (2012–), even amidst increasingly contentious political conversations about women's sexual rights.

Chapter 5 continues a consideration of the postfeminist romance cycle's fluctuation between female dependency and autonomy, but expands the framework to consider industrial context. Focusing on the films of two of the most prominent writer-directors of the contemporary era, Nancy Meyers and Nicole Holofcener, it argues that there are illuminating connections between the representation of romance and the mode of production in which a filmmaker works. Meyers's Hollywood films have huge budgets and construct a particular brand of lifestyle fetishism unquestionably mixed with heterosexual romance. By contrast, Nicole Holofcener's small budget, independent films contemplate the connections between money and romantic relationships. Meyers, in *It's Complicated* (2009), combines a satisfying romantic catharsis with the consumption of material goods, while Holofcener, in *Friends with Money* (2006), deviates from typical romantic structures and calls attention to what lies beneath acts of consumption.[53] By illustrating that 'having it all' can mean different things to different women (both real and fictional), we can see some variations on the structural and discursive characteristics that typify different concepts of romance.

All of these case studies trace the ways in which the postfeminist romance cycle films are dynamic and complex vehicles through which some of the central issues facing contemporary women are rehearsed and negotiated. Close narrative analyses of film and other forms of media help us parse the false binaries that unite these films, and thus reveal how they deal with multi-layered concerns where politics meet personal choices, and fantasy meets reality. Or, to return to our opening example, where we see traces of Friedan's 'feminine mystique' mixed with Sandberg's 'leaning in.' Romance functions, in the words of Northrop Frye, as a 'wish-fulfillment dream' that, despite the great changes that may 'take place in society . . . will turn up again, as hungry as ever, looking for new hopes and desires to feed on.'[54] This book illustrates the specific hopes, desires and contradictions that romance has fed on for the last thirty years and how, through its reliability, the narrative structure of romance continues to create new hopes and desires to be fed on in the future. In other words, we will see that the romance film is not merely symptomatic or reflective of the postfeminist era's political and cultural shifts; it is inextricably linked to these changes.

NOTES

1. Betty Friedan, *The Feminine Mystique* (New York: Norton Books, 2001), p. 58.
2. Sheryl Sandberg, *Lean In: Women, Work and the Will to Lead* (New York: Borzoi Books, 2013), pp. 4–8.

3. American studios produced most of the films that I discuss in my case studies. The few postfeminist romance films that did not originate in Hollywood – including *Me Myself I* and *In the Cut* – were international coproductions that received wide distribution in the United States, usually through the major studios.
4. Yvonne Tasker and Diane Negra, 'Introduction: Feminist politics and postfeminist culture', in Y. Tasker and D. Negra (eds), *Interrogating Postfeminism: Gender and the Politics of Popular Culture* (Durham, NC: Duke University Press, 2007), p. 4.
5. Diane Negra, *What a Girl Wants: Fantasizing the Reclamation of Self in Postfeminism* (New York: Routledge, 2009), p. 5.
6. Susan J. Douglas, *Enlightened Sexism: The Seductive Message that Feminism's Work is Done* (New York: Times Books, 2010), p. 5.
7. Tasker and Negra, 'Feminist politics', p. 2.
8. Gina Bellafante, 'Feminism: it's all about me', *TIME*, 28 June 1998.
9. A March 2013 *Atlantic* article comments on the tough times that have befallen the romantic comedy in recent years concluding that 'the easy profitability of the past decade was the worst thing to happen to the romantic comedy – an invitation to stale formulas and ridiculous conceits alike – and a few lean years might do the genre good.' Christopher Orr, 'Why are romantic comedies so bad?: The long decline from Katharine Hepburn to Katherine Heigl', *The Atlantic*, March 2013, 42–3.
10. Lori Gottlieb, *Marry Him: The Case for Settling for Mr. Good Enough* (New York: Dutton, 2010), p. 42.
11. Amanda Ann Klein, *American Film Cycles: Reframing Genres, Screening Social Problems and Defining Subcultures* (Austin: University of Texas Press, 2011), p. 6.
12. David Shumway, *Modern Love: Romance, Intimacy and the Marriage Crisis* (New York: New York University Press, 2003), p. 3.
13. Klein, *American Film Cycles*, p. 9.
14. Raphäelle Moine, *Cinema Genre* (Malden: Blackwell, 2008), p. 29.
15. David Bordwell, Kristin Thompson and Janet Staiger, *The Classical Hollywood Cinema: Film Style and Mode of Production to 1960* (New York: Columbia University Press, 1985), p. 16. In a 1979 interview with Janet Bergstrom, Raymond Bellour states, 'If you think about it, you notice that after a certain situation posed at the start as a problem or as an enigma, the film gradually leads to a final solution which allows the more or less conflicting terms posed at the beginning to be resolved, and which in the majority of cases takes the form of marriage. I've gradually come to think that this pattern organizes – indeed, constitutes – the classical American cinema as a whole.' Janet Bergstrom, 'Alternation, segmentation, hypnosis: interview with Raymond Bellour – an excerpt', in Constance Penley (ed.), *Feminism and Film Theory* (New York: Routledge, 1988), p. 187.
16. Indeed, there are a great many commonalities in how people account for the essential components of romance plots. For instance, in *The Hollywood Romantic Comedy*, film scholar Leger Grindon outlines romantic comedy in terms of its narrative 'moves'. These moves consist of: (1) unfulfilled desire; (2) the meeting; (3) fun together; (4) obstacles arise; (5) the journey; (6) new conflicts; (7) the choice; (8) crisis; (9) epiphany; (10) resolution. On the other side of the cultural spectrum, mass-market book author Kim Adelman, author of *The Ultimate Guide to Chick Flicks*, also writes of what she calls romance's 'steps'. In her first, and appropriately named, chapter, 'From Meeting Cute to the Ultimate Happy Ending: How to Create the Perfect Romance,' she outlines the steps of this 'perfect romance': (1) create a sympathetic heroine; (2) offer up a love-worthy hero; (3) don't forget the best friend; (4) something's wrong with the heroine's life; (5) they meet; (6) toss in impediments to the romance; (7) they dance; (8) pack in as many memorable moments as possible; (9) the hero employs the three magic words; (10) achieve

the ultimate happy (or unhappy ending). When looking at them side by side there is clearly a collective acknowledgment of a successful formula at work. Leger Grindon, *The Hollywood Romantic Comedy: Conventions, History, Controversies* (Malden: Blackwell Publishing, 2011), pp. 9–10, and Kim Adelman, *The Ultimate Guide to Chick Flick: The Romance, The Glamour, The Tears, and More!* (New York: Random House, 2005), pp. 7–17.

17. See Stanley Cavell, *Pursuits of Happiness: The Hollywood Comedy of Remarriage* (Cambridge, MA: Harvard University Press, 1981).

18. Catherine Preston, 'Hanging on a star: the resurrection of the romance film in the 1990s', in Wheeler Winston Dixon (ed.), *Film Genre 2000* (Albany: SUNY Press, 2000), p. 238.

19. Celestino Deleyto, 'Between friends: love and friendship in contemporary Hollywood romantic comedy', *Screen*, 44: 2 (Summer 2003), 168.

20. Celestino Deleyto, *The Secret Life of Romantic Comedy* (Manchester: Manchester University Press, 2009), p. 29

21. Shumway, *Modern Love*, p. 158.

22. See Karen Hollinger, *In the Company of Women: Contemporary Female Friendship Films* (Minneapolis, University of Minnesota Press, 1998); Suzanne Ferriss and Mallory Young (eds), *Chick Flicks: Contemporary Women at the Movies* (New York: Routledge, 2008); Diane Negra, *What a Girl Wants: Fantasizing the Reclamation of Self in Postfeminism* (London: Routledge, 2009).

23. For instance, in *Romantic Comedy* (New York: Routledge, 2010), Claire Mortimer describes the genre as, 'a hybrid of the romance and comedy genres, featuring a narrative that centers on the progress of a relationship, and being a comedy, resulting in a happy ending.' Kathrina Glitre contends 'While romance treats the affair seriously, romantic comedy is more light-hearted.' Kathrina Glitre, *Hollywood Romantic Comedy: States of the Union, 1934–1965* (Manchester: Manchester University Press, 2006), p. 9. And for Leger Grindon, 'The plot of most romantic comedies could be presented with the earnestness of melodrama, but the humorous tone transforms the experience. The movie assumes a self-deprecating stance which signals the audience to relax and have fun, for nothing serious will disturb their pleasure.' Leger Grindon, *The Hollywood Romantic Comedy: Conventions, History, Controversies* (Malden: Blackwell Publishing, 2011), p. 2.

24. Tamar Jeffers McDonald, *Romantic Comedy: Boy Meets Girl Meets Genre* (London: Wallflower Press, 2007), p. 10.

25. Ibid.

26. Bruce Babington and Peter William Evans, 'Preface', in B. Babington and P. W. Evans (eds), *Affairs to Remember: The Hollywood Comedy of the Sexes* (Manchester: Manchester University Press, 1989), p. 4.

27. Deleyto, *The Secret Life*, p. 29.

28. Ibid.

29. Rick Altman, *Film/Genre* (London: British Film Institute, 1999), p. 11.

30. David Bordwell, *The Way Hollywood Tells It* (Berkeley: University of California Press, 2006), p. 121.

31. Ibid. pp. 163.

32. Ibid. p. 161.

33. Ibid. p. 49.

34. Jim Collins, *Bring on the Books for Everybody: How Literary Culture Became Popular Culture* (Durham, NC: Duke University Press, 2010), p. 133.

35. Negra, *What a Girl Wants*, p. 4.

36. Virginia Wright Wexman, *Creating the Couple: Love, Marriage and Hollywood Performance* (Princeton: Princeton University Press, 2003), pp. 12–13.

37. Cavell, *Pursuits of Happiness*, p. 2.
38. See Thomas Wartenberg, *Unlikely Couples: Movie Romance as Social Criticism* (Boulder: Westview Press, 1999), and Virginia Wright Wexman, *Creating the Couple*.
39. Klein, *American Film Cycles*, p. 20.
40. Tamar Jeffers McDonald, *Romantic Comedy: Boy Meets Girl Meets Genre* (London: Wallflower Press, 2007), p. 44.
41. See Frank Krutnik, 'The faint aroma of performing seals: the "nervous" romance and the comedy of the sexes', *Velvet Light Trap*, 26 (1990), and Jeffers McDonald, *Romantic Comedy*.
42. Flora Davis, *Moving the Mountain: The Women's Movement in America since 1960* (Urbana: University of Illinois Press, 1991), pp. 286–7.
43. Ibid. p. 287.
44. Preston contends: 'Between 1960 and 1969 there were an average of 7 romances released a year. In the 1970s that figure went down to 5 per year. In 1980 the production of romances began to rise and between 1984 and 1989 an average of 20 were released each year. Between 1990 and 1996, the annual average rose to 26, peaking at 40 in 1991.' 'Hanging on a star', p. 229.
45. Steve Neale, 'The big romance or something wild?: Romantic comedy today', *Screen*, 33: 3 (Autumn 1992), 287.
46. Mimi White, 'Representing romance: reading/writing/fantasy and the "liberated" heroine of recent Hollywood films', *Cinema Journal*, 28: 3 (Spring 1989), 42.
47. White, 'Representing romance', p. 41.
48. Angela McRobbie, *The Aftermath of Feminism: Gender, Culture and Social Change* (London: SAGE, 2009), p. 12.
49. Ibid. p. 12.
50. Negra, *What a Girl Wants*, p. 4.
51. Tania Modleski, *Loving with a Vengeance: Mass Produced Fantasies for Women* (Hamden: Archon Books, 1982), and Janice Radway, *Reading the Romance: Women, Patriarchy and Popular Culture* (Chapel Hill: University of North Carolina Press, 1984).
52. Chapter 3's final case study was originally published as '"Misty Water-Colored Memories of the Way We Were" postfeminist nostalgia in contemporary romance narratives', in Vicki Callahan (ed.), *Reclaiming the Archive: Feminism and Film History* (Detroit: Wayne State University Press, 2010). © Used with the permission of Wayne State University Press.
53. A version of Chapter 5's case study of Nicole Holofcener's *Friends with Money* was originally published as 'Independence at what cost?: economics and female desire in Nicole Holofcener's *Friends with Money* (2006)', in Hilary Radner and Rebecca Stringer (eds), *Feminism at the Movies: Understanding Gender in Contemporary Popular Cinema* (Abingdon: Routledge, 2011). Republished with permission of Taylor and Francis Group LLC Books; permission conveyed through Copyright Clearance Center, Inc.
54. Northrop Frye, *Anatomy of Criticism* (Princeton: Princeton University Press, 1957), p. 186.

1. 'BOTH GLAD AND SORRY': ROMANCE CYCLES AND WOMEN'S POLITICS

As we have seen, the postfeminist romance cycle has a reliable, known set of conventions that mythologizes the redemptive qualities of love and heterosexual coupling. It is by relying on and adhering to this known formula or structure that it negotiates historically contingent shifts in the Hollywood film industry, and the social and political terrain for women over the last thirty years. In this chapter, we will look more closely at what the postfeminist romance cycle has inherited from the romance film cycles that have preceded it, and what makes it unique. Close case studies of three female-centered films, the classic romance film *Kitty Foyle*, the 'feminist' romance film *An UnMarried Woman*, and the postfeminist romance film *27 Dresses*, demonstrate how their respective eras of romance negotiate women's personal and political issues within the confines of classical or post-classical filmmaking.

Most studies of romance place films from different historical periods in separate chapters with their continuities merely implied or discussed in passing. Here the commonalities as well as the differences reveal how much Hollywood romance has stayed the same and the subtle but important ways that it has changed. Indeed, these three seemingly different films have a great deal in common. They all focus on strong and autonomous female protagonists who try to balance personal fulfillment with professional aspirations, ideas of fantasy with reality, and the past with the present. Whether by choice or circumstance, the protagonist is put in a position where she must overcome dreams and patterns that have shaped her past and opt for a different kind of future. This decision is intertwined with a wish for a romantic partner.

Where these films differ is in the ways in which they use narrative structure and aesthetics to tell this story. They also received different responses from critics who are inclined to read the romance portrayed within the film as both a barometer of the genre at that time, as well as a reflection of its socio-political and industrial context. Choice as it relates to women's personal lives becomes intertwined with choice as positioned within the film's romantic narrative, often leaving the viewer, as a *Kitty Foyle* reviewer comments, 'both glad and sorry' about her ultimate fate.

The Classical Romance Film: *Kitty Foyle*

The classical romance period (1934–68)[1] spans thirty plus years and has a surplus of exemplar films. Yet, *Kitty Foyle*, made at the height of this era in 1940, is an illuminating film because it is both typical and atypical of classical romances. Typical, because it focuses on love and coupling and abides by a three-act plot trajectory wherein most narrative obstacles are resolved through the heterosexual romantic relationship. It is atypical because of its implicit and explicit discourse on social and political issues that are specific to the eponymous female protagonist and broadly applicable to women of the early twentieth century in which the film is set. Most of these issues originate in the Christopher Morley novel from which the film is adapted, specifically the illicit affair between the lower class female protagonist Kitty (Ginger Rogers) and her upper-class lover, Wyn (Dennis Morgan). However, the film version sees the controversial nature of this relationship, and its class issues, overshadowed by the heterosexual love triangle.

The film's most significant element of distinction is a self-contained sequence that serves as a prologue to Kitty's story. Added in the screenwriting stage, the prologue consists of a five-scene episodic history lesson that shows how the suffragette movement (frequently referred to as first-wave feminism) affected women's social and political progress. This sequence makes *Kitty Foyle* stand out from its contemporaries because it speaks to a political history outside of the narrative that is only peripherally related to the narrative. Therefore, the film does not simply reflect its social and political milieu but provides commentary on women's political progress. However, as I will show, the film's primary narrative manages to absorb, if not overwhelm, the sequence's content which ultimately makes it intrinsic to the film's discourse on women's choices, rather than the anomaly that *Kitty Foyle* appears to be initially.

The novel version of *Kitty Foyle* is episodic in structure with Kitty reflecting on her past and present circumstances while telling a linear story about her life. When adapting the novel into a screenplay, screenwriter Dalton Trumbo adopted a flashback structure through which Kitty in 1940 reflects back on the previous eleven years in order to come to a decision about her love life. She needs to choose between two men: Wyn, her impetuous upper-class lover of many years, or Mark (James Craig), a hard-working, practical doctor who has just proposed marriage to her.

The flashback scenes begin when Kitty is fifteen. She comes from a working-class neighbourhood in Philadelphia and lives with her supportive but cantankerous Irish father. She is obsessed with upper-class Philadelphia society 'Main Liners' and in particular with an annual party called the Assembly where this upper-crust group gathers for a night of dinner and dancing. Young Kitty talks of her Cinderella-inspired fantasies about being rescued from her lower-class 'ashes' by a rich suitor, sentiments that are met with playful teasing by her father. Time passes, and Kitty's voiceover tells us that at the onset of the Depression, she 'had to trade in a few of those dreams for a volume of Gregg Shorthand.' After earning a business degree, she becomes a secretary to a dashing member of the elite, Wynnewood Stafford VI, who runs a failing magazine about Philadelphia high society. The two fall in love, but Kitty soon realizes that her father's warnings about the naiveté of her childhood fantasies about love are sage, and that she and Wyn's class differences will likely prevent him from making a serious commitment to her.

After Kitty comes to this realization, and her father passes away, she leaves

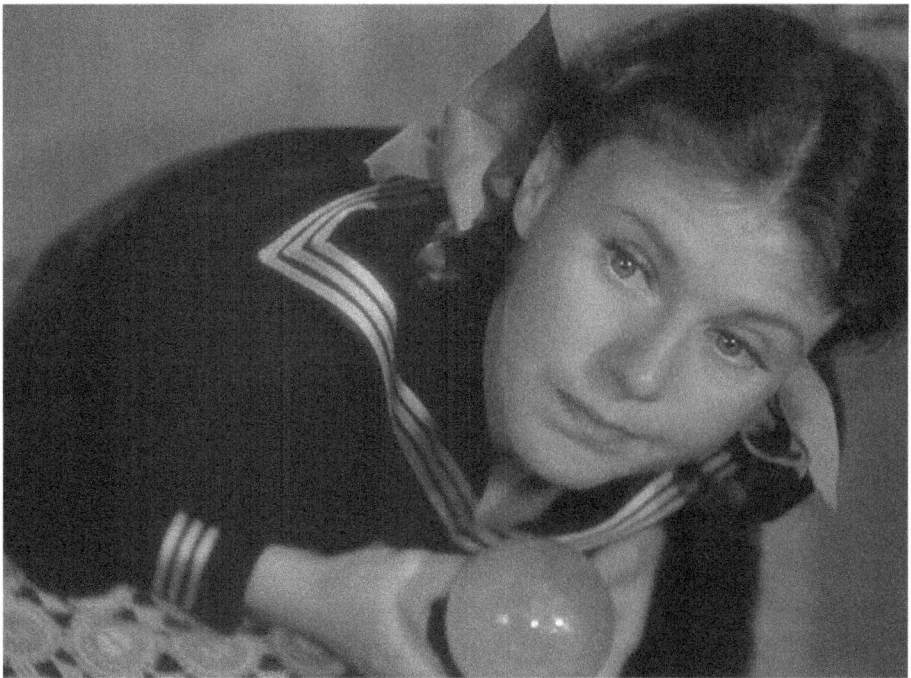

Figure 5   Young Kitty (Ginger Rogers) in *Kitty Foyle* (Wood, 1940).

Philadelphia to start a new life in New York as a salesgirl in an upscale department store. However, wherever she goes, Wyn continues to find her and persuade her to rekindle their relationship. The first reunion is on the night of the annual Assembly ball. Wyn makes Kitty's Cinderella dreams come true by filling her small apartment with flowers and purchasing her a beautiful gown. They have their own private ball at a supper club and dance until 5 a.m. Wyn then proposes marriage over breakfast, and they get married in an off-screen ceremony. The two go home to tell his family the news and they insist that Kitty attend finishing school before she is introduced into proper Philadelphia society. She leaves the house in disgust, recognizing the futility of the marriage. Soon after their separation, Kitty discovers that she is pregnant. She hears from Wyn but realizes that he is contacting her to let her know of his engagement. Kitty decides to have the baby on her own, but loses it in childbirth.

In the midst of these reunions and separations with Wyn, Kitty meets Mark, who is portrayed as Wyn's opposite: he is frugal, very practical and committed to his work, and interested in marrying Kitty. He works hard and takes great strides to make sure that Kitty is not a 'gold-digger' by insisting that they spend their first date in her extremely tiny apartment playing cards, instead of dining out.

The film maintains the structure of the novel, and includes most of its major plot points, with a few notable exceptions. Most significantly, per Joseph Breen's insistence, the screenplay sees Kitty lose her child through an unidentified birth-related complication, rather than from an abortion like in the book. As Lea Jacobs has written, this change was made in order to cast Kitty and Wyn's illicit affair in a negative light. She argues that the inclusion of the flashback structure, and its framing narrative in which Kitty must choose between Wyn and Mark, is also part of the film's strategy in containing the source material's controversial content.[2] Many films of this era, particularly those from the noir and women's film cycles, made use of flashbacks and voiceovers, but *Kitty Foyle* adds a new twist to this format. It visually presents two versions of Kitty – one, who is looking in the mirror, and the other, the reflection in the mirror – having a conversation. One version is packing her bags and inclined to continue her love affair with Wyn, and the other is cautioning against this choice. This conflict motivates the voiceover that guides the flashback.

This technical choice was noted in several stories about, and reviews of, the film. Frederick Othman claimed the technique entailed 'as much machinery as we've ever seen on a movie set.'[3] Melrose Gower of *The Washington Post* wrote of a similar use of narrator in *Outward Bound* (Milton, 1930) and *Strange Interlude* (Leonard, 1932) but declared that 'modern screen history reveals no other picture in which the screen has introduced a character's other self.' He goes on to argue 'usually, women's stories, so-called, are written objectively by someone on the outside looking in. But Kitty Foyle tells her own story subjectively, from the inside looking out.'[4] Indeed, the mirror/ flashback approach is integral to the film for two intertwined reasons. First, it is the structuring device that allows for the film to render its ultimate verdict on Kitty's affair with Wyn. Jacobs has argued that this approach to framing the narrative is characteristic of how the Production Code Administration's (PCA) self-censorship of the film industry regulated female sexual power. For Jacobs, 'these textual processes . . . served as a mechanism for absorbing and negotiating material which, in the period, was constituted as "difficult" or "dangerous."' *Kitty Foyle*'s narrative economy 'produces the sense of the inevitability of the final moment of closure' where Kitty ultimately decides to choose a traditional marriage rather than continue to pursue an affair with a married man.[5]

The mirror/flashback technique, along with the voiceover that guides the film's narration, is also integral to the film because it serves as the primary way in which the viewer connects with Kitty as a character. As Gower contended, Kitty is speaking her own story, as opposed to being spoken about. This alignment of Kitty's strong and even admirable qualities with the decision to choose a romantic partnership that will bring her love, marriage and children is how the film and the PCA achieve this expected and satisfying resolution. In other words, we want Kitty to choose Mark because the film's system of narration makes us feel like this is the better choice for her, irresistible as Wyn may be.

Certainly, no other romance film makes use of this particular mirror technique. Yet *Kitty Foyle* does share many other affinities with the contemporary films with which I will compare it. It forges a close understanding of a female protagonist who strives to succeed in both the professional and personal spheres and whose struggles in both of these areas are navigated through the lens of the romance structure. Kitty is sensible yet idealistic, strong yet vulnerable. The appeal of these coexisting qualities is furthered by Ginger Rogers's performance, which earned her the best reviews of her career and an Academy Award for Best Actress. Mae Tinee of *The Chicago Daily Tribune* wrote it was 'her best performance up to date,'[6] and Mary Harris of *The Washington Post* claimed that she 'slings her saucy hat right into the middle of the ring as America's foremost competitor for Garbo's crown.'[7] Known primarily for her musicals with Fred Astaire, Rogers's ability to play both comedy and drama, and make herself relatable to a wide range of audiences (even with a newly dyed head of hair, a topic of much discussion at the time of the film's release),[8] bears similarities to the star discourses in and around Jill Clayburgh and Katherine Heigl that I will discuss in later sections. Rogers's star persona and performance are essential to the film's success.

Ginger Rogers is also instrumental in navigating the film's shifts in tone from tragedy, as when Kitty comes to terms with the death of her child, to comedy, when she is engaged in romantic witty repartee. This balance between the serious and the lighthearted embodies the broader category of romance that I discuss throughout this book. Jacobs places *Kitty Foyle* into a group of films that she calls the fallen woman cycle, which are primarily dramas. But the film also takes on the tone of a romantic comedy in more than a few scenes. Presumably, this sensibility is a result of Donald Ogden Stewart's contributions to the screenplay. Stewart was the screenwriter for many of the most highly regarded romance films of the period, including *Holiday* (Cukor, 1938), *Love Affair* (McCarey, 1939), and *The Philadelphia Story*. In addition to contributing dialogue for the more dramatic romance scenes, one assumes that he also added the comedic interactions that are featured throughout the film, augmented by Roy Webb's jaunty score.

For instance, in an early scene between Kitty and Wyn, a gag using a Dictaphone serves as a tool for flirtation. Kitty tells Wyn that when she plays back his voice on the Dictaphone, he sounds just like actor Ronald Colman. She leaves the room, and he speaks into the Dictaphone, attempting to make his voice sound debonair and distinguished like the British actor. We cut away to Kitty at her desk. When, later in the scene, Kitty reenters Wyn's office to play his recent dictation, she finds that he has recorded himself making overtures toward her in Colman's voice. Much to their mutual embarrassment, she hears him recite the following as if it was a Shakespeare sonnet: 'Roses are red, violets are blue, Ms. Foyle has nice legs, I love you.'

Another obviously comedic scene is one that portrays Kitty and Mark's first date. She is planning for a night on the town, but when he arrives, he insists that they play cards in her one-room apartment. This affront to dating etiquette inspires Kitty's two roommates, Pat and Molly, to attempt to 'throw her a lifeline' and force Mark out of the apartment by making him uncomfortable with their intimate domestic arrangement. They walk out into the living room in robes with cold cream on their faces and almost stumble over him while trying to locate reading material. Their efforts are of no use. Mark and Kitty stay in the main room for hours, while Pat and Molly spend the evening stuck in the small bathroom.

The film's humorous, serious and entertaining elements are all positioned within, and resolved by, the film's romance structure. None of them are unique in themselves but when presented together, they make for a complex interplay between comedy and drama, social commentary and censorship, revealing the contradiction inherent in the presentation of class elevation as both impossible and beguiling.[9] What critics and scholars have neglected to discuss in depth is how the film's prologue sequence also contributes to the film's eclectic tone.[10] The episodic sequence provides a historical backdrop for Kitty's white-collar working-girl story and seems to be disconnected from the film's narrative. However, its bold socio-political commentary can also be seen to be 'resolved' by Kitty's narrative dénouement, which even further cements the significance of the film's 'happy ending' moment of closure.

It is assumed that Trumbo's addition of the prologue sequence in the adaptation stage was intended to accompany the novel's subtitle: 'The Natural History of a Woman.' The sequence scenes use intertitles, written on a graphic of needlepoint canvas, and have little to no diegetic sound, with most of the information being communicated through broad gesture-laden acting reminiscent of silent films. The first intertitle appears immediately after the film's credit sequence. It reads: 'This is the story of a white-collar girl. Because she is a comparative newcomer to the American scene, it is fitting that we briefly consider her as she was in 1900.' We cut to a scene circa 1900 that sees a woman embark on a streetcar filled with men. As soon as she enters the car, several men stand up, take off their hats, and offer her their seat. She accepts one man's offer, and sits down looking satisfied.

The following scene shows the same woman on her front porch being courted by a man, playing a mandolin. Her father soon comes out to remind them of the late hour, and after the father leaves, the gentleman caller moves in to kiss the girl. She is aghast at his forwardness and in order to appease her, he gets down on his knee to propose. She appears excited. He appears terrified.

Figure 6   The prologue sequence in *Kitty Foyle* (Wood, 1940).

The next scene features the gentleman caller, who is now the woman's husband, return to their house and place his earnings on the woman's lap. She deposits the money, minus a coin for the husband, into a jar in a nearby cabinet. The husband then looks at what the woman has been needlepointing, and we see a close-up of the needlepoint canvas (which resembles that on the intertitle cards) that says 'Baby.' He is thrilled.

The next intertitle marks a shift in tone. It reads, 'But this was not enough.' We cut to a street scene that shows a group of suffragettes, with the woman from the previous scenes sitting front and center, riding in cars with large campaign signs. The signs read 'Climb Aboard the Band Wagon for Woman's Suffrage,' 'Give Women the Right to Vote,' and 'Let the Hand That Rocks the Cradle Guide the State.' This is followed by the sequence's final intertitle card, which says: 'And so the battle was won. Women got their equal rights.' We then return to a streetcar scene that mirrors the opening sequence. However, this time the woman is not offered a seat, and a man actually elbows her out of the way to get to a vacant seat ahead of her. She appears disheartened but resigned.

The prologue is quite extraordinary for its self-contained commentary on the progress of women in the early part of the twentieth century. Certainly, it

Figure 7   The prologue sequence in *Kitty Foyle* (Wood, 1940).

Figure 8 The prologue sequence in *Kitty Foyle* (Wood, 1940).

has bearing on the film's historical context as it shows how the 'white collar' woman such as Kitty came to be. However, it also predicts Kitty's efforts to find a balance between the personal sphere accomplishments that we see predate women's suffrage, like love and a family, and the sense of autonomy and power available in the public sphere. The entire sequence implies that the only thing that is gained from such reconciliation is that women are treated just as poorly as men, and are no longer on the receiving end of polite and deferential behavior. A cursory interpretation of the prologue casts a critical and mocking eye on the women's suffrage movement. As Mary Ann Doane has argued, the sequence evinces 'a nostalgia for a time before "women's suffrage."'[11] However, the fact that screenwriter Trumbo, a noted liberal, was the one to add this to the film does cause one to question whether to take this critical tone at face value.

But whether one interprets the sequence to be funny or insulting, or both, its commentary on women's issues gets absorbed into *Kitty Foyle*'s exposition. Eventually, her happy ending sees her choose the right domestic path with a man whose actions resemble the prologue sequence's domestic scenes. Although she makes Mark's acquaintance while she is at work, he is associated primarily with domestic spaces and/or conversations about domesticity.

Mark courts her in an appropriate old-fashioned manner through proper dates (the first of which, as we discussed, is chaperoned by her roommates), and like the man who dutifully turns his money over to his wife, his conversations with Kitty are dominated by discussions of class and economics. Even his proposal sees him mention that he has 'a lot of money tied up in that little hoop [the engagement ring].' One can assume that Mark's frugal and down-to-earth ways would receive the approval of Kitty's father (who dies before Mark enters the picture) who warns against Kitty's tendency to equate love and class elevation.

In short, Kitty's ultimate path toward her happy ending mirrors the domestic arrangement seen in the pre-suffragette sequence of the prologue. The film seems to be reinforcing the idea that marriage and family is enough. The presumed satisfaction that a woman gains from this traditional path is contrasted with Kitty and Wyn's relationship that, despite its beginnings in Kitty's home, primarily takes place in the public sphere. Wyn is only seen occupying private domestic spaces briefly and woos Kitty in the public spaces such as the office of the magazine, in Gionos, and other restaurants. The Poconos getaway is the only scene in the film when we see Kitty and Wyn remain in a domestic space for any extended period of time. However, they spend only one night here and our glimpse of this space is limited to a brief establishing shot of the fireplace. What we see are medium and close-up shots of the two lovers' faces as they cuddle in front of the fire. The film suggests that this place is significant because it is where they consummate their relationship, with the sexual act implied through a fade out. However, they pass through the Poconos briefly, and do not dwell. Consequently, the film's verdict on Kitty's affair with Wyn is imbued with the prologue's attitude about non-domestic spaces. Just as the white-collar girl's entry into the public leads to disrespect, Kitty's role as Wyn's lover is, as the conversation between Kitty's two selves tells us, 'a pretty unsatisfactory role . . . even under the best circumstances.'

Interpreting *Kitty Foyle* in this way is not intended to suggest that this well-scripted and exquisitely acted film offers only a simplistic reading where female empowerment enabled by the suffragette movement is pitted in stark contrast to love, fantasy, and domestic fulfillment. The film works far more complexly than this. It is merely to illuminate how classical Hollywood narrative and aesthetic techniques successfully contain these issues within the structure of the romance, even when attempting to use an unconventional sequence to make a political point. As Matthew Bernstein has argued, 'Kitty Foyle's choice highlights the 1940 heroine's typical dilemma of whom to marry, without, again, questioning the desirability of marriage for American women.'[12] Both Bernstein and Jacobs contend that the film's entire premise is based on women's choices – both Kitty and the woman in the prologue – but renders these choices as inevitable and predetermined.

What we are left with is a satisfying resolution but one that elicits residual curiosity about the path not taken. Mary Harris's review of the film captures this feeling perfectly: 'The ending leaves beholders both glad and sorry. Too bad there isn't some way of lining the narrow path with primroses or vice versa.'[13] To be sure, Harris's sentiments about *Kitty Foyle* are familiar. Feeling both 'glad and sorry' about a film's presentation of an either/or scenario for her protagonist deciding between the 'primrose path' or the 'narrow way of conventional virtue' sums up the narratives of many a romance text. However, as we have seen, the fact that Kitty chooses the latter, more practical option makes the film a product of its historical and industrial context. We will look at how this idea of choice changes in subsequent historical periods.

THE 'FEMINIST' ROMANCE FILM: *AN UNMARRIED WOMAN*

An UnMarried Woman was released as the second-wave feminist movement was in full swing and the American film industry was in the midst of a significant period of transformation. Beginning in the mid-1960s, Hollywood saw major changes in its economic infrastructure, its system of self-regulation, the demographics of its audience, and the sensibilities of its filmmakers, and all of these had a profound effect on its depiction of romance and sexuality. The change from the Production Code Administration to the MPAA ratings system in 1968 gave filmmakers more leeway in how they represented sexual and violent themes. This was an overdue development, and one which saw struggling studios reap significant profits, as European films such as France's *A Man and a Woman* (Lelouch, 1966) and Britain's *Blow-Up* (Antonioni, 1966) were already introducing American audiences to a visual vocabulary in which sexual interaction was represented openly and honestly.[14] A new generation of filmmakers, some of whom trained at film schools or had a background in television, used this more lenient system, and this vocabulary gleaned from European cinema, to make more explicit films that would appeal to the growing youth demographic, which was at the forefront of Vietnam War protests, the civil rights movement, and the women's liberation movement. It is out of this context, which predated but eventually coexisted with the rise of the blockbuster era, that a different type of romance film emerges in Hollywood; what I will call the 'feminist' romance film.

At the same time that we identify and characterize the 'feminist' romance film, we must simultaneously acknowledge the limitations of this label. While 1970s Hollywood saw many remarkable new developments, films with strong female protagonists were not among its innovations. Of the cultural influences reflected in these films, feminism is probably inscribed in the least explicit terms, but felt in the ways in which the traditional romance conventions seen in the classical period were made strange or interrogated. This issue is taken up by Brian Henderson in his seminal article 'Romantic comedy today: Semi-tough or impossible?' that I discuss at more length in Chapter 4. Henderson argues that the romantic comedy saw a drastic transformation in the 1970s in response to changing sexual mores. He argues that when films highlight, rather than repress sexual gratification, the genre becomes impossible to maintain.[15] Steve Neale and Frank Krutnik responded to Henderson's points with a less fatalistic tone, declaring that the 1970s did not signal the death knell for romantic comedy but rather saw a new cycle of romance emerge that they called the 'nervous romance.' In these films, they state,

> There is a reluctance about commitment to a heterosexual union in an age where divorce and marital disruption are prevalent, but there is also a contrary pull which is strongly marked by fantasy, hearkening for an 'old fashioned' security in heterosexual romance (rather than sex).[16]

Neale and Krutnik's reading of the 1970s nervous romance as being caught simultaneously in the past and the present describes the nature of the change in romance that I have described. However, neither they nor Henderson consider at length the important role that feminism plays in films of this era, which was one of many movements that led to the changing political tide of the 1970s and the changing nature of representations of romance of which these authors speak. As my analysis of *An UnMarried Woman*'s critical reception evinces, the public certainly interpreted the film as a direct response to the women's movement.

While we acknowledge the degree to which *An UnMarried Woman* reflects attitudes about feminism, I must also call attention to my use of scare quotes. They indicate the hesitancy with which I name this subgroup 'feminist.' There is nothing to suggest that *An UnMarried Woman* was intended to be explicitly political in itself. In fact, the film has been interpreted as decidedly antifeminist. Michael Ryan and Douglas Kellner have argued that it displays a male perspective in its 'insistent focus on Erica's relations to men,' expunging 'all radicalism from feminism and repackag[ing] it as a "new woman" or "corporate" feminism.'[17] David Shumway, on the other hand, interprets the film as 'neither the remarriage to Martin [Erica's ex-husband] that we would expect from a studio-era film nor even a marriage to someone new. Rather it is the story of a woman's development as an independent person.'[18] This question of whether the film instantiates a discourse of dependence or independence should be familiar to us by now. *An UnMarried Woman* sees this either/or question taking on a different shape than it did in *Kitty Foyle* since the film's discourse in and around Erica's choice between these two options is not framed tightly by its narrative structure in adherence to the classical model. Rather, her future path is left ambiguous, and the verdict on her choice, or lack thereof, is rendered in the film's critical reception.

As we will see, *An UnMarried Woman* is just different enough from a classical film like *Kitty Foyle* to elicit debate about the balancing act it maintains between dependence and independence. Its episodic structure, along with its contentious critical reception, point to the elasticity of the romance form to account for explicitly political discourses that are in direct conversation with transformations in women's lives. It loosely follows, and ultimately deviates from, the traditional romance narrative structure, but falls short of being radical in representing Erica as a woman whose choices remain intertwined with this structure. The film sees traditional romance structures merge with politically progressive ideas and most remarkably, leaves its central questions unanswered at its conclusion. When comparing it to the equally complex but still very classical *Kitty Foyle*, in which Kitty's choice seems predetermined, its ambiguous, neither-happy-nor-sad ending seems even more notable.

An UnMarried Woman begins on an average day in Erica (Jill Clayburgh) and Martin's (Michael Murphy) sixteen-year marriage. The state of affairs appears to be happy. The couple engages in a morning jog, a bout of lovemaking, and intimate and witty repartee with their rambunctious fifteen-year-old daughter. A couple of days later, out of the blue, Martin tells Erica that he has been having an affair with another woman, and he wants out of the marriage. She is devastated by the news and struggles to establish a new identity as a single woman. The rest of the film sees Erica continue her part-time job at an art gallery and commiserate with her eclectic group of girlfriends, who are going through their own respective life crises. She pursues therapy and

Figure 9   Erica (Jill Clayburgh) in *An UnMarried Woman* (Mazursky, 1978).

eventually begins to date. She meets and begins a relationship with Saul, an emotionally mature British artist (Alan Bates), who wants to settle down with her. The film ends with Erica expressing ambivalence about pursuing the relationship and choosing not to join Saul in his move away from the city. The concluding scene sees her walk away from Saul's apartment by herself, as she fumbles with an extremely large canvas that he has given her as a gift.

An UnMarried Woman's spare visual style, its awkward, seemingly improvised dialogue sequences and Jill Clayburgh's star persona infuse the film with a sense of realism that was well-received by critics at the time of its release. Much of the praise revolved around the film's writer-director, Paul Mazursky, who had a string of highly regarded films during the 1970s, including *Bob and Ted and Carol and Alice* (1969), *Blume in Love* (1973), and *Next Stop, Greenwich Village* (1976). Upon the release of *Woman*, *The New York Times*'s Janet Maslin lauded Mazursky as being 'particularly clever in showing the way things can go wrong for no good reason.' She continues, 'One of the most likeable things about Mr. Mazursky's movies is his acknowledging the bewildering way in which unimportant-sounding problems cause such real pain.'[19]

Mazursky's knack for creating entertainment out of unimportant problems, and seemingly unmotivated reasoning, finds its perfect match in actress Jill Clayburgh, arguably the decade's quintessential 'natural' and idiosyncratic star. She was featured extensively in the few romance films made during this period, including *Silver Streak* (Hiller, 1976), *Semi-Tough* (Ritchie, 1977), *Starting Over* (Pakula, 1979), and *It's My Turn* (Weill, 1980). As a 1978 *Washington Post* style profile on the star characterized her: 'Clayburgh is a woman's woman. She is every woman's idea of what she would like her best friends to be. She is comfortable, friendly, open, intimate, straight, smart, funny, confiding. She doesn't mind laughing at herself, exposing her vulnerabilities, empathizing.'[20] Gene Siskel put it in a slightly less flattering way: 'She looks like a conventional Hollywood bombshell who can't quite get it all together.'[21]

Siskel is definitely on to something when he strikes a contrast between Clayburgh and a 'conventional Hollywood bombshell' because it is exactly her unique blend of star quality mixed with an accessible everydayness that is at the heart of *An UnMarried Woman*'s sensibility. If the film did not depict Erica as a 'woman's woman,' 1970s style, then presumably it would not have tapped into its cultural zeitgeist as successfully as it did. That said, Siskel's comments, and the sentiments that he expresses in his review, are illustrative of the desire for, or simply the basis of comparison for, an 'old-fashioned security' in the classical romance model of which Steve Neale and Frank Krutnik speak. Even the female characters within the film express a longing for the magical qualities of classical Hollywood film. Midway through the film Erica and her friends talk about the strength of old Hollywood actresses like Bette Davis, Greta Garbo, Katharine Hepburn, and Joan Crawford who they pit in contrast to their therapy-dependent, self-esteem-deficient generation. Her friend laments: 'where are all of wonderful women that were in the movies in the old days?'

While Siskel saw *An UnMarried Woman* as a platform for Clayburgh's lack of togetherness, other critics saw it as her ideal role. The *Boston Globe*'s Bruce McCabe states that Clayburgh gives a 'superior performance' in the film because 'until Paul Mazursky, the creator of "Woman" came along, no one had conceived a role for her.'[22] He continued, 'Clayburgh's dominance of "An UnMarried Woman" may be the best evidence we have that Hollywood has rediscovered women . . . I can't remember when I saw a film so attuned to the feminine mood and instinct.' He later surmised, '"An UnMarried Woman" is that rarity, the woman's story seen through the eyes of an intelligent man.' The other major reviews of the film similarly posited a dynamic in which a 'feminine mood' or sensibility based in Clayburgh's performance comes into contact with Mazursky's authorial flair for social critique, which is realized through conventional representations of women's genre forms. David Sterritt remarked that the film's plot is 'the stuff of soap operas and melodramas, but Mazursky doesn't raise the issue [Martin's betrayal of Erica through infidelity] for frivolous reasons.'[23]

What these critics convey are conflicted expectations of what a romance film made during this era should look like, which echo Ryan/Kellner and Shumway's disagreement about the film's feminist potential. Unlike Siskel, McCabe and Sterrit are eager to dismiss the 'frivolous' excesses that are inextricable with women's pictures from an earlier period, and soap operas of the contemporary period. They express a palpable longing for a dose of the 'real' (in Clayburgh and from Mazursky) that is capable of absorbing the well-worn thematic territory of the classical Hollywood romance film. McCabe's insistence that only an 'intelligent' man can capture this type of verisimilitude of women's experience points to some broader gendered discourses engaged in and by the film that are intertwined with ideas of what 'real' women want, how they look and behave in the late 1970s.

Indeed, the film elicits discordant perspectives from those who want it to be a conventional film that ties up its loose ends at its conclusion, presumably with Erica settling down with Saul, and those who revel in its quirky often aimless exploration of the complexities inherent in what Pauline Kael called 'a sensitive empathetic case for a modern woman's need to call her soul her own.'[24] Returning to Siskel again, his disagreement with what critics like Kael praise about the film is far from subtle. In his review entitled 'An issue is overdone in "Woman"' Siskel writes:

> But it is difficult to accept a movie that so clearly applauds a woman's independence, that so clearly forces its central character to be independent in the face of a more attractive choice – interdependence with a terribly attractive man she meets toward the end of the film.[25]

Two intertwined sentiments are at work here. First, there is Siskel's explicitly stated assumption that a relationship with the 'terribly attractive' Saul is a better choice for Erica than remaining on her own. And second, there is his more implicit contention that that the film's deviation from the expected happy ending (with the heterosexual couple intact) makes it difficult to accept. Siskel blames the fact that Erica cannot 'run to a man' on the film's 'trendiness,' by which one assumes he means its reflection of feminism and the rising divorce rate. Unlike most of the film's critics who applaud the film's realist sensibility, Siskel believes that the film overplays the independence card at the expense of more satisfying romance narrative conventions.

Resistance to the film's representations of independent women came from other sources as well. In a 'Feedback' piece in the *Los Angeles Times* writer and actress Victoria E. Thompson argued that the film is exploitative, cliché-ridden, and 'all too common' for her taste. As a counterpoint to Siskel's argument, Thompson's biggest complaint is that the film is too focused on Erica's romantic trajectory, and not enough on her friendships and professional pursuits:

> In *An UnMarried Woman*, Erica and her cronies have been rejected by their mates. They spend a lot of time talking to one another about their conditions. They feel sorry for themselves and for each other – but face themselves? No. They have not in any way given up their desperate attempt to attract the 'tired men.' . . . Never in the film are we shown what Erica's function is at the gallery where she works. Is she interested in or involved with the world of art? No woman is shown as creative or active in any way. Ultimately, the thing that succeeds in bringing Erica out of her depression is . . . another man.[26]

Anticipating Ryan and Kellner's analysis, Thompson finds the film too hesitant to examine what independence looks like outside of the boundaries of a heterosexual romance framework. For her, the film is not too real, but too dependent on the clichés that have dominated female-oriented romance films for decades. Two weeks after this piece appeared, veteran producer Robert Radnitz wrote a response, taking issue with Thompson's characterization of the film, and describing her as 'the kind of person who would flail at a Romeo for being overly compulsive, at Natasha for being overly sweet, etc.'[27] According to Radnitz, Thompson's desire to see Erica represented as a creative and active woman puts her in a category of 'the kind of people' who, he assumes, must resist all romances, even those written by Shakespeare and Tolstoy.

The discourse surrounding *An UnMarried Woman* demonstrates that the film hit a cultural nerve. It was in the right place at the right time, with the right actress and writer-director to explore some of the most important issues of its era. Certainly, both critics and scholars seemed to agree that it differs greatly from classic romance films. However, it was too different for some people, not different enough for others. Their contentious debates surrounding either/ or questions of whether Erica is confident or insecure, happier with Martin or Saul, alone or in a relationship, and whether the film's ambiguous ending is positive or negative remind us of the interpretive debates around *Kitty Foyle* yet these remain more open-ended. *An UnMarried Woman*'s structure cannot quite recuperate or absorb the tensions it raises. In short, the film can be seen as feminist because it elicited a heated extra-diegetic political debate about women and Hollywood storytelling even if it falls short of representing a politically motivated exploration of these intersections.

The Postfeminist Romance: *27 Dresses*

Our case studies thus far have shown us that, while no film's discourse is simple or fixed, the classical and feminist romance films evidence an obvious connection to the industrial and cultural expectations of their respective historical periods. The postfeminist romance is more unwieldy in this regard because it reflects the very conflicted position of its historical period, which, as we have seen, is constantly negotiating where traditional conceptions of women's roles align with their unprecedented social autonomy. This hybridity is also reflected in the degree to which the postfeminist romance is caught somewhere in between the classical and feminist narrative models that we have examined thus far, recalling both *Kitty*'s presentation of a choice between the 'primrose path' and 'conventional virtue,' and *An UnMarried Woman*'s presentation of a choice between dependence or independence. In some cases, the postfeminist romance film adopts the looser, episodic realist style of *An UnMarried Woman* but most return to the classical model in which, per Jacobs' description, 'textual processes' 'absorb and negotiate difficult material.' The new social realities facing women in the late twentieth and early twenty-first century even further complicate the model because there is also the choice *not* to choose any of these paths, or at least delay the choice until much later in life than was the norm in the 1940s and 1970s.

The typical postfeminist romance follows the structure that I laid out in the Introduction but has its own distinctive features. It is focused on a woman who is single (or in an unsatisfying relationship), strong and independent, and usually professionally accomplished. However, as opposed to being satisfied,

she remains emotionally and psychologically unfulfilled, and missing an unidentified 'something.' The film is quick to imply that this 'something' is the
perfect romantic partner. The hardened female character frequently voices her
doubts about the role of romance in her life and bemoans the lack of quality
men from which to choose. Inevitably the text introduces a man who piques
her interest and a love relationship unfolds, ultimately providing a much-
needed and much-desired salve for her weary female psyche or what Diane
Negra has called an 'enchantment effect.'[28]

This man often challenges her in some way, usually through verbal sparring
or debate, and causes her to take a deep look at herself and the choices that
have led her to this point. He is generally pitted against another man, who is
the safer choice, either because he will secure her social status, or because he
seems better 'on paper.' While initially our protagonist is immune or resistant
to the charms of her preferred love match, she eventually realizes the right
course of action, and the two come together at the end of the film.

After examining *Kitty Foyle* and *An UnMarried Woman* we know that these
characteristics share a great deal in common with previous generations of
romance films. As we discussed in the Introduction, where the biggest point of
differentiation lies is in the contemporary film's implication that the woman's
bad luck, both romantic and otherwise, is a product of some problem that
she has for which the film must find a solution. And, this problem is linked to
her aforementioned social and political status. She is *too* 'fill in the blanks':
whether it's too independent or too dependent, too selfish or too selfless, too
invested in romance, or not invested enough in romance. Both the problem and
the resolution for her problem have their roots in this character's conflicted
allegiance to both the past and the present, ideas of fantasy and reality, sexual
curiosity and concerns about promiscuity, and independence and dependence.
The means for negotiating these different allegiances is also torn between a
resolution based in the structure of classical romance film (and fairy tales) in
which every problem has a solution and the feminist conception of romance in
which independence is valued highly and alternative options beckon.

Because she exists in a universe in which these contradictory messages
abound, the contemporary female protagonist shows signs of *An UnMarried
Woman*'s 'doesn't have it together'-ness by being in a permanent state of flux.
The protagonist is generally confused, imperfect, insecure, and vulnerable, a
state of being that Diane Negra has labeled 'abject singlehood.'[29] Identification
is forged with even more depth with our protagonist when she is set apart
from, or in contrast to, another woman (or women) who appears to proceed
with her life with none of these problems and follows a traditional 'script' by
adapting her behavior and 'costume' to meet a good man, achieve a happy
relationship, and a seemingly blissful and secure domestic environment. This
more perfect woman is often a source of envy and disdain for our less polished

female protagonist. The fact that our central character is less than perfect makes her seem more regular and endearing.

The postfeminist romance film rarely presents an ambiguous or open-ended narrative structure. It usually offers a closed system like *Kitty Foyle* but unlike the classic film, the socio-political issues that get raised within the narrative do not always get resolved, even when there is a happy ending. The postfeminist romance film is always about more than the romance. It is about the social and political hot button issues that get negotiated, sometimes contained, but frequently and egregiously unresolved, that are intertwined with the romance. However, in contrast to the fiery critical response to *An UnMarried Woman*, critics of these contemporary romance films rarely find anything political in them. They are written off as frivolous and formula-based. When one looks at the films as a group it is obvious that they are dealing with the most potent issues facing women today, including but not limited to, anxieties about women's biological clocks, their sexual promiscuity, their increasing professional power, their economic independence, their consumption, their over-emotional behavior, and of course, their over-attachment to women's-oriented entertainment.

The Pew Research Center statistics cited in the Introduction reflect the reality of women's growing prominence in the public sphere, fostering anxiety about the issues identified above. This anxiety results in another retrograde cultural narrative to be circulated that tempers this evidence of progress. These two narratives circulating in tandem create a dynamic in which women are made to feel like they have to choose one path or the other – the either or the or – when in fact this binary has been fabricated. Because most of these anxieties revolve around women's personal choices, the romance becomes the perfect forum in which to represent them. The following passage from neo-conservative feminist Danielle Crittenden provides a transparent snapshot into how these types of either/or dynamics are created and perpetuated. It is worth quoting at length because it succinctly hits on many of the hot-button discursive messages we see circulating in the postfeminist romance:

> What a woman is aware of, at around the age of twenty-six or twenty-seven, is a growing, inchoate dissatisfaction, a yearning for more, even if her life is already quite full. Her apartment feels too quiet, her work, no matter how exciting or interesting, is less absorbing, and her spare time, unless packed with frenetic activities, almost echoes with loneliness – think of an endless wintry Sunday afternoon unbroken by the sound of another voice . . . Alas, it is usually at precisely this moment – when a single woman looks up from her work and realizes she is ready to take on family life – that men make themselves most absent. This is when the cruelty of her singleness really sets in, when she becomes aware of the fine

print in the unwritten bargain she has cut with the opposite sex . . . she cannot be blamed for believing, at this point in her life, that it is men who have benefited most from women's determination to be independent.[30]

Crittenden presents a particularly ominous either/or scenario that posits a twenty-something single woman's personal and professional choices as implicitly counterproductive to romantic fulfillment. The social environment that Crittenden describes is one where women remain unmarried until their late twenties by choice because they are interested in fostering a sense of autonomy through their careers, friendships, and personal pursuits. She implies that these women, whether they like it or not, will begin to desire a husband, family and children by a culturally preordained age – twenty-six or twenty-seven. She describes this as a completely organic and natural process wherein a woman will find herself wanting to pursue a relationship or fall in love not because she chooses to have a partner in her life but because she is overcome with 'the cruelty of her singleness.' A woman's determination to be independent and those 'endless wintry Sunday afternoon[s] unbroken by the sound of another voice' are deemed in stark contrast to a readiness to 'take on family life' (presumably filled with quick-paced Sundays surrounded by a cacophony of children's voices). The extremity of Crittenden's statements might serve her ideological ends but it also effectively serves the opposite purpose, which is to make transparent the fact that most women's realities fall somewhere in between her two extremes.

Anthea Taylor's work on the figure of the single woman in postfeminist culture speaks directly to the type of rhetoric perpetuated by Crittenden. She argues that 'being a straight single woman, particularly for a prolonged period, is often seen as a failure to perform heterosexuality adequately or appropriately,'[31] and that the single woman is 'written out (or worse) of the dominant narratives of this signifying economy.'[32] Given the preponderance of these types of cultural messages, it is no surprise that the postfeminist romance film reflects a decidedly and explicitly conflicted discourse about the intersections of personal autonomy, professional decisions, and romantic relationships.

The film *27 Dresses* is an excellent case study for wading through some of the ways in which these films represent contentious and conflicted refrains. It is, in many ways, a prototypical contemporary romance film. It did good business, earning $76,808,654 at the domestic box office but was generally lambasted by the critics, who saw it as too cliché-ridden.[33] As *USA Today*'s Claudia Puig writes, 'It is an uninspired romantic comedy that adheres slavishly to the conventions of the genre.'[34]

Indeed, the film presents a narrative structure reminiscent of a classic film like *Kitty Foyle* that predetermines a happy ending for Jane (Katherine Heigl), its protagonist. Her obsession with weddings is rewarded at the film's conclusion in which she is finally able to plan her own nuptials. Furthermore, Jane's characterization is reduced to this obsession, which limits the depiction of her independence as a twenty-first-century, twenty-something woman. Jane can have it all but the plot reduces what she wants to a very limited set of options. Thus, we will see that she is independent and dependent at the same time, in addition to being simultaneously girlish and womanly. She is fixated on images of her parents' wedding from the past in addition to the embellished accounts of real-life weddings that she sees in the Commitments section of the newspaper. In this way, 27 Dresses negotiates a significant number of politically situated questions about women's choices in a highly entertaining package.

From its opening sequence, 27 Dresses portrays Jane's two intertwined 'too' problems: she is too selfless, putting others needs before her own, and she is too obsessed with weddings. These problems are introduced through the flashback sequence that opens the film, which shows Jane at eight years old. This particular sequence, accompanied by a voiceover from the adult Jane, shows young Jane at her cousin Lisa's wedding. A day that 'changed her life.' In the act of taking her sister Tess to the bathroom (which her distraught, recently widowed father cannot manage to do), she comes across the distressed bride who is trying to deal with a tear in her gown. Jane is able to fix the dress to Lisa's satisfaction, and her voiceover tells us that this is when she 'fell in love with weddings.'

This opening scene establishes Jane's childhood notions of weddings as integral to the formation of her adult personality. The representation of childhood as providing a moral compass for the choices that a character should make in his or her adult life recurs frequently in the postfeminist romance cycle. Diane Negra and Amanda Lotz have both written extensively about this retreatist trend in contemporary fiction films and network television shows during the 1990s and 2000s that sees women either reflecting back on their childhoods for insight on their adult lives or actually physically returning to their hometowns in order to temporarily or permanently escape their urban, career-driven lives. They argue that media texts that depict the lure of 'folksy' small-town life such as the television shows *Providence* (1999–2002), *Gilmore Girls* (2000–7), *Judging Amy* (1999–2005) and the films *Sweet Home Alabama* (Tennant, 2002), *Hope Floats* (Whitaker, 1998), and *The Runaway Bride* (Marshall, 1999) are a hallmark of the postfeminist era.[35] This retreatist discourse suggests that the lessons we learn as we grow from adolescents to adults deter us from making healthy decisions about love.

In *27 Dresses* this snapshot of a wedding in which young Jane helps to solve Lisa's problem while also taking care of Tess is the film's shorthand for communicating Jane's most significant character traits. In other words, the sole purpose of our brief and one-time glimpse into Jane's childhood tells us all we need to know about who she is. We may recall that childhood, and childhood fantasies about love, also played a significant role in *Kitty Foyle*. There are two interesting points of distinction between the two portrayals that are worth exploring.

First, *Kitty Foyle*'s flashback to Kitty as a fifteen-year-old is instrumental in introducing the film's complex discourse on the intersections between love and economics. The snow globe that appears in this first scene serves to visually represent her girlish fantasies about love and class elevation. The globe's prominent function as the visual cue that signals the passage of time always serves to remind the viewer of this earlier scene. Jane's flashback also establishes that her ideas of love are wrapped up in an extravagant institutional display of wealth. The wedding, or what Chrys Ingraham has called 'the wedding industrial complex,' is a common preoccupation of contemporary women's culture, with numerous films and other media texts focused on every minute detail of the experience.[36] However, in contrast to *Kitty Foyle*, class and economics are deemed inconsequential in *27 Dresses* just like they are in most postfeminist romance films. The upper-middle-class status of the film's characters is passed off as normal and expected.

Another telling point of contrast between *27 Dresses* and *Kitty Foyle*'s childhood flashbacks is that in *27 Dresses* this scene serves not simply to depict Jane as a young girl but to associate her look and her behavior with that of a young girl. In *Kitty Foyle*, the flashback is a foundation upon which the film builds incrementally and organically. The younger version of Kitty is played by Ginger Rogers who is simply made to look younger through makeup, hair and costume. In this way, the young Kitty is seamlessly connected to older Kitty. She is always Ginger Rogers. In *27 Dresses* an eight-year-old actress plays the young version of Jane and the film cuts from her image to that of the adult Jane, played now by Katherine Heigl. Thus, it is difficult not to see the young version as coexistent with the older version. Jane's close association

Figure 10   Young Jane (Peyton List) in *27 Dresses* (Fletcher, 2008).

with her eight-year-old self becomes an integral part of her characterization. This conflation of girls with grown women, and vice versa, is another trait of the postfeminist romance that I discuss at more length in Chapter 4.

The sentiments of the childhood flashback scene are punctuated in its transition into an image of Jane trying on a wedding dress, and admiring herself in a mirror. She is complimented for how beautiful she looks but we soon learn that this is not her dress but that of a friend whose wedding Jane is planning. The film then moves into a montage sequence in which Jane's selflessness and devotion to weddings is made clear. She is participating in not just one but two weddings in a single evening on opposite sides of town. Here the film seems to be both celebrating and mocking wedding culture. Despite the fact that each wedding reflects a different style – one is a traditional, elegant affair in Manhattan, the other an eclectic intermarriage between a Jewish woman and Indian man in Brooklyn – they are still remarkably similar. With the film's score mixed with the diegetic song, Michael Jackson's 'Don't Stop Until You Get Enough,' the montage sees Jane move back and forth between Manhattan and Brooklyn in a cab that she has hired for the evening. She changes from her traditional purple bridesmaid's dress to a sari and back again, in order to be present for each reception's key moments, including the cutting of the cake, dancing the electric slide, and the bouquet toss. Her quick dash in and out of the Manhattan wedding catches the attention of Kevin (James Marsden), a writer for the *New York Journal*'s Commitments column, who is there to write a story about the event.

This opening sequence, in tandem with the flashback childhood sequence, reveals Jane's 'problem' persists into adulthood. She is invested in planning others' weddings but not in her own love life. In fact, both brides dedicate toasts to her and describe in painstaking detail all of the steps of the planning process with which Jane helped. Her dedication and work ethic is made abundantly clear when we are introduced to Jane's professional environment. She is an executive assistant for an environmentally conscious outdoor sports company for the handsome and accomplished CEO (Edward Burns) – with whom she also happens to be in love. She is devoted to him, remembering small tidbits about his life and finishing his sentences. Jane's unrequited love for this handsome, yet safe and boring, man is common in films throughout the romance canon: think Bruce (Ralph Bellamy) from *His Girl Friday*, among many others. This safe character serves as a counterpoint to the wittier and more dynamic male character Walter Burns (Cary Grant), whom the female protagonist would rather be with. *Kitty Foyle* notwithstanding, the romance film almost always promotes the idea that the female protagonist's choice of love interest should be based in love and passion, not pragmatism. In *27 Dresses*, Jane's devotion to the bland but handsome George establishes a semblance of a love triangle, with Kevin taking on the dynamic male character role (this dynamic takes on heightened proportions with the appearance of Jane's sister, Tess (Malin Akerman)).

This love triangle serves two additional functions that have specific relevance to the postfeminist romance film more generally. First, Jane's devotion to George is intertwined with her professional career. She is shown to be a fantastic assistant, but this proficiency is chalked up to her crush, and not to her abilities. Her talent for planning other people's weddings is also seen to be a sign of her strong work ethic, organizational skills and smarts. However, this aptitude is also intertwined with her ideas about romance and similarly diminished in the narrative. In this way, her position as a professionally successful woman is not rendered significant in itself but only important insofar as it is inseparable from her romantic life.

The second way in which the love triangle, specifically, Jane's crush on George, exemplifies the postfeminist romance is that it further supports Jane's characterization as a young girl, keeping the film firmly planted in the safe, chaste confines of the PG-13 landscape. As I noted in the Introduction, in most contemporary romantic comedies, sex is referred to but never seen. As I will discuss in more detail later, the scene in which Jane does have sex with Kevin is seen to be a product of excess consumption of alcohol, and covered up by a well-placed edit. Jane's best friend, Casey (Judy Greer), who is conveniently also her coworker, is pitted in contrast to the sexually chaste Jane. She is sexually active, for example, seeing her role as a bridesmaid in the opening scene's Manhattan wedding as an opportunity to meet a man with whom she has a thirty-six-hour tryst. She offers Jane healthy doses of adult reason, frequently calling attention to the degree to which Jane's professional life, sexual life, and romantic life are too intertwined. Early in the film, she asks Jane to: 'tell me that crazy crush is the reason you work as hard as you do, 'cause it's upsetting.'

After the film introduces Jane's problems, they are brought to the forefront most acutely and then solved through the film's subplots involving Jane's sister Tess and Kevin, the Commitments reporter. Jane and Kevin have a classic 'meet cute' moment at the Manhattan wedding where he helps her to her feet after an overzealous wedding bouquet catcher knocks her out. They engage in quick-witted banter that sees Kevin's cynicism about love and weddings come into conflict with Jane's enthusiasm for them. After they share an uncomfortable cab ride, Kevin accidentally intercepts Jane's datebook and sees the large number of weddings she has attended over the previous year. He proceeds to pitch a feature story to his editor about Jane's serial bridesmaid status in the hopes that it will save him from the 'taffeta ghetto' of the style section. She agrees. He gets close to Jane, and gathers information about her, by agreeing to feature her sister's wedding in his column. While Jane is surprised that jaded Kevin is the author (writing under a pseudonym) of her much-beloved Commitments, she agrees to let him accompany her on various wedding-related errands. She soon learns that there is a reason for his resistance to romantic love: his former wife left him for his college roommate. The two get stuck in a rainstorm in a remote area and after much alcohol, and a bar sing-along to Elton John's 'Bennie and the Jets', they kiss, and then proceed to have sex in Jane's car. The film cuts to the next morning when Jane learns that Kevin has betrayed her by writing about her behind her back.

Tess fulfills the aforementioned archetypal role in the postfeminist romance film as the 'perfect' woman with whom Jane is contrasted. As the childhood flashback sequence suggests, Jane is the caretaker and Tess is the one who is taken care of. Tess is a model and thus portrayed as the more conventionally attractive of the two sisters, with costume and hair design (that sees Heigl's normally blond hair dyed brown) functioning to make Jane look dowdy in comparison. This common trope forges even closer association between the presumed female spectator and Jane. She is the 'everyday' woman, whereas Tess is the idealized perfect model-type whom the viewer is supposed to both idolize and resent. Much like the discourse surrounding Ginger Rogers and Jill Clayburgh, Katherine Heigl is seen to anchor the film with her down-to-earth qualities. In her *Philadelphia Inquirer* review, Christy Lemire writes, 'Heigl has such an intriguingly different presence for a rom-com heroine . . . there's nothing cutesy about her – nothing self-conscious.'[37] And *The Boston Globe*'s Wesley Morris states, 'Heigl is not a goddess. She's very appealing but not chic or cool, which for so-so romantic comedies is an advantage. She isn't slumming, so you believe in her.'[38]

George is attracted to Tess immediately and the two engage in a whirlwind courtship that sees him proposing within weeks of making her acquaintance. Even in the midst of these painful circumstances, Jane remains selfless and helps the two plan their wedding. This becomes an even more difficult task

Figure 11   Jane (Katherine Heigl), Tess (Malin Akerman) and George (Edward Burns) in *27 Dresses* (Fletcher, 2008).

once Jane realizes that Tess is performing the role of George's perfect woman. She pretends to love the outdoors, be a vegan, and love animals despite the fact that none of these things is true. Eventually, Tess's deceit becomes so unbearable to Jane that she 'outs' her sister for who she truly is, and not who she is portraying herself to be for George. The manner in which the film pits accessible Jane against a more perfect, but ultimately more superficial, Tess is illustrative of a recurrent paradox found in the postfeminist romance. The film seems to champion authenticity and that one should be true to oneself, and not pose or perform to find love. However, at the same time, the costume design and product placement that surrounds Jane and the wedding culture with which she is enamored enables the film to sell a heavily commercialized idea of romance.

Once Jane makes her first selfish decision by revealing her sister's true nature to George, Jane's selflessness problem is solved. She finally kisses George, now a single man again, and recognizes that there is no sexual spark, a realization that consequently frees herself from her chaste, childish crush. At the same time, she quits her job and is free to pursue a professional situation that is separate from her love life. And, she begins to understand that while she felt humiliated by the publication of her story in the newspaper, it ultimately functioned as a wakeup call for her. In perfect adherence to the resolution stage of the romance structure, she runs to find Kevin at a wedding that he is covering. She makes it on the boat just in time, and gets on the PA system to declare her love for him. The film ends with Jane's dream realized: she finally gets to plan her own wedding and make all of the brides for whom she was previously a bridesmaid wear the dress from their own wedding.

These case studies have demonstrated how *Kitty Foyle*, *An UnMarried Woman* and *27 Dresses* use both comedic and dramatic elements to frame their female protagonist's choices within the context of the romance narrative structure. In *27 Dresses*, postfeminist culture's most potent concerns become seamlessly integrated into the romance story. Even the film's seemingly benign thematic elements reveal cultural anxieties that exist just beneath the surface, revealing that the idea of choice for women outside the film can sometimes be in tension with the idea of choice within the film. But certainly one example cannot reveal the full landscape of the postfeminist romance cycle. We can only grasp its complexities by examining the subsequent case studies of films and recognizing their patterns and the tensions with which they engage.

NOTES

1. Clearly, Hollywood made romance films before 1934, but the year is regarded as a pivotal one for the genre for multiple reasons. This was the first year that the Production Code Administration began to regulate content in Hollywood thoroughly, thus affecting the representation of love and sexuality. This saw a turning

point in romantic comedy wherein Hollywood began to produce films that have been most influential on the romance structural and discursive model upon which later classical and contemporary texts rely. *It Happened One Night* (Capra, 1934) is one of the first films of this classic era. Lea Jacobs has written that because of the PCA's influence, 1934 also saw a dramatic shift in women's films in which the narratives are 'relatively more unified: they appear to proceed inevitably and "naturally" toward the final moment of closure.' Lea Jacobs, *The Wages of Sin: Censorship and the Fallen Woman Film: 1928–1942* (Madison: University of Wisconsin Press, 1991), p. 148.

2. Karen Weingarten has written about the novel's explicit racial discourses. In the novel, Kitty's father hires an African-American maid who is 'presented as a somewhat of a "Mammy" figure, one who is foremost classified by belonging to her race.' The novel also emphasizes Mark's Jewish heritage, which initially turns off Kitty. As Weingarten describes it, 'While Mark is educated and ambitious – a seemingly ideal suitor – Kitty feels repulsed by him, a reaction she attributes to his Jewishness.' These parts of the book are also conspicuously absent from the screenplay. Karen Weingarten, 'Bad girls and biopolitics: abortion, popular fiction, and population control', *Literature and Medicine*, 29: 1 (Spring 2011), 81–103.

3. Frederick C. Othman, 'Reporter finds Ginger Rogers upset by mirror, hair, rumor', *The Washington Post*, 31 October 1940.

4. Melrose Gower, 'Movie version of Kitty Foyle introduces new technique', *The Washington Post*, 29 September 1940.

5. Jacobs, *The Wages of Sin*, p. 149.

6. Mae Tinee, 'Ginger Rogers is at her best in "Kitty Foyle"', *Chicago Daily Tribune*, 1 January 1941.

7. Mary Harris, 'Ginger Rogers scores a hit as "Kitty Foyle" at RKO-Keith's', *The Washington Post*, 1 January 1941.

8. Articles written in anticipation of *Kitty Foyle*'s release by Hedda Hopper and Frederick Othman discuss Rogers's controversial decision to dye her hair brunette during the filming of *Lucky Partners* (Milestone, 1940) and express their, and the public's relief, that she changed it back to a lighter color for *Kitty*. Othman, 'Reporter finds Ginger Rogers upset', and Hedda Hopper, 'Hedda Hopper's Hollywood', *Los Angeles Times*, 11 September 1940.

9. Matthew Bernstein, '1940 – Movies and the reassessment of America', in Wheeler Winston Dixon (ed.), *American Cinema of the 1940s* (New Brunswick, NJ: Rutgers University Press, 2006), p. 31.

10. Jacobs mentions the prologue sequence parenthetically, referring to it as 'a putative historical prologue on the "white collar girl."' Jacobs, *The Wages of Sin*, p. 140.

11. Mary Ann Doane, *The Desire to Desire: The Woman's Film of the 1940s* (Bloomington: Indiana University Press, 1987), p. 105.

12. Bernstein, '1940 – Movies and the reassessment', p. 31.

13. Harris, 'Ginger Rogers scores a hit'.

14. Thomas Schatz, 'The new Hollywood', in Jim Collins, Hilary Radner and Ava Preacher Collins (eds), *Film Theory Goes to the Movies* (New York: Routledge, 1993), p. 14.

15. Brian Henderson, 'Romantic comedy today: semi-tough or impossible?', *Film Quarterly*, 31: 4 (1978), 11–23.

16. Steve Neale and Frank Krutnik, *Popular Film and Television Comedy* (London: Routledge, 1990), pp. 171–2.

17. Michael Ryan and Douglas Kellner, *Camera Politica: the Politics and Ideology of Contemporary Hollywood Film* (Bloomington: Indiana University Press, 1988), p. 144.

18. David Shumway, *Modern Love: Romance, Intimacy and the Marriage Crisis* (New York: New York University Press, 2003), pp. 167–8.
19. Janet Maslin, 'Critics notebook: new Mazursky', *The New York Times*, 13 March 1978.
20. Sally Quinn, 'An unmarried movie stars view from the top', *The Washington Post*, 9 April 1978.
21. Gene Siskel, 'An issue is overdone in "Woman"', *Chicago Tribune*, 17 March 1978.
22. Bruce McCabe, 'Jill Clayburgh steals Unmarried Woman', *Boston Globe*, 7 April 1978.
23. McCabe, 'Jill Clayburgh steals'.
24. Pauline Kael, 'Empathy and its limits', *The New Yorker*, 6 March 1978. http://archives.newyorker.com/?i=1978-03-06#folio=038.
25. Siskel, 'An issue is overdone'.
26. Victoria E. Thompson, '"UnMarried Woman": a feminine view', *Los Angeles Times*, 9 July 1978.
27. Robert Radnitz, 'In defense of "an Unmarried Woman"', *Los Angeles Times*, 23 July 1978.
28. Diane Negra, *What a Girl Wants: Fantasizing the Reclamation of Self in Postfeminism* (London: Routledge, 2009), p. 6.
29. Ibid. p. 61.
30. Danielle Crittenden, *What Our Mothers Didn't Tell Us: Why Happiness Eludes the Modern Woman* (New York: Touchstone Books, 1999), pp. 66–8.
31. Anthea Taylor, *Single Women in Popular Culture: the Limits of Postfeminism* (Basingstoke: Palgrave Macmillan, 2012), p. 22.
32. Ibid. p. 20.
33. See http://boxofficemojo.com/movies/?id=27dresses.htm.
34. Claudia Puig, 'Bridesmaid Heigl is a stitch in "27 Dresses"', *USA Today*, 18 January 2008.
35. See Amanda D. Lotz, 'Same story, different channel: returning home and starting over in protagonist-centered female dramas', in *Redesigning Women: Television after the Network Era* (Urbana: University of Illinois Press, 2006), pp. 118–43, and Diane Negra, 'Postfeminism, family values and the social fantasy of the hometown,' in *What a Girl Wants*, pp. 15–46.
36. There have been numerous postfeminist romance films that take weddings or wedding culture as their focus, including *Bride Wars* (Winick, 2009), *Something Borrowed* (Greenfield, 2011), *Bridesmaids* and *The Bachelorette* (Headland, 2012). Reality television has also seen a veritable explosion of programs that deal with weddings and wedding culture, including the Learning Channel's *Say Yes to the Dress* and *Four Weddings*, and virtually all of WE's (Women's Entertainment Network) programming – including, *Bridezillas, My Fair Wedding, Platinum Weddings, Girl Meets Gown,* and *Rich Bride, Poor Bride*. See Chrys Ingraham, *White Weddings: Romancing Heterosexuality in Popular Culture* (New York: Routledge, 2008).
37. Christy Lemire, '27 Dresses', *Philadelphia Inquirer*, 25 January 2008.
38. Wesley Morris, 'Wedding bell blues take a toll on "27 Dresses"', *Boston Globe*, 18 January 2008.

2. PRAGMATISM VS. SENTIMENTALITY: AMELIORATION IN THE POSTFEMINIST CYCLE

To get a snapshot of the function of film in the contemporary cultural conversation about women's relationships consider the following 2012 story featured on the feminist website Jezebel, entitled 'Meet the so-called nice guys of OK Cupid.'[1] The story discusses a Tumblr blog created by a disenchanted female user of the online dating site OK Cupid that superimposes innocuous quotes from men's dating profiles over their pictures, highlighting the juxtaposition of words and visuals.[2] Both the original Tumblr site, and the Jezebel story about it, suggest that men disingenuously describe themselves as 'nice guys' on their online dating profiles to play on a recurring trope in the romance genre wherein the nice but boring male friend character is overlooked by the female protagonist, only to be revealed be her best love match at the end of the film. In other words, the two sites contend that the OK Cupid men are adopting vocabulary and conjuring archetypal representations from oft-seen romantic films as a tool to persuade potential female love interests that they are the ideal mate.

A female reader with the screen name rokokobang responded to the Jezebel story in the following way:

> Maybe I'm crazy, but I feel like women are actually bombarded with the whole 'The nice nerdy quiet shy guy right in front of you – HE"S the one you should be with!!!' via movies and television. I know I always felt this way growing up, and it led me to stay in a super shitty relationship with a guy because he had me convinced he was the nice nerd, when in fact he treated me like shiiiiiit. But I had known him since we were little! We

were good friends! He wasn't the popular guy, he was a film geek! He MUST be the guy I'm supposed to be with!! Maybe I'm just way more susceptible to movies and TV than most people . . .

Other users responded to rokokobang's comments with words of commiseration:

This is spot on. I too was heavily influenced by romantic comedies. It took me a long time to realize: sometimes the nerd is the jerk and the hot jock is the sweet guy. – vivavariety

I think there's this premise out there that it should somehow be easier than you're finding it to find someone. He's around the corner! You just need to do X! Shave this! Stand here! No, stand like this! But, in reality, it should be a challenge to find compatibility on your terms, once you understand yourself and what you want/value, that is. Divorce rates are around 50%. I'd imagine that the remainder aren't all happy, healthy relationships. And the TV/movie formula does little to dispel the formulaic nonsense that is supposed to pass for finding compatibility. – Huxtablesweater

This story, and the response it received, reveals a great deal about the function of film in romance, and romance in film, and the degree to which this relationship has permeated how women talk and think about their own relationships. First, it shows the complex intermediality that makes up this landscape. A website – Jezebel – references a Tumblr page, which is critiquing an online dating site – OK Cupid – where members are implicitly referencing fictional media texts. Amidst this series of references, it becomes clear that the primary point of origination of this nice guy trope, and the complicated female response to it, is the romance film.

Over the last thirty years, women's identification of fictional romantic films and other media texts as the source of inspiration for or negotiation of their real-life relationship problems has become ubiquitous and free-flowing. Rokokobang and her fellow Jezebel commentators are a part of a continuum that includes fictional characters like *Romancing the Stone*'s Joan Wilder (Kathleen Turner), a romance novelist who gets to experience the type of romantic adventure about which she has previously only written in her books, and *27 Dresses*'s Tess's obsession with the weddings that she reads about in the Commitments section. They also have something in common with real writer Lori Gottlieb who, as I will discuss later in this chapter, blames romantic comedy films such as *Broadcast News* and *When Harry Met Sally* for her unrealistic expectations about men and relationships in her 2011 self-help book *Marry Him: The Case for Settling for Mr. Good Enough*. While serious film critics still largely denigrate romance films, the stigma once associated with admitting their influence on one's real perceptions of relationships has all but disappeared. Now this ambivalence about romance is integrated into the media, creating a perpetual loop of fiction feeding reality and reality feeding fiction. Film remains the most powerful and significant medium through which romance narratives can be found and its discourses circulated. However, to truly grasp the influence of the postfeminist romance cycle, one must also look beyond film and examine its broader cultural impact.

The transmedia discourse found in the texts that I will analyze in this chapter further illuminates both the pleasures and pitfalls that accompany the ameliorative function of the postfeminist romance. As the opening Jezebel example illustrates, this group of media texts present a binary in which women are overly immersed in fiction and fantasy, parlaying the pleasure gained from viewing (or reading) romance media as a salve or escape from real life burdens. Men, on the other hand, are presented either as opportunistically appropriating this therapeutic discourse to serve their own ends or offering a practical anecdote to women's idealism through their down-to-earth 'authentic' discourse. Thus, these case studies reveal not just how romance functions remedially in postfeminist film and media but also how deeply ensconced in gender binaries this discourse is. More than perhaps any other cluster of texts under examination in this book, the 'happily ever after' ending begins another cycle of texts in other media that negotiate or reflect back on the same concerns. In this way the postfeminist romance's cyclicality is not medium specific but truly a fluid process where real life and fiction collide.

Analyzing how the postfeminist romance seeps beyond film and into other media demonstrates Jason Mittell's argument that generic discourses can have a very broad reach. In *Genre and Television*, he contends, 'Since genres are formed through intertextual relationships between texts, then the discursive enunciations that link texts under a categorical rubric become the site and material for genre analysis.'[3] In the course of outlining a theoretical approach to television genres specifically, Mittell makes a broadly applicable point about genres more generally, particularly those that emerge in the contemporary transmedia era. That is, they should be understood not as closed, inflexible entities but as culturally operative. This broad perspective in tandem with our focus on both comedies and dramas enables a more thorough account of the relationship between film and other media texts' structures, their discursive patterns, and how they participate in wider conversations about women's relationship to romance.

Chick Lit Meets Jane Austen in *The Jane Austen Book Club*

Because romance's appeal falls somewhere in between reality and fantasy, the postfeminist cycle always endorses the notion that one should choose one's heart over one's head. Countless films within the cycle posit that love can make an otherwise sane individual engage in spontaneous and impulsive actions. It can also provoke a person to embark on an activity that is in opposition to his or her character. In other words, romantic coupling based in logic and forethought is vilified and that which is impulsive and defies convention is championed. For instance, films such as *Legends of the Fall*, *Four Weddings and a Funeral* (Newell, 1994), *The Bridges of Madison County* (Eastwood, 1995) and *The Horse Whisperer* (Redford, 1998), pose passionate love against safe, conventional and traditional love, which is seen as stifling and lacking in true passion. When there is a choice between these two options, the film consistently renders the practical choice as the wrong one. This trend also manifests itself in a protagonist choosing someone who he or she is shown initially to detest and who, logically, seems a wildly inappropriate match. This characteristic of the postfeminist cycle is on display most vividly in films that evoke what I call the 'idea of Jane' Austen. She is the figurehead and her novels the inspiration for our first group of texts, which use the cultural mythology surrounding Jane Austen and her novels to instantiate a therapeutic discourse in which 'female' ideas of sentimentality associated with the past are pitted against the 'male' practicality associated with the present.

The phenomenally popular category of literary fiction known as 'chick lit' is a good place to begin our discussion of the therapeutic discourse of the 'idea of Jane' because, besides film, it is the most significant media form through which Austen-philia takes form during the postfeminist period. The following passage from Hester Brown's 2008 chick-lit novel, *The Little Lady Agency in the Big Apple*, is representative of how this literary category creates a pleasurable effect by blurring the boundaries between fact and fiction, using Jane Austen as inspiration:

> Gabi is a great girl . . . but God in Heaven, she was driving me insane . . . I don't know whether it was some sort of phase she was going through, but honestly she wanted me to be this Mr. Darcy figure and boss her around and tell her what to do . . . it was *unnatural* . . .[4]

The Mr. Darcy reference here is, to some degree, a throwaway line. It is assumed that the reader knows that he is the male protagonist of Jane Austen's *Pride and Prejudice*, and understands the reference to what type of character he is: bossy, insolent, and uncommunicative. The passage is amusing and knowing and serves an important function: it links the reader of *The Little Lady in the Big Apple* to a broader conversation about women's relationship to fiction, and the effect that this has on modern social relationships. First, it points to how the female character about whom the line is spoken – Gabi – is fixated on a type of man that resembles a fictional character from a 200-year-old novel. Second, Gabi's preoccupation with this fictional 'Mark Darcy figure' is deemed 'unnatural' by her ex-boyfriend who is speaking the line. The passage seems designed to call attention to the very practice of literary fandom that the book intends to elicit from its reader.

'Chick lit' novels like *The Little Lady Agency in the Big Apple* are unquestionably influential on the postfeminist romance film cycle more generally because they do not just invite this collapse between fiction and reality but are self-conscious about the degree to which this boundary has been blurred. To be able to work in a reference to a piece of English literature in a mass-market trade book points to the fluidity and permeability of any previously intact boundaries between high art and low art, real people and fictional characters, and past and present modes of courtship and amorous behavior.

That female-focused, female-oriented fiction is pleasurable and offers an escape from the everyday pressures of one's life is not new. It has been integral to studies of the Harlequin and Mills and Boon romance series, which have been in publication since 1949 and 1908, respectively. Scholars have identified many differences between these older romance books and chick lit, the most significant of which is the characterization of the female protagonist. Whereas the classic Harlequin romance novel 'glorifies the distance between the sexes' and sees 'the heroine's sexual inexperience' contributing to 'this excitement'[5] Suzanne Ferriss and Mallory Young see the chick-lit genre as defined by its sense of 'realism,' appealing to contemporary sensibility that 'jettisons the heterosexual hero' often seen in these earlier series, 'to offer a more realistic portrait of single life, dating and the dissolution of romantic ideals.'[6] The chick-lit protagonist is usually experienced in ways that these earlier fictional romance heroines were not and 'flawed, eliciting readers' compassion and identification simultaneously.'[7] As we might recall from our case study of *27 Dresses*, this level of identification is essential to the postfeminist romance narrative's efficacy.

Chick lit's formula of appealing to women on this 'realistic' level has proven to be wildly successful. Since hitting the mainstream in the late 1990s, the genre has seen a tremendous popular response. Ferriss and Young report that in 2002 chick-lit books earned publishers more than $71 million in book sales.[8] This success sparked numerous sales of books as film properties including the two *Bridget Jones* films, Laura Zigman's *Animal Husbandry* (made into the 2001 Tony Goldwyn film, *Someone Like You*), Jennifer Weiner's *In Her Shoes* (adapted in 2005), Lauren Weisberger's *The Devil Wears Prada* (adapted in 2006), Karen Joy Fowler's *The Jane Austen Book Club* and Emma McLaughlin and Nicola Kraus's *The Nanny Diaries* (both adapted in 2007), *Something Borrowed* (adapted in 2011), and *I Don't Know How She Does It* (adapted in 2011) among many others.[9]

Chick-lit novels, like films in the postfeminist cycle, are appealing because of their basis in a realistic depiction of a humorously flawed female character with concerns that are specific to the postfeminist period, but here these concerns are deeply intertwined with fictional texts from a past historical period with vastly different romantic norms. *The Little Lady Agency in the Big Apple* may make a passing reference to Mr. Darcy but the extremely popular *Bridget Jones's Diary* series of books offers a loose appropriation of the entire plot line of *Pride and Prejudice* – most notably the use of the Mr. Darcy character (played by the same actor – Colin Firth in both the wildly popular BBC adaptation and the *Bridget Jones* films). Stephanie Harzewski has argued that, '*Bridget Jones's Diary* additionally serves as a historical marker and index into the Austen-philia and Darcymania of the last decade, a cottage industry encompassing a staggering number of fictional offshoots of Austen-inspired stationary and board games.'[10] With the chick-lit genre emerging at the same time as Hollywood's first adaptations of Austen novels in fifty years (the only classical Hollywood film adaptation of Austen's work was the 1940 version of *Pride and Prejudice* starring Laurence Olivier and Greer Garson), including the films *Sense and Sensibility* (Lee, 1995), *Mansfield Park* (Rozema, 1995), *Emma* (McGrath, 1996), and *Pride and Prejudice* (Wright, 2005), it is clear that Jane Austen, and other 'romance of manners' authors serve an important function in the working through of postfeminist cultural anxieties.

Adaptations, remakes and revisionist texts like these Austen films predominate in the postfeminist romance cycle, including films based on the novels of Emily Brontë, E. M. Forster, Henry James, and Edith Wharton. Led by the critically acclaimed films of producer Ishmail Merchant and director James Ivory, including *A Room with a View* (Ivory, 1985), *Howards End* (Ivory, 1992), and *The Remains of the Day* (Ivory, 1993), these 'romance of manners' films depict romances that are, in some way, inhibited by the social and historical circumstances of the, mostly British, characters. (It is revealing in this regard that one of the team's lesser-known early films, made in 1980, is called *Jane Austen in Manhattan*.) Jim Collins has discussed this wave of adaptations as a signal of changing audience tastes and the rise of a popular literary culture in the 1980s:

> Just as the bestseller status of Tolstoy and Faulkner novels may be attributed to the ways in which they have been redefined by Oprah Winfrey's Book Club, the cinematic versions of Austen and James novels represent a comparable reframing that changes the picture quite drastically – they *are* different novels, and not just because they have been transformed into images. They are different experiences now that they've been given value and function within a particular taste culture.[11]

Collins offers the framework of a growing 'taste culture' to provide an explanation for the rise in popularity of the aforementioned films and the successful

BBC television Austen adaptations of the 1990s. These 'romance of manners' texts are no doubt appealing because, while restrictive, the courtship rituals of a vastly different historical period seem somehow charmingly preordained.

The degree of insight that these classic texts are capable of providing for women is also made evident in the frequency with which their structures are appropriated in romance texts set in the contemporary period, including *Bridget Jones's Diary*, *Clueless* (Heckerling, 1995) and *Bride and Prejudice* (Chadha, 2004), and the British television series *Lost in Austen* (2008; also currently being adapted into a film). In addition, there is an entire subgenre of chick-lit books that explicitly refer to Austen in their titles, including Laurie Viera Rigler's *Confessions of a Jane Austen Addict* (2008) and Shannon Hale's *Austenland* (2008), Laurie Brown's *What Would Jane Austen Do?* (2009) and Beth Pattillo's *Jane Austen Ruined My Life* (2009) and *Mr. Darcy Broke My Heart* (2010), among many others. Jane even creeps into a 2010 YouTube mashup video called *Jane Austen's Fight Club*, in which the mise-en-scène and female characters typical of an Austen film adaptation meet the plotline of David Fincher's *Fight Club* (1999).

The pervasiveness of the 'idea of Jane' demonstrates how the ideas and plot structures of these classic novels can be just as easily appropriated when telling a contemporary love story, which is seen as a testament to the timelessness of romantic love and how it transpires. In the midst of this upsurge in Austen's popularity, a 1995 *People* magazine article asked:

> If Jane Austen were alive today, would she provide husband-hunting tips on *Good Morning America*? Perform a 'Stupid Human Trick' for Letterman? Or remain discreetly at home, surrounded by a small gossipy circle, sipping – as her heroines sometimes do – a soothing glass of Madeira wine? Dearest Jane, make it a double. Austen, a literary favorite for almost 200 years, got Hollywood-hot in 1995, racking up enough screen adaptations to rival John Grisham.[12]

The circulation of popular discursive ideas about Jane Austen and the period during which she wrote reveals less about her historical moment than it does about ours. As many articles on the Austen film adaptations have asked, why do we crave Jane now? The *People* article suggests that it is because Austen's heroines 'take the world by storm . . . because of their intelligence,' thus appealing to the autonomous bent of contemporary female spectators.[13] Sue Parrill argues that the Austen adaptations are engaging because they remind women that they have gained more choices in how they pursue romantic relationships. However, she adds that they may have the opposite effect, reminding women that they live in a world in which traditional courtship is a vestige of the past.[14]

In *What Our Mothers Didn't Tell Us* Danielle Crittenden supports Parrill's latter point and argues that Jane Austen has something to teach us about the current state of male-female relationships in the United States. She suggests that women would be better off if we were to return to 'standards of behavior' lost during the sexual revolution.[15] Crittenden cites a friend's response to the 1995 adaptation of *Emma* to support her case. After screening the film, her friend lamented, 'There are no Mr. Knightleys!' thereby suggesting that contemporary men do not live up to the same standards as Austen's heroes. Crittenden replies, there are 'no more Emma Woodhouses either,' implying that women are equally as responsible for the disintegration of traditional rules of courtship as men.[16] Only if all women refrain from giving away their sexuality freely will men change their behavior. Crittenden's idealized view of Austen's characters is held in stark contrast to what she refers to as prime time's '*unglamorous* [her italics] single, thirtyish female characters neurotically brooding about their thwarted love lives.' She continues, 'To the lonely urban women, the times before the sexual revolution suddenly do not look so bad.'[17]

This comparison sees Crittenden look not just to the past, but the fictional past, as a barometer for appropriate female behavior in the present. Jane Austen's iconic characters are complicated but honorable, whereas contemporary fictional characters are uncomplicated, unglamorous and neurotic. Women's historical advances are hindering, rather than helping, their pursuit of the kind of romance about which Jane Austen wrote. Certainly, Jane Austen and the bygone relationship practices she depicts have the potential to provide pleasurable entertainment, particularly with what Collins calls the adaptations' 'excessive mise-en-scene' including lush settings, meticulous costume design, and large casts studded with highly regarded British actors. However, the regularity with which these texts about the past are appropriated to illustrate something about the present is curious.

Clearly, for Crittenden the 'idea of Jane' has less to do with the meaning of Austen's texts within their own historical context and more to do with how she perceives the texts will serve her ideological argument. However, her appropriation of the 'idea of Jane' in this manner is quite commonplace. The invocation of Austen's 'brand' in the contemporary period is rarely situated in detailed knowledge about her books, her life, or the historical context in which she wrote. And, surprisingly, with the exception of *Becoming Jane* (Jarrold, 2007), Austen's unmarried status generally goes unmentioned.

Instead, her books' stories, character types, and the social mores and historical periodization that they detail are condensed into a basic mythology. This mythology then gets recycled and romanticized, as a means through which to wade through the differences between women's social and economic power then and now. The contemporary world is deemed overly complicated, whereas everything associated with Jane Austen's world is presented as refreshingly simple. The fictional past is consistently deemed preferable over the real present. This is a recurring conceit in the postfeminist romance, and a type of viewing position that, like *Sleepless in Seattle*, other women get, and men do not understand. As the narrator in *The Jane Austen Book Club* puts it, 'each of us has a private Austen.' Clearly cultural discourses reinforce this idea. A 2010 *Wall Street Journal* article, 'Jane Austen 2.0', goes as far as to say that 'Ms. Austen's tales of courtship and manners' even 'resonate with dating-obsessed and social-media-savvy 21st-century youths.'[18]

The proposition that Jane Austen is a therapeutic agent for a contemporary culture gone astray is at the heart of *The Jane Austen Book Club*, first published as a book in 2004, and adapted into a film in 2007. The story is loosely based on the plots of all of Austen's books but also imbued with the idea of Jane Austen as a sort of corrective or panacea for its female characters' problems. As the character of Bernadette (Kathy Baker) states, the film positions Austen as 'the perfect anecdote to life.' *The Jane Austen Book Club* introduces dual layers of engagement – it satisfies women's desire to consume romance fiction both within and outside of the text, as well as satisfying the desire to be a part of community of women – and in the case of this text, one man – who are doing the same. Thus, contemporary viewers can establish a 'relationship' with the chick-lit novel text of *The Jane Austen Book Club*, the film text, and then by extension the Austen books read within both texts. In other words, there are several layers of fiction being used to convey ideas about the nature of real women's lives. The film's visual design, and particularly its opening sequence, suggests that these problems are brought on by the increasingly mechanized nature of society, and its narrative implies that this mechanization has also wreaked havoc on romantic relationships. The 'idea of Jane' then serves as a form of individual and group therapy, and the sentimentality it evokes tempers the overly practical and mechanistic attitudes that have proved detrimental to women's happiness.

The film's opening succinctly presents the qualities of contemporary life that might drive one to escape into this far-removed fictional world. It opens on a black screen with the Austen quote, 'Is not general incivility the very essence of love?' and then transitions into a complex soundscape (featuring the overlapping sounds of people talking, a radio DJ, cell phones ringing, a jackhammer, general traffic noise) and quickly edited establishing shots that show just how uncivil, if not oppressively mechanized, contemporary life has become. This montage sequence, accompanied by the non-diegetic song 'New Shoes' by Paolo Nutini (in which the singer also speaks of 'something missing in my day to day life' that needs fixing), introduce the protagonists in and around a world that is not only dominated by technology, but increasingly dysfunctional technology – street signs, cars, cell phones, laptops, treadmills, stores' antitheft alarms, an airport luggage carousel, a copy machine, leaf blowers, elevators, and ATM machines. All are seen to disrupt the routine of everyday life and inhibit interpersonal interaction.

The only character immune to this mishmash of technological overload is Bernadette (Kathy Baker), who is first seen in a long shot participating in a yoga class and does not mind it when she accidentally bumps into the man standing next to her. This opening credit sequence is instrumental in establishing the film's point of view that interpersonal relationships are crucial for its female characters' happiness. Here Bernadette's association with the playful and tactile proximity to other individuals in her yoga class is contrasted with the frustration and affective distance that is elicited by the machines that dominate the other scenes. Bernadette, who embraces her 'inner Jane' and initiates the book club, seems to possess some sort of timeless wisdom, and she transcends the physical distance that technology perpetuates; a virtue that the other characters initially lack.

The premise of the titular book club is that each of its six members is responsible for one Austen book, and each character's narrative arc resembles the plotlines of that novel. The film is broken up into chapter-like sections that are demarcated by graphics that cue the viewer into what month it is, and which book the club is reading, along with a short montage sequence that shows the characters absorbed in said book. Bernadette initially starts the club as a way to distract Jocelyn (Maria Bello) after the death of her beloved dog, whose funeral is the centerpiece of the scene subsequent to the credits. Jocelyn's insistence on the ritual is honored by some and mocked by others, and this contrasting response establishes the tone for the film's vying discourses of rational versus the sentimental, and the present versus the past.

Figure 12   Sylvia (Amy Brenneman) in *The Jane Austen Book Club* (Swicord, 2007).

In this early sequence, Sylvia's (Amy Brenneman) husband Daniel (Jimmy Smits) is clearly positioned on the side of the rational present, as he mocks Joceyln's attachment to her dogs (despite the fact that she is a dog breeder), and sees it as a symptom of her sad single life. He argues that Jocelyn has misplaced affection that would be better channeled into a conventional form of love for a human, rather than animal, family. Daniel's sentiments establish Jocelyn's romantic status as a problem that the film must solve. His narrow attitude about love's many permutations is met with playful disdain by Sylvia and profound disgust by his gay daughter, Allegra (Maggie Grace), who reminds him that women can indeed find happiness outside of the boundaries of traditional heteronormative contexts.

The next few scenes establish reasons why characters other than Jocelyn come to need the book club. Sylvia and Prudie (Emily Blunt) are both in the midst of marriage problems. Daniel reveals to Sylvia soon after the funeral that he is having an affair and plans to leave her for another woman. Prudie's husband Dean (Marc Blucas) is uncommunicative, chooses a business trip to a basketball game over a trip to Paris with Prudie, and believes that 'Austen is the capital of Texas.' Favoring one's libido (in the case of Daniel) or work (in the case of Dean) over romance and fidelity are deemed an affront to the Austen code of conduct (recalling Crittenden's friend's lament over the lack of modern-day Mr. Knightleys). In *The Jane Austen Book Club*, Austen's novels function as a how-to manual of sorts for the characters. They also provide a vocabulary that bonds them together in a collective effort to escape all that is wrong with the day-to-day grind, and escape into a simpler world where the romantic order was more transparent and circumscribed. The film initially renders this language as the domain of female heterosexual women, but this changes, and is challenged to a degree, as the narrative progresses.

The two outsiders – Allegra and Grigg (Hugh Dancy) – are deemed such because they are outside of the heterosexual female demographic. They are also, not coincidentally, less familiar with the author's work than other members, and consequently do not exhibit the requisite reverence for Austen. Grigg is a heterosexual man who joins the club to get closer to, and try to win the affections of, the seemingly disinterested Jocelyn. Austen is new to him, as is the broader literary genre into which her books fall. Allegra goes through the same romantic trials and tribulations as her heterosexual counterparts. Where she is most disruptive is in her active disregard for her fellow group members' unflinching admiration of the Austen texts. In particular, her queer reading of *Pride and Prejudice* elicits a lot of eye-rolling. She has the gall to offer an alternative interpretation of a dialogue scene between Charlotte and Lizzy in which Charlotte states that she is not as romantic as Lizzy. Allegra suggests that the word romantic here might be code for heterosexual, and that what Charlotte is saying is that she's not straight like Lizzy. This interjection is not taken much further after the women dismiss such an unorthodox reading. However, perhaps accidentally, the film seems to highlight the degree to which the discourse of romance that circulates around Austen is code for a specific brand of female heterosexual desire.

Grigg's difference is marked by his gender but also by his love of the traditionally male-dominated literary genre of science fiction. Like Allegra, he struggles with the language of Jane that is so familiar to most of the club members. At one point, he attempts to diffuse the tension caused by Sylvia's emotional eruption by equating the plotline of *Mansfield Park* to *The Empire Strikes Back* (Kershner, 1980) and *Return of the Jedi* (Marquand, 1983), much to the confusion of the women. (This is reminiscent of the *Sleepless in Seattle* scene in which Sam (Tom Hanks) and Greg (Victor Garber) use guy-genre-speak to talk about *The Dirty Dozen* (Aldrich, 1967).) However, once Grigg learns Austen-speak, he is able to woo Jocelyn, who also does some compromising by capitulating to reading his science-fiction books. And, of course, once Daniel and Dean familiarize themselves with Austen, they too find happiness and are able to reconcile with their wives.

While *The Jane Austen Book Club* may adopt a more circuitous route to get to its point, it calls to mind Crittenden's earlier argument about what Jane Austen can teach us about contemporary gender relations. Should we assume that *The Jane Austen Book Club* shares Crittenden's stance on women's devolving grasp of the social mores advanced in Austen's oeuvre? That is unclear. But what is a more interesting observation for the study at hand is the fact that in both contexts, fiction is the great mediator between the harsh reality of the present and idealized ideas of the past. When fiction is as central to Crittenden's critical political writing as it is to the reader characters in *The Jane Austen Book Club*, to the readers of *The Jane Austen Book Club*, and to the viewers of the film adaptation, then 'all Jane Austen all the time' takes on a decidedly complex function.

SELF-HELP MEETS *SEX AND THE CITY* IN *HE'S JUST NOT THAT INTO YOU*

The 'idea of Jane' as circulated in chick-lit novels, and their direct or loose film adaptations, posit Jane Austen as a remedy for those disenchanted with a contemporary way of life. The self-help genre, which offers an explicitly therapeutic discourse, has also become increasingly popular during the postfeminist period and served as inspiration for the postfeminist romance cycle. A 2006 Marketdata Enterprises study estimated that $693 million was spent on self-help books in 2005, which indicated a growth of 8.3 percent per year over ten years: significantly higher than the growth of book sales in the industry overall.[19] The past fifteen years have seen several self-help books transcend the confines of the genre and assume a prominent place in the cultural discourse in and around romance. Three of the most culturally influential books in this regard have been Ellen Fein and Sherrie Schneider's *The Rules: Time Tested Secrets for Capturing the Heart of Mr. Right* (1995), Greg Behrendt and Liz Tuccillo's *He's Just Not That Into You: The No-Excuses Truth to Understanding Guys* (2004), and Lori Gottlieb's *Marry Him: The Case for Settling for Mr. Good Enough* (2010). They all target the increasing number of women who wait until later in life to marry, offering advice on how to date and pursue relationships without compromising their self-esteem or personal growth.

The stated intention of all three books is to empower their female reader to take control of her life. And thus, like many postfeminist romance texts, the foundation upon which they rely is that she is doing something wrong in her search for a lasting romantic relationship. As Anthea Taylor has argued in her exhaustive analysis of the self-help genre, 'a number of these manuals reveal how postfeminism works to shape the public stories in circulation around women's singleness, stories which help delimit how it is possible to *be* (or in some cases, *not* to be) a single woman in the contemporary West.'[20] The books suggest either implicitly or explicitly that women are either too resistant to, or too active in their embrace of, traditional courtship models. This inescapable either/or dynamic has led them to a series of unsatisfying relationships. As we will see, all of the books rely on romance's well-worn discursive refrains and regularly cite classic and contemporary romance media for evidence to support their advice. Just as they create an intertextual and transmedia discourse by borrowing from other media texts, they also contribute to this discourse by being the subject of popular blogs and by their authors' appearances on female-skewing popular television shows such as *Oprah* and *The Today Show*.

Aside from John Gray's *Men Are From Mars, Women Are From Venus*, Ellen Fein and Sherrie Schneider's *The Rules* is arguably the most culturally significant self-help book of the last thirty years. It does not borrow as explicitly from fiction as the other two books in this section but its authors' philosophy of courtship gives the impression of having been gleaned from 1960s Doris Day sex comedy films. The premise of *The Rules* is that feminism did women a disservice by convincing them that personal satisfaction can be found outside of a long-term romantic relationship or marriage. According to Fein and Schneider, women's focus on their careers has caused their personal lives distress because they mistakenly use their business savvy rather than their innate femininity when pursuing romantic relationships. The authors recommend that women take their professional acumen and put it to good use. Specifically, they should assume a retrograde position in courtship rituals by being elusive and playing hard to get. In other words, women should be aggressively passive. As the book contends, 'Women who call men, ask them out, conveniently have two tickets to a show, or offer sex on the first date destroy male ambition and animal drive. Men are born to respond to challenge. Take away challenge and their interest wanes.'[21] The introduction sums up how the authors manage to effectively combine the discourses of regressive and progressive views of women into their hodgepodge kernels of wisdom:

> Modern women aren't to talk loudly about wanting to get married. We had grown up dreaming about being the president of the company, not the wife of the president. So, we quietly passed *The Rules* on from friend to friend, somewhat embarrassed because they seemed so, well, '50s. Still we had to face it: as much as we loved being powerful in business, for most of us, that just wasn't enough . . . We didn't want to give up our liberation, but neither did we want to come home to empty apartments . . . We needed *The Rules*![22]

The authors' ambivalence about 1950s cultural mentality that is the foundation of *The Rules* echoes the tension between past and present seen in *The Jane Austen Book Club*. Fein and Schneider argue that women's approach to courtship in the prefeminist era was extremely effective. However, the authors simultaneously acknowledge the importance of progressive feminist liberation, which, in their view, is best exercised by choosing to adopt this prefeminist position. As Anthea Taylor has argued, this approach fits with the ways in which 'self-help writing has appropriated feminist discourses in ways that are consonant with the broader cultural logics of postfeminism.'[23] Achieving the sentiment of love through an unsentimental business-like strategy inspires the thirty-five rules that make up the book. Some of these include: 'Rule #4: Don't Meet Him Halfway or Go Dutch on a Date,' 'Rule #5: Don't Call Him and Rarely Return His Calls,' 'Rule #7: Don't Accept a Saturday Night Date after Wednesday,' 'Rule #27: Do *The Rules*, Even when Your Friends and Parents Think It's Nuts,' and 'Rule #31: Don't Discuss *The Rules* with Your Therapist.' As rules 27 and 31 reveal, following *The Rules* not only involves ignoring your own intuition about the validity of the book's husband-nabbing strategies, but it also encourages its reader to ignore the voices of her closest confidants.

Fein and Schneider's philosophy has grown from a single book to an empire. They have published multiple follow-up titles, including one on finding love on the Internet, and another on how to make your marriage work, *Rules* style. According to their website, they also run a consulting business, charging $150 to answer a 'quick' e-mail question, and phone consultations ranging from $150–$350. Thus, they not only disseminate love advice through books, they transcend the author-reader divide by making themselves quite literally accessible to everyday women who want to get customized feedback for their specific dilemmas.[24]

As a single mother by choice, self-help author Lori Gottlieb comes at romance from a somewhat different vantage point than Fein and Schneider. But her book, *Marry Him: the Case for Settling for Mr. Good Enough* published in 2010, and adapted from a 2008 *Atlantic Monthly* article of the same name, makes the same fundamental argument as the earlier book. That is, women in their thirties and forties are single because they have been too sentimental in their pursuit of love. Gottlieb's premise is that women are their own worst enemies because they reject men with minor flaws in the hopes of finding Mr. Perfect. Her thesis is made quite explicit in the title of her third chapter: 'How Feminism Fucked Up My Love Life.' Gottlieb's language bears a striking resemblance to that used by Fein and Schneider,

> The truth was, every one of my single friends wanted to be married, but none of us would admit how badly we craved it for fear of sounding weak or needy or, God forbid, antifeminist . . . We didn't want yet another Sunday brunch with the girls. We wanted a lifetime with The Guy.[25]

As Gottlieb goes on to argue, it is not just feminism but fictional romance texts that are to blame for this problem. This craving for 'The Guy' that she deems antifeminist stems from her habitual spectatorship of films and television shows.

In another succinctly named chapter, 'The Romantic Comedy That Predicted My Future,' Gottlieb describes how her adult life choices came to mirror the trajectory of Jane, the fictional protagonist (played by Holly Hunter) in *Broadcast News*. The film's conclusion sees Jane reject relationships with both of her potential love interests: her best friend Aaron (Albert Brooks), who is in love with her, and Tom (William Hurt), a handsome yet superficial news anchor to whom she is attracted but finds to be vacuous. Gottlieb interprets Jane's single, childless status in the film's epilogue (that sees the three characters reunite after seven years) to be the result of Jane's misguided choice to wait for Mr. Right, as opposed to choosing a relationship with one of these two perfectly decent men.

Gottlieb holds firm in her opinion about Jane despite the fact that in this concluding scene, Jane informs Aaron and Tom that she is in a promising new relationship. Gottlieb argues, 'What are the odds that this relationship will work out, given that she's probably been in several relationships in the past seven years that seemed promising but didn't pan out?'[26] Gottlieb thus reads Jane's decision to reject both of her potential suitors and wait for a better, more suitable match as a bad choice. And, she even goes as far as to dismiss the relationship in which Jane finds herself at the end of the film as having no potential to be that suitable match.

These observations reveal as much about Gottlieb's larger argument as they do about her engagement with the structure of the postfeminist romance. Rather than support her argument that Jane is too choosy, her response to *Broadcast News* seems to reflect her disappointment with the film's ambiguous conclusion, where we are not assured of Jane's happy ending. Rather than read this subtly played last sequence as a sign that Jane may have indeed finally found a great match, Gottlieb sees it as evidence of Jane's failure and a cautionary tale for her readers.

Later in the chapter, Gottlieb outlines the lessons she should have learned from *When Harry Met Sally*. She writes that she was in her twenties, she interpreted Sally and Harry's coupling as a sign that Sally had lowered her standards. However, when speaking from the vantage point of her older self, she recognizes that she should have been searching for the practical guys like Harry all along. Gottlieb's method of reading the fictional romance beyond its textual boundaries does not stop at film but also includes television. She claims the female protagonists of shows like *Ally McBeal* (1997–2002), *Caroline in the City* (1995–9), *Sex and the City*, and *Grey's Anatomy* (2005–) convinced women like her that it was okay to date a series of guys and talk to your friends about them because there was always the assumption that 'she'd [the female protagonist] end up with her true love at the end.'[27] While providing hours of enjoyable entertainment, Gottlieb surmises that these fictional shows taught her destructive and overly sentimental relationship behavior. Specifically, that all of the men – who appeared at the time to be not quite right – may have been just fine if she had not been holding out for somebody better.

Gottlieb's book might be easily dismissed as silly and too wrapped up in fictional pretense to be taken seriously (although the publication of her work in the respected *The Atlantic* might counterbalance this claim). Nonetheless, it is remarkable how effectively she codifies the anecdotal cultural discourse that surrounds both feminism (feminism is anti-romance) and media romance (fantasy scenarios gleaned from romance film and television are filling women with overblown ideas about love). Indeed, the cultural currency of Gottlieb's perspective was immediately evident when *Marry Him* became countless media outlets' *subject du jour*. On NBC's *The Today Show*, Meredith Vieira claimed that Gottlieb's theory had 'caused quite a stir.' The 'stir' to which she refers was presumably the response the book received from mainstream journalists and bloggers. For example, pandagon. net's feminist political blogger Amanda Marcotte slammed Gottlieb's argument, suggesting that she encourages women 'to see ourselves as items on sale, and to assess the bids we're getting on our "price" realistically, instead of thinking our asses are so expensive.'[28] On the other side of the spectrum, salon.com's review of the book claims, 'At its best, "Marry Him" is a sensible, old-fashioned plea to look past the superficial, to discard the toxic fantasy of romantic comedies and think realistically about what makes a solid partnership.'[29]

By positioning the reverie of romantic comedies in opposition to the practical reality of settling for someone who is just good enough, Gottlieb is perpetuating and benefitting from the very discourse that she critiques in the book. If she preaches the gospel of practicality, there is a higher likelihood that women will seek out fiction, which promises something better. On the flipside, without the unrealistic expectations that fictional film and television texts promote, few would buy Gottlieb's book and it would not have achieved best-seller status. In other words, she is supporting the dialectic at the heart of this chapter, which is to keep the therapeutic flow of discourses between fiction and reality flowing seamlessly.

The cultural discourse in and around an earlier, different strain of self-help book, *He's Just Not That Into You*, has an even more explicitly established continuum with fiction. The book was written by Greg Behrendt and Liz Tuccillo, two *Sex and the City* contributors – the latter, a writer, the former, a consultant – and inspired by an episode from the show's sixth season. The episode features a scene in which Miranda regales Carrie and her boyfriend Jack about a date she went on the evening before. She tells them that she thought it went well and was therefore surprised when her date refused an invitation back to her apartment. When Miranda asks Jack for the male perspective on things, he tells her that it was obvious that the guy 'just wasn't that into you.' While Carrie is mortified at Jack's blunt assessment of Miranda's dilemma, Miranda is relieved, claiming that if she had been aware of how simple male behavior actually is, she could have avoided years of therapy. She takes the dose of reality in her stride and begins to apply it, albeit misguidedly, to a date later in the episode.

Behrendt and Tuccillo clearly anticipated that other women share Miranda's misguided ideas and wrote *He's Just Not That Into You* to help clarify male behavior. Consequently, the book's content is built around scenarios that all have one thing in common – if they are happening, the man in question is just not into you. For instance, 'He's Just Not That Into You if He's Not Asking You Out,' 'He's Just Not That Into You if He's Not Having Sex with You,' 'He's Just Not That Into You if He Doesn't Want to Marry You.' The repetition of the book's title therefore functions as a sort of mantra, working as a reality check against whatever fantasy-based scenarios play out in women's heads. The theme that underlies the book is that women are so eager to find a man who is relationship-worthy that they willingly overlook his negative traits and stay with him much longer than they should. As Tuccillo sums up in her introduction:

Just like on any other day, one of the women on staff asked for feedback on the behavior of a man whom she liked. He was giving her mixed messages – she was confused . . . on this day, we had a male consultant in the room . . . Greg listened intently to the story and our reactions, and then said to the woman in question, 'Listen, it sounds like he's just not that into you.' We were shocked, appalled, amused, horrified, and above all, intrigued. We sensed immediately that this man might be speaking the truth . . . All these years I'd been complaining about men and their mixed messages; now I saw they weren't mixed messages at all. I was the one that was mixed up.[30]

As Tuccillo makes clear, the book's premise results from a real, typical session of girl talk amongst *Sex and the City*'s female writers that would be familiar to many women readers. And thus, its readers are placed in the same category as the real women writers: a group who needs help figuring out how to value themselves and quit pursuing men that are not worth their time. In other words, the book's conceit is that women's romantic, idealistic approach is in need of a remedy by way of a rational male perspective. Indeed, Behrendt's voice dominates the book, with Tuccillo merely offering a short side note at the end of each chapter. This formula did not stop it from being a runaway best-seller.

In a fascinating twist, the film adaptation of *He's Just Not That Into You* and its related promotional materials deviate from this rational perspective, reinforcing and further perpetuating the sentimental, fantasy-based ideas that the book was designed to debunk. It is exactly the kind of loop of fiction leading to reality and reality leading to fiction that we have seen in our previous examples. Presumably, the screenwriters and producers determined that it was too challenging to follow the book's reality-check model while maintaining an upbeat tone. Thus, the film is a strange hybrid that sees the structural and discursive model of the postfeminist romance infused with the book's insights about idiosyncratic male behavior.

In the vein of the ensemble films, *Love Actually* (Curtis, 2003), *Valentine's Day* (Marshall, 2010), and *New Year's Eve* (Marshall, 2011), *He's Just Not That Into You* features the intertwined stories of a large, star-studded cast of characters whose narratives resemble the 'he's just not that into you if . . .' chapters. These different plot lines are intercut with 'person on the street' interviews that feature everyday people disseminating wisdom or regaling an invisible interviewer with tales of woe about relationships gone wrong. These sequences imply that love's trials and tribulations, particularly those that stem from men's less than admirable behavior, are a widespread phenomenon to which everyone can relate. The film begins its exploration of these common concerns by turning to a scene from childhood for insight. The scene depicts a typical park interaction between a young girl and boy wherein the boy tells the girl that she 'smells like dog poo.' The scene cuts to the little girl crying to her mother, with the mother responding in a manner that, as Gigi's (Ginnifer Goodwin) voiceover tells us, will 'program' her young daughter. The mother consoles her daughter by telling her that the boy is saying and doing those things 'because he likes you.' As the voiceover goes on to say, this leads to 'us' (the presumed female audience) being encouraged to think that 'if a guy acts like a total jerk, that means he likes you.'

The film then transitions into a montage consisting of seven scenes featuring groups of women from various ethnic and social backgrounds, including Japanese women shopping, African tribal women sitting in front of huts, army cadets, and sorority sisters, all reassuring each other that there must be some excuse for why a man is treating her friend badly. 'He likes you too much. You are too pretty and too awesome. He can't handle it.' In other words, in this opening sequence, the film strives to make viewers feel connected not simply to the trials and tribulations of the film's cast, but to the broad range of everyday women (and some men), who have been misguided enough to believe that a guy or girl was into us, when he or she was not. In this way, like a good self-help book, the film uses specific 'case studies' to make broader, more global, generalizations about how the reader or viewer can solve a common problem.

One of the most transparently contradictory case study plot lines involves the 'He's not that into you if he's not marrying you' storyline that involves Beth (Jennifer Aniston) and her long-term boyfriend Neil (Ben Affleck), a couple who live together but have consciously decided not to marry. The two live a seemingly happy life in a waterside Baltimore condo that they bought together, and Neil is portrayed to be a helpful, supportive partner. It is only when she learns of her younger sister's engagement that Beth becomes dissatisfied with her and Neil's relationship status. After her attempts to convince Neil to take the marriage plunge are unsuccessful, she breaks off their relationship. There are several scenes throughout the film that depict Beth's family reminding her of her abject single status, including an awkward rehearsal dinner toast made by one of her cousins. Beth is shown to remain strong in the face of this cajoling, and seems to be 'learning' and improving her life according to the guidelines originally put forward in Behrendt and Tuccillo's book.

However, the allegiance to the book's original premise stops there. The film does not show Beth move on to pursue another relationship with a guy that is 'into her' and would be interested in marrying her. Rather, after her father has a heart attack, she begins to recognize that being in a solid relationship with Neil, who provides invaluable support during her time of need, is more important than marriage. This would seem to be happy ending enough, but the film takes this one step further by having Neil go on to propose to Beth. Clearly, this trajectory follows the postfeminist romance structure closely, but

Figure 13   Neil (Ben Affleck) and Beth (Jennifer Aniston) in *He's Just Not That Into You* (Kwapis, 2009).

for this reason, it also completely contradicts the message that the source material conveys. It implies that if a guy like Neil is not marrying you, he might be into you, but you might need to read a different self-help book – namely, *The Rules* – to get that coveted proposal.

The film of *He's Just Not That Into You*'s attempt to be all things to all viewers – practical and sentimental, general and specific, realistic and fictional – extended into its promotion as well, using both male- and female-associated media forms to appeal to potential viewers. One example of this effort was a YouTube video circulated at the time of the film's release entitled '10 chick flick clichés that you won't see in *He's Just Not That Into You*.' The video seems designed not only to attract a male audience but to capitalize on YouTube's power as a form of what Henry Jenkins has called 'spreadable media.'[31] Its content intends to bridge the gender gap that romance generally fosters but also the gap between YouTube's real, participatory viewership, and the seemingly impenetrable fantasy world of romance texts. The video stars three of the film's male costars, Bradley Cooper, Justin Long, and Kevin Connolly, who make a plea to the film's potential male viewers. It starts with the three addressing the camera directly, and after telling them that they are the stars of *He's Just Not That Into You*, Long states quickly:

> Now, hold the phone. I know what you guys out there are thinking. You're all thinking to yourselves, 'oh, fantastic, another chick flick, this is just what I need. I just started dating this girl, she's going to drag me to go see it. This sucks!'

Cooper follows up,

You're safe seeing this film, we're here to tell you you might even enjoy it. *He's Just Not That Into You* is not your typical chick flick. Connolly adds, We'd like to present ten chick flick clichés that are not in this movie.

Each cliché is represented by a scene in which the actors parody the style and manner in which it plays out in other chick flicks. The clichés include the following:

10. There are no makeover montages.
9. There is no singing into random objects.
8. There is no quirky best friend (or sardonic best friend, or sassy best friend).
7. There is no scene where someone has a one-night stand and then shows up to work the next day and finds out that they actually slept with their new boss.
6. No one in this movie slides down a wall while crying, and as a subset of that, no one is ever laughing and crying at the same time.
5. There are no elderly folks who say anything inappropriate.
4. Nobody chases anybody down to stop them from going somewhere or to stop them from doing something. Not in an airport, not in a train station or at a wedding. Nowhere.
3. There is no shot where heads fall into frame and land on pillows.
2. There is no speech where, in order to win her over, a guy tells a girl all of the little details that he likes about her.
1. There is no falling in love montage.

The content and style of each scene and the piece as a whole offers an astute nod to romance's structural elements that are discussed throughout this book. The video also works on many other levels, not the least of which is the latent homoerotic connotations invoked by the actors fluidly moving in and out of 'feminine' roles, reminiscent of the slate of 'bromance' films that became popular during this period. What is most compelling about the video for the purposes of this discussion is that that the actors' tone and approach to typical female-associated material resembles Behrendt's original discursive style. It returns to the approach wherein a rational male voice repudiates the expectations that a male audience might have about the romance fantasy perpetuated by the film (and films like it). Cooper, Long, and Connolly are seemingly trying to make this film palatable to a male audience through a male-skewing media form. However, this gesture even further parodies and distances them from the 'typical' chick flick, which parallels Behrendt's position as a male figure who is reasonable and distanced from typical feminine conversations.

ONLINE DATING MEETS ADVERTISING IN *MUST LOVE DOGS*

The use of YouTube as an ironic and hip promotional vehicle to attract, or perhaps further repel, a broader audience for *He's Just Not That Into You* is evidence of how the Internet's immediacy has effectively challenged boundaries that were previously distinct, particularly that between public and private space. This is nowhere more evident than the increased prominence of online dating, which has boomed since the late 1990s. A 2011 study by Stanford sociologist Michael Rosenfeld found that for heterosexual couples who met in 2009, 22 percent met their partners online, making it the third most common means of finding romance (after being introduced by friends, and approximately tied with meeting in a bar, restaurant or other public place).[32] In a November 23, 2003 *New York Times Magazine* cover story article entitled 'Love in the time of no time,' author Jennifer Egan examined the dynamics of this behemoth phenomenon. She outlines how Internet dating's dynamics loosely parallel those found in traditional courtship and dating models. However, the personal profile where an individual reveals and sells characteristics about him or herself to other members of that online dating community is unique to the form, with many online daters inadvertently referring to their profile as an 'ad.'[33]

The idea of selling oneself in the same way that one might sell a commodity undergirds online dating's entanglement of the past and the present, fiction and reality, to the same degree as other, more entertainment-based romance media. First, it reinforces the false binary between serendipity and premeditation. In a culture that consistently celebrates the accidental and fortuitous as being more authentic ways of finding love, the act of branding oneself on one's online profile in order to attract a worthwhile love interest strikes some as overly calculated. However, such a practical approach also recalls antiquated models of courtship, much like those found in Jane Austen's novels, wherein romantic mating was frequently based on class, social status, and the dowry or fortune that one would bring into a marriage, and not on the type of romantic connection that we celebrate today.[34] However, as we have seen, the Jane Austen mentality that circulates in the media tends to ignore this more pragmatic reality. The advertising for Internet dating sites accommodates these opposing tendencies, balancing ideas of control with those of fate and destiny, while films that feature Internet dating tend to evade the deliberateness of the process, in favor of a more conventional emphasis on the binary between pragmatism and idealism.

Television advertisements for the two most successful American dating sites eharmony.com and match.com actively deflate the negative connotations of online dating's unromantic nature by appropriating aesthetics reminiscent of postfeminist romance films. Eharmony's advertistments are particularly skillful at playing up the serendipitous possibilities available once the site matches you with compatible partners based on your responses to a lengthy questionnaire. The company's founder, clinical psychologist, Dr Neil Clark Warren, teamed up with a University of Southern California research professor to develop a copyrighted compatibility matching system that predicts future success based on several 'key dimensions of personality.'[35] The system uses your questionnaire to determine these dimensions, so it is more likely that the people with whom you are matched are compatible with the 'real' you, rather than the person whom you might sell yourself to be if left to your own devices.

It probably comes as no surprise that eharmony's commercials do not broadcast the fact that a computer formula is used to determine their clients' love matches. Instead, they embrace, in consolidated form, the same structural and discursive elements seen in fictional romance films. A particularly ubiquitous series of advertisements produced by the donat wald + haque agency that ran on television in the late 2000s crystallized eharmony's delicate approach to these issues. They each tell the story of a couple that met on eharmony, and have gone on to have a successful relationship, most of which led to marriage. The production values in these spots are high and the 'characters' are attractive, appearing polished yet realistic and spontaneous. Each individual commercial follows a structural pattern that addresses: (1) What the couple thought about love before they joined eharmony, (2) Why eharmony is different than most dating sites, (3) How their lives have been changed by finding each other on eharmony.

The 'Lee and Ann Marie' spot from this campaign begins on a slow motion shot of Lee, bouncing a soccer ball by himself, with a soulful organ playing in the background. His voiceover tells us, 'The thing is, you don't know it 'till you have it.' Then it cuts to a medium shot of Lee and Ann Marie sitting on a couch, as if they are being interviewed. Lee addresses someone off-camera, while Ann Marie looks on lovingly, and continues, 'Because I had heard that in the past, there was always people like "she's not right for you," "you'll know, you'll know," and me being like (he rolls his eyes), okay.' Ann Marie then interjects, "Well, we know." And, Lee follows up, "*This* is what they were talking about." Next we see Lee and Ann Marie in a long shot embracing with an overlaid caption reading 'Lee and Ann Marie: Matched October 2, 2006.' And then a combination of shots of Lee and Ann Marie by themselves and together, some in slow motion, some cutting back to the original medium shot on the couch. Lee states: 'Ann Marie changed my life. She is extremely happy, lighthearted, doesn't let things get to her. And, I learn from that. I am jealous of that but she's bringing it into my life.' And then in a final shot that features the two kissing, an overlaid caption reads: 'Married: May 3, 2008,' he continues, 'Ann Marie allows me to be who I am. As long as I have her, that's it.'

In addition to selling Lee and Ann Marie's love, the commercial's aesthetics

Figure 14   Television advertisement for eharmony.com.

are also selling what we might call the 'mise-en-scène of wealth' that I will discuss at length in Chapter 5. The open airy loft spaces and urban settings, not to mention the lighting and clothing of the two participants, imply an upper-middle-class milieu. The advertisements promote the idea that Internet dating is an investment that will pay off in happiness and perhaps, elevated class status. The ad also strives to debunk some of the commonly held misperceptions about Internet dating. The Lee-Ann Marie narrative demonstrates that being organized and practical in your attempts to find love can still lead to a relationship based in fate, that makes you 'know' what true love feels like. And, perhaps most importantly, you will be matched based on the 'real' you – not who you might pretend to be on another dating website. In short, the eharmony brand wants to sell you the best combination of these factors by finding the consumer the most satisfying love match his or her money will buy.

This complex negotiation between the real or authentic self and the fantasy performance of self is a particular point of preoccupation for films that depict Internet dating. The postfeminist romance film reveals a palpable ambivalence about the Internet's mechanized quality and either sidesteps its repercussions or ultimately depicts it as a vehicle for dishonesty or inauthenticity. Nora Ephron's 1998 *You've Got Mail*, a loose remake of Ernst Lubitsch's 1940 film *The Shop Around the Corner*, is a great example of this attitude, although it does not involve Internet dating per se. Instead, it portrays two booksellers, Kathleen (Meg Ryan) and Joe (Tom Hanks), who are pitted against each other in their professional lives but fall in love with each other's Internet selves through e-mails and online chats. Kathleen claims that she met Joe's avatar through an online chat room into which she accidentally stumbled. In other words, she was not actively looking for love on the Internet but found it serendipitously. Jane Austen resurfaces yet again in *You've Got Mail* when Kathleen places a copy of *Pride and Prejudice* on the table during her first arranged meeting with the real person behind the avatar with whom she has become smitten. When Joe shows up instead of her online friend (at this point he realizes her online identity but she does not recognize his), they engage in a bitter banter about the Austen book, wherein she claims to have a more authoritative perspective on its plot.

Kathleen's firm allegiance to an old-school approach to the bookselling business that foregrounds interpersonal contact and quirky main-street sensibility is associated with a wholehearted and naive embrace of the ideals as espoused by the 'idea of Jane.' Much like the dysfunctional dehumanizing machines that open *The Jane Austen Book Club*, Kathleen resents Joe's more corporate and streamlined approach to the book business. Significantly, it is the scene during which they discuss Jane Austen when Joe realizes that he must make Kathleen fall in love with his real self and out of love with his fantasy Internet self. In other words, the Internet here is not quite a hindrance to true love, but it must be eliminated in order for that love to be consummated. Joe's desire for Kathleen to see him as less of a corporate suit and more of a softer, dog-loving neighborhood mensch mirrors *Emma*'s Mr. Knightley's desire for Emma to see him as a romantic interest rather than a friend.

A similar dynamic of Internet dating as a false performance plays out in the later film, *Must Love Dogs*. The film sees two newly divorced singles, preschool teacher Sarah (Diane Lane) and boatmaker Jake (John Cusack), pushed into the online dating world by their friends and family members. Jake, who has recently gone through an emotionally debilitating divorce, is deeply invested in old-school authenticity, even in his job as a boat builder. While his wood boats, which he refers to as 'time machines,' do not provide a particularly smooth ride on the water or much of an income for Jake, he emphatically stands behind their superiority to the 'Tupperware, computer designed fiberglass composite things' that most people want to buy. Jake's antiquated, old-school, antitechnology, anticapitalist approach to life is seen as 'real' and romantic, which is posed against the artifice and performance of the Internet. The film implies that Jake is not an actual user of PerfectMatch.com and only answers Sarah's ad because his friend, Charlie (Ben Shankman), somehow comes across it while surfing for Internet porn. In fact, Jake's only real use of technology in the film is his repeat viewings of *Dr. Zhivago* (Lean, 1965) on his television, which he believes portrays what true love should be. In an interesting reversal of the *Sleepless in Seattle* gender dynamic that I discuss in the next chapter, Jake forces Charlie to watch the film with him on a weekend afternoon.

Sarah is ambivalent about capitulating to her family's insistence that she begin Internet dating but eventually gives in and uses the profile that her sister has authored for her, entitled 'must love dogs.' This profile presents her falsely, with a decades-old photo, a description of herself as voluptuous, and implies that she owns a dog, which she does not. This idea of performing a role is emphasized in a montage sequence that chronicles Sarah's dating escapades, in which she morphs her appearance for every date, changing her clothes, her hair and her attitude. The sequence humorously implies that there is a different Sarah on every date that adapts to each man's personality (and often the venue where their date takes place). It clearly pits the inauthenticity of these many Sarahs with the 'real' imperfect Sarah who is accessible and awkward, and fumbles her way through interactions with Jake. In their first meeting scene, which takes place in a quiet park (in contrast to the busy mise-en-scène of the previous dating sequence) Jake blasts Sarah for misrepresenting herself in her profile, but admits that he prefers the true version of her. And, after a few successful dates in which the two stumble through the stages of courtship, Jake discovers that Sarah has lied to him about dating another man – the father (Dermot Mulroney) of one of Sarah's young students – who has also been falsely performing the role of perfect Dad to seduce Sarah.

In perfect accordance with the steps of the romance structure as outlined in the Introduction, after this problem stage, Sarah comes to a realization that she is ready to shed the falsity of her dating self and admits that she wants real love. The film's dénouement sees her enact the aquatic equivalent of employing a rapid form of transportation by hopping on a boat with a female crew team so that she can chase after, and declare her love for, Jake, who is taking his time machine boat out for a last spin (before turning it over to a wealthy man who wants to turn it into a piece of décor). After overcoming her fear of

Figure 15 Sarah (Diane Lane) and Jake (John Cusack) in *Must Love Dogs* (Goldberg, 2005).

water and diving into the river after Jake's boat, she tells him, 'You asked for honesty. It scared the hell out of me. I was afraid of letting you see the real me.' The conclusion is satisfying because it instills the idea that underneath everyone's performative fantasy self or online avatar, lies a truly authentic individual capable of finding and succeeding at 'true' love.

The multifarious media texts that we have analyzed throughout this chapter reveal the postfeminist romance cycle's spectrum of discourses in and around reality and fiction, past and present, practicality and romanticism. Media scholars have always been interested in how fictional ideas of romance affect the vocabulary with which we talk about our everyday lives, but now in many contexts the fictional and the everyday are one and the same, and this tendency is being even further promoted in and by new media forms. These case studies have demonstrated only a few of the many ways in which fictional fantasy and real-life pragmatism are gendered, with women, and women's-oriented media, consistently placed on the side of performance, fantasy, and sentimentality while men are positioned as practical onlookers who can fix their problems through down-to-earth authentic discourse. As we have seen, even if the conclusion of the films suggests that one perspective emerges as the better of the two, neither side wins out over the other in the broader transmedia conversation to which they give life. In fact, the ongoing, cyclical interdependency of the two discourses of fiction and everyday life is a hallmark of postfeminist culture. The next chapter examines the temporality of this interdependency in more depth.

Notes

1. See http://jezebel.com/5969737/meet-the-so+called-nice-guys-of-okcupid?tag=on line-dating.
2. The tumblr site http://niceguysofokc.tumblr.com/ was deleted soon after the Jezebel story was published on December 19, 2012.
3. Jason Mittell, *Genre and Television: From Cop Shows to Cartoons* (New York: Routledge, 2004), p. 13.
4. Hester Brown, *The Little Lady Agency in the Big Apple* (New York: Pocket Star Books, 2006), p. 451.
5. Ann Barr Snitow, 'Mass market romance: pornography for women is different', in Ann Snitow, Christine Stansell and Sharon Thompson (eds), *Powers of Desire: the Politics of Sexuality.* (New York: Monthly Review Press, 1983), p. 250.
6. Suzanne Ferriss and Mallory Young, *Chick Lit: the New Woman's Fiction.* (New York: Routledge, 2006), p. 3.
7. Ibid. pp. 3–4.
8. Ibid. p. 2.
9. Ibid. p. 2.
10. Stephanie Harzewski, *Chicklit and Postfeminism* (Charlottesville: University Of Virginia Press, 2011), p. 61.
11. Jim Collins, *Bring on the Books for Everybody: How Literary Culture Became Popular Culture* (Durham, NC: Duke University Press, 2010), p. 137.

12. *People Magazine*, 25 December 1995. Accessed via the web: http://www.people. com/people/archive/article/0,,20102443,00.html.
13. *People Magazine*, 25 December 1995.
14. Sue Parrill, *Jane Austen on Film and Television: a Study of the Adaptations* (Jefferson: McFarland & Company, 2002), p. 7.
15. Danielle Crittenden, *What Our Mothers Didn't Tell Us: Why Happiness Eludes the Modern Woman* (New York: Touchstone Books, 1999), p. 41.
16. Ibid. p. 40.
17. Ibid. p. 39.
18. *The Wall Street Journal*, 6 December 2010. Accessed via the web: http://online.wsj. com/article/SB10001424052748704594804575649041609261602.html.
19. See http://www.prweb.com/releases/Marketdata/Enterprises/prweb440011.htm.
20. Anthea Taylor, *Single Women in Popular Culture: the Limits of Postfeminism* (Basingstoke: Palgrave Macmillan, 2012), p. 143.
21. Ellen Fein and Sherrie Schneider, *The Rules: Time-tested Secrets for Capturing the Heart of Mr. Right* (New York: Warner Books, 1995), p. 7.
22. Ibid. pp. 1–2.
23. Taylor, *Single Women*, p. 147.
24. See www.therulesbook.com.
25. Lori Gottlieb, *Marry Him: The Case for Settling for Mr. Good Enough* (New York: Dutton, 2010), p. 44.
26. Ibid. p. 34.
27. Ibid. p. 40.
28. See http://www.rawstory.com/rs/2010/02/02/pandagon-what_about_love/.
29. See http://www.salon.com/life/feature/2010/02/07/lori_gottlieb/.
30. Greg Behrendt and Liz Tuccillo, *He's Just Not That Into You: the No-Excuses Truth to Understanding Guys* (New York: Simon Spotlight, 2004), p. 1.
31. Henry Jenkins, *Convergence Culture: Where Old and New Media Collide* (New York: New York University Press, 2006), p. 275.
32. Michael J. Rosenfield and Reuben J. Thomas, 'Searching for a mate: the rise of the Internet as a social intermediary', *American Sociological Review*, 77: 4 (2012), 531.
33. Jennifer Egan, 'Love in the time of no time', *The New York Times*, 23 November 2003.
34. Ibid.
35. See http://www.eharmony.com/about/eharmony/.

3. PAST VS. PRESENT: TEMPORALITY IN THE POSTFEMINIST CYCLE

Katie, the female protagonist played by Barbra Streisand in the 1973 romance film *The Way We Were*, is presumably the subject speaking the lines from the film's theme song. In the song, she expresses ambivalence about the role of time in the process of making sense of romance. She suggests that events from the past, in this case, a romance from the past, can only be seen via 'misty water-colored memories,' which obscure the clarity of the events as they really occurred and diminish the intensity of the emotion that accompanied them. She goes on to question, 'Could it be that it was all so simple then, or has time rewritten every line?' suggesting the muddled distinction between a memory of the past as it really happened, and the sort of revisionism inherent in recollection that transforms the historical and personal past to fit one's own present subjectivity.

This notion of 'the way we were' suggests that romance is simultaneously specific and universal, timely and timeless. It is a form that has remained constant throughout history but that has also maintained its ability to reveal a great deal about historically specific social and political tensions, particularly those that hold significant ramifications for women such as Katie, who is representative of both the primary players as well as the primary consumers of romantic fantasies. The song's expression of ambivalence toward time and its close association of fictional subject Katie with real person Barbra Streisand bring to mind Chapter 2's discussion of the postfeminist romance's proclivity to break down distinctions between fiction and reality and past and present. *The Way We Were*'s setting in the oft-romanticized World War II and postwar era, its basic flashback structure, and the lyrics of its prescient theme song are examples of how issues of temporality, history, and subjectivity often become inextricably intertwined in romance texts. This chapter looks at a cluster of films and an episode from one television show in the postfeminist romance cycle in which 'timelessness' is no longer just a thematic element but serves an increasingly prominent and explicit narrative function.

The intersection between women, questions of history, and romance has been at the heart of scholarly work on melodrama, women's films, and soap operas. In her seminal study of the women's film *The Desire to Desire*, Mary Ann Doane argues that the typical love story presents time as non-progressive, cyclical, and dependent on the female protagonist's waiting for 'phone calls or letters.'[1] For the female protagonist of Doane's 1940s women's films, such as *Back Street* (Stevenson, 1941) and *The Heiress* (Wyler, 1949), time passes without anything of significance occurring. These, 'ordinary' love stories, 'rather than activating history as mise-en-scene, as space,' – such as that which occurs in epic romantic films, *Gone with the Wind* (Fleming, 1939), *Reds* (Beatty, 1981) and *Dr. Zhivago* – 'inscribe it as individual subjectivity closed in on itself.'[2] Therefore, these love story films are situated outside the arena 'in which history endows space with meaning.' The women within them are not in a position to create change or make events happen but 'live in a state of expectation which is never fulfilled or fulfilled only in imagination.'[3]

The media texts in this chapter were produced in a drastically different historical and political context than Doane's films but they reveal a similar tension. They suggest seemingly limitless options for their female protagonists at the same time that they imply a historically situated containment of them within the psychic spaces of subjectivity, memory, and nostalgia. They offer a compelling glimpse into the many ways in which contemporary culture sees female subjectivity oscillate between traditional positions of immobility and waiting (as described by Doane) often associated with the past, and mobility and progress associated with the future.

The first two case studies of what I call the 'Time Travel as Matchmaker' and 'What-If' narratives focus on postfeminist romance films that present some form of time travel, whether real or imagined, in which the spectator of the text, or a character within the text, is transported to another historical time, either literally or figuratively. To be sure, the act of glimpsing another time and place, and understanding how it is both similar to and different from one's own time and place, is one of the many pleasures offered by film and media spectatorship. However, as I will argue, the nature of this representation and the pleasure it elicits in these films, takes on complex connotations when realized in the postfeminist era, which, as Diane Negra and Yvonne Tasker have contended, also 'evidences a distinct preoccupation with the temporal.'[4] Each group of texts' presentation of time travel raises timely questions about gender dynamics and the stakes at issue when characters, and spectators, invite the collapse of boundaries between past and present. Specifically, my focus will be on whether or not the narratives' depiction of time travel limits or expands women's – both women characters and women spectators – options. The implications of this temporal position are made even clearer when comparing films that have similar structures but protagonists of different genders.

The third case study of 'the Nostalgia Narrative' examines an episode of *Sex and the City*, entitled 'Ex and the City', and the film *Sleepless in Seattle* to focus on how nostalgia becomes representative of a broader postfeminist cultural trend – also seen in other media forms and neo-conservative feminist writing – in which the reflection on, or imitation of, the prefeminist period (both real and fictional) is implicitly (and often, explicitly) encouraged as a means of resolving complex postfeminist quandaries, specifically those related to female identity and romantic relationships. Expanding on Chapter 2's case studies, both texts illustrate how nostalgia functions as a sort of therapeutic discourse through which women, individually and collectively, negotiate their ambivalence about their role in contemporary culture. They want to be autonomous, professionally successful, and economically independent individuals while simultaneously desiring traditional love narratives in which their identity becomes associated with the promise of heterosexual coupling and marriage.

Time Travel as Matchmaker: *Somewhere in Time* and *Kate and Leopold*

> Theoretically speaking, if you go to the past in the future, then your future lies in the past. That is a picture of you in the future – in the past.
> Stuart Besser (Liev Schreiber) in *Kate and Leopold*

In *Somewhere in Time* and *Kate and Leopold*, romantic love is such a powerful force that it empowers and enables people to quite literally transcend temporal and historical boundaries. Both films introduce a means through which characters can transport themselves either backward or forward in time in order to satisfy their curiosity about another historical period and/or a person from that period. While *Kate and Leopold*, the more recent of the two films, engages in lengthy explanations – in the vein of the *Back to the Future* films – as to how such time travel is possible (at least within the scientific world of the film) these details are not really integral to these narratives. What is important is what the time travel reveals, which is that romantic love transcends historical barriers. In its purest state, it remains – or rather, should remain – untouched by the cultural and political mores that accompany particular historical periods. *Somewhere in Time* and *Kate and Leopold* explicitly suggest that turn-of-the-century America (the historical past referenced in both films) offers love that is far easier and simpler than that of the contemporary world. Much like texts that engage with the 'idea of Jane' as discussed in Chapter 2, both *Somewhere in Time* and *Kate and Leopold* idealize romance and relationships based in modes of socially imposed courtship wherein gender roles were far more restrictive. The two films arrive at vastly different conclusions about the implications of time travel for the sake of love.

Somewhere in Time tells the story of a playwright, Richard Collier (Christopher Reeve), who on the evening of the successful production of his first play in college, is approached by a mysterious elderly woman who gives him a watch and begs him to 'come back to me.' Richard has never seen this woman before and shrugs off the incident as a freak occurrence. Eight years later, we see Richard, now a successful writer, afflicted with writer's block as a result of a recent romantic breakup. For inspiration, he visits his old college and stays at the local Grand Hotel. After admiring a painting of a young woman in the lobby of the hotel, he learns that she is an old stage actress named Elise McKenna. He soon discovers that she also happens to be the elderly woman who approached him with the watch years before. Upon discovering this coincidence, Richard becomes obsessed with Elise, and decides he must learn how to travel back in time to find her.

Richard eventually comes across a book by his old philosophy professor called 'Travels Through Time.' When he asks the professor about the concept of time travel, the professor tells him that he must 'disassociate [himself] from the present,' and remove everything in the room that reminds him of it. Richard tries this technique, unsuccessfully, but is more determined to time travel after he sees his name in the hotel's 1912 log. Eventually he suc-

Figure 16   Richard (Christopher Reeve) and Elise (Jane Seymour) in *Somewhere in Time* (Szwarc, 1980).

cessfully returns to the past and falls in love with Elise (Jane Seymour), but he is abruptly pulled out of his travels because he does not remove every present-day item from his surroundings, specifically a 1979 penny. When Richard returns to the present day he is so fatigued (the professor warns him that it is one of the effects of a self-induced hypnotic time travel) and depressed at the prospect of losing Elise that he starves himself to death. The last scene of the film sees him following a 'white light' and reuniting with Elise.

Kate and Leopold takes place in Manhattan in the contemporary period of 2001. Kate (Meg Ryan) has recently ended her relationship with long-term boyfriend Stuart (Liev Schreiber), a scientist whose obsession with time travel caused him to be a less than doting partner. At the beginning of the film, Stuart proves his theories about time travel by jumping off the Brooklyn Bridge at exactly the right moment, sending him back in time to turn-of-the-century New York. While visiting the past, he takes pictures with a tiny camera at a social gathering, which manages to capture the attention of Leopold (Hugh Jackman), a restless duke and fellow amateur scientist who is dreading his impending arranged marriage. Leopold follows Stuart forward to the year 2001, takes up residence in his apartment, and becomes acquainted with a contemporary New York City way of life. In the midst of Leopold's requisite comic difficulties in adjusting to modern living (everyone else thinks that he is merely an actor playing a part), he wins the affections of Kate and the friendship of her brother Charlie (Breckin Meyer). His chivalrous ways are attractive to the siblings; he teaches Charlie how to woo a women the 'old-fashioned' way and courts Kate with poetry and romantic dinners until she eventually falls in love with him.

Kate is a no-nonsense, successful career woman who is on the verge of a big promotion at her market research company. Between her bad relationship history with Stuart and her difficult upbringing, we are led to believe that Kate's life has been challenging. Her cynicism initially causes her to be skeptical of Leopold's old-fashioned pursuit of her affections, as she has been hardened by her life experiences. Eventually, her tough outer shell cracks and she begins to acknowledge that Leopold's vintage world view is a panacea for the many struggles that she has faced.

At the conclusion of the film, Stuart transports Leopold back home to his own time, leaving Kate to celebrate her hard-won promotion alone. Soon, Stuart notices that Kate has suddenly appeared in the pictures from his first trip into the past, and he rushes to tell her that her love for Leopold has made it so she is destined to live with him back in the 1870s. At first, Kate refuses Stuart's offer to transport her to the past, as she is on the verge of accepting her new position. However, she ultimately decides that she does not want the job after all and that her true desire is to share her life with Leopold.

Figure 17   Kate (Meg Ryan) and Leopold (Hugh Jackman) in *Kate & Leopold* (Mangold, 2001).

Both *Somewhere in Time* and *Kate and Leopold* present circular narrative structures in which historical time can be traversed easily. The contemporary period in which both films are set is dominated by work-related stress and disappointing romantic relationships, and the past is depicted as slower, less demanding, and filled with romantic potential. While *Somewhere in Time*'s ending is downbeat, it ultimately implies a 'happy ending' in that Richard and Elise will be together in some eternal post-mortem time. The conclusion of *Kate and Leopold* is also 'happy' but has more complex implications. Certainly, the viewer wants to see Kate find a partner that will satisfy her emotional needs in the way that Leopold can. That said, her decision to relinquish her circa 2001 social and economic power in exchange for a life in 1876, where she would be Leopold's wife but presumably have no social power, does raise some questions about the cost of her romantic fulfillment. She can choose whichever historical definition of 'woman' that she prefers.

This intersection between fluctuating female identity and history recalls Denise Riley's discussion of how women *know* or *feel* their womanhood temporally. She argues that women do not always have awareness of themselves as 'women' but only realize their position by 'some secondary stage of reflection induced by something else.'[5] This 'something else' of which Riley speaks is a cultural or political circumstance that forces a woman to recognize how she is defined at that historical moment. In other words, 'woman' does not have meaning unto itself, but its definition fluctuates depending on historical context.[6] She sums up:

It is not only that concepts are forced into new proximities with one another – but they are so differently shot through with altering positions of gender that what has occurred is something more fundamental than a merely sequential innovation – that is, a reconceptualisation along sexed lines, in which the understandings of gender both re-order and are themselves re-ordered.[7]

Regardless of whether the woman recognizes herself as 'woman' in positive or negative terms, her place in historical time does ultimately subject her to a fixed societal perception of what the term means. What Riley alludes to but does not develop in detail is the idea that in certain periods of history, society struggles with the definition of 'woman' so actively that traditional notions of femininity widely circulate and serve as a constant reminder of what she is 'supposed to' look and act like. This process forces the woman into recognition of her femininity with more frequency than Riley describes. Kate's character is an embodiment of Riley's argument. She must consider her position as a woman in 2001 and weigh that against what it would be in 1876. She makes the choice to return to 1876 without hesitation. However, the film's turn of events that sees Kate appear in Stuart's time-travel pictures (Stuart's attempt at explaining how this occurred is detailed in the quote that opens this section) implies that Kate does not really have a choice. She must go back, and is destined to live in the past.

Somewhere in Time and *Kate and Leopold* make literal within their structures what epic films within the postfeminist cycle like *Out of Africa* (Pollack, 1985), *Titanic*, and *Australia* (Luhrmann, 2008) merely gesture toward, which is the desire to return to a past time where true love resides. These films' editing and production design serve to demarcate the past time from the present time, but there is no visual marker for the films' ideological implications. Both Richard and Kate prefer the past to the present, and lose their present-time selves, either through death or time travel. Richard's ending is rendered tragic, Kate's ending is rendered happy. But, what lies beneath this happy ending? Let us consider what it would look like if the genders were reversed in these films. If a female character like Kate was placed in Richard's scenario, and the film kept its tragic ending, her death from heartache would not be markedly different from Richard's. On the other hand, if we put Richard in Kate's shoes, and he traveled back to the 1870s to be with the woman he loves, the narrative would have vastly different political connotations. Richard's social position would not change. He would maintain roughly the same power that he has in contemporary period in 1876, but Kate's social status will most certainly be drastically different. The degree to which gender difference functions in these temporally engaged narratives becomes even further crystallized in the What-If films.

THE 'WHAT IF?' NARRATIVE: *ME MYSELF I* AND *THE FAMILY MAN*

This isn't really my life, it's just a glimpse.

Jack Campbell (Nicholas Cage) in *The Family Man*

In the previous section, characters' compulsion to literally travel through time in order to be with the ones that they love has varying implications for their ultimate fates – Richard dies as a result of his quest, and Kate travels to a past era where her identity as a woman will be reframed. The What-If films, on the other hand, contain their exploration of different life choices within the context of possible forking paths into the future. They have one temporal setting as a point of departure and do not return to a historical time that predates the period of the film. These films explicitly reflect the preoccupations of a contemporary culture in which men and women wait until later in life to get married, and the pursuit of a fulfilling and lucrative career is a top priority. They explore how these choices – or often the random acts of fate and timing that decide for us – can result in one's life heading in one direction versus another. A character's choice to prioritize either career or love at the expense of the other becomes the impetus for the films' representation of two possible life paths, but in all cases, for better or worse, love is always presented as the better, or more appropriate, choice. This allegiance to love is expected given the genre, but in this subset of texts, women's professional and personal choices are interrogated in a way that complicates our reflection on the ramifications of historical progress on their range of options.

While the What-If films examine the importance of choice, another popular postfeminist film, *Sliding Doors*, contemplates the idea that timing – good or bad – can determine the fate of a person's life. In doing so, the film operates under different assumptions about the vast difference between positive and misguided decisions. It suggests that random occurrences and fluke events can significantly transform our life path in ways of which we are often unaware. A seminal forking-path film, to which *Sliding Doors* is particularly indebted, is Krzysztof Kieslowski's *Blind Chance* (1987), which presents three possible versions of its protagonist's life that hinge solely on whether or not he is able to catch a train to Warsaw. Similarly, *Sliding Doors* presents two versions of Helen's (Gwyneth Paltrow) life that depend on whether or not she catches a London tube train. Much like Tom Twyker's 1998 *Run Lola Run*, *Blind Chance* presents Witek's three possibilities one after the other in three separate segments. Each begins with Witek's struggle to make the train, but vary based on his success. *Sliding Doors*, on the other hand, shows both possible variations on Helen's life simultaneously, cross-cutting back and forth between them throughout the film.

The film begins as single narrative, the beginning of which sees Helen fired from her job. Forced to leave work earlier than expected, she walks to the tube to catch a train home. In variation #1, wherein Helen makes her train, she meets a fellow traveler named James (John Hannah), who in both versions of the narrative is presented as an ideal love match. In this first variation, Helen returns to her flat in time to catch her unsuspecting boyfriend Gerry (John Lynch) in bed with another woman. Helen leaves Gerry and willingly begins a new chapter in her life. Her first decision is to get a chic new haircut and dye job, which conveniently serves as the visual cue that allows the viewer to distinguish between the two Helens throughout the rest of the film. She starts her own successful business and pursues a romance with James. They fall in love, and she gets pregnant, but then has an accident and dies.

In version #2 of Helen's life, she misses the train and consequently, does not discover Gerry's infidelity. She chooses to work at two waitress jobs to support him in his professional pursuits. However, after learning of the affair toward the end of the film, she breaks off their relationship, but soon finds that she is pregnant with his baby. She also has an accident, which she survives but takes the life of the child. On her way out of the hospital at the end of the film she meets James in an elevator where they have an interaction (which mirrors the version #1 train interaction), implying that they may end up together after all.

Three potential implications can be drawn from *Sliding Doors*'s representation of the two alternate versions of Helen's life. First, while Helen's struggle for autonomy takes more time in one version than the other, the film implies that because she possesses innate confidence and initiative, it is just a matter of time before she finds it within herself. Second, both paths rely on the premise that she is a professional failure and the degree to which she is able to turn her professional life around is predicated entirely on the success or failure of her romantic life. And third, regardless of which version of her life she lives, Helen is destined to be in a relationship with James. In this case, the primary romance of the film is fated, and Helen will find this love regardless of the path her life takes.

In the article 'Film futures,' David Bordwell discusses 'forking path' narratives like *Sliding Doors*, which, he observes, generally only introduce 'two or three alternative chains of events . . . but not twenty or sixty, let alone an infinite number.'[8] Bordwell argues that film narratives that use the forking-path concept cannot successfully present an unlimited range of narrative possibilities (such as those introduced by the work of Jorge Luis Borges), because they are limited by cinematic conventions. In introducing seven conventions of forking-path narratives in his article, Bordwell contends that these films stay grounded within the limits of what is formally representable, and do not stray into the territory of the incomprehensible.[9]

The degree to which *Sliding Doors* explores the concept of the forking path establishes it as a satisfying romance film that poses the question of 'what if,' but really refers back to the same landscape in both scenarios. While there are two possible variations of Helen's life, they both include the same cast of characters and locations, as well as the accident serving as denouement. Most importantly, both paths only include two possible love options – the cheating boyfriend or the trustworthy James. In other words, her choices are seemingly limitless, but in order for the film's narrative structure to be comprehensible, they have to be limited to what is representable.

Another pair of What-If films, *Me Myself I* and *The Family Man*, loosely adopt the narrative 'gimmick' of the 1946 Frank Capra classic *It's a Wonderful Life*, in which the protagonist, George Bailey (James Stewart), is given the opportunity to see what the people closest to him and the town in which he lives would have been like had he never been born. However, *It's a Wonderful Life* does not explore how George's life would have differed had he made different choices, such as going to college as opposed to staying at the Building and Loan or marrying Violet (Gloria Grahame) instead of Mary (Donna Reed). Rather it presents a Bedford Falls existence completely devoid of George Bailey's presence. This is in contrast to the more contemporary permutations of the 'what if' structure, *Me Myself I* and *The Family Man*, which give the characters a glimpse into the lives they could have had if they had they made different personal and professional choices. These films tell almost exactly the same story but from the different perspectives of a woman and a man. They introduce interesting questions about the degree to which time (or timing) is related to one's ultimate success in life. They also make important claims about which type of life choices will elicit happiness and personal satisfaction and which will not. As in the previous comparison between *Somewhere in Time* and *Kate and Leopold*, these distinctions have subtly different connotations depending on the gender of the protagonist.

Me Myself I begins with scenes of individual adolescent girls talking in direct address to the camera about what they want to do with their lives. Some mention specific careers, others mention getting married, one girl even talks about being concerned about the timing of her marriage – she does not want to do it too early, or too late. In the next scene we see Pamela Drury (Rachel Griffiths), a thirty-something reporter, who is in the midst of writing a story about these young girls' hopes and aspirations, and is the person to whom they are speaking. Pamela's office décor, which includes numerous awards, makes it clear that she is a successful journalist but it soon becomes clear that she is less successful in her personal life, with no romantic prospects. After a bad blind date on the eve of her birthday, she drowns her sorrows in wine and pornography, and soon finds herself sifting through a box of old pictures. When she comes across a photo of an old boyfriend, Robert, she asks, 'Why did I let you go?' Pamela's alcohol-induced depression and loneliness becomes so dire that a couple of scenes later she attempts suicide by filling the bathtub with water and then dropping the hairdryer into it. She

Figure 18   Pamela (Rachel Griffiths) in *Me Myself I* (Karmel, 1999).

ultimately does not succeed because the hairdryer unplugs before it reaches the tub.

The day following her suicide attempt a hung-over Pamela is crossing the street and is hit by a car driven by . . . herself, or the alternate version of herself that stayed with, and married, Robert. The two Pamelas have coffee together, and then alternate Pamela (for the sake of clarity, I will refer to this version as Pamela 2) leaves our original Pamela (Pamela 1) to find out what a professional life without marriage and kids looks like. The plot follows Pamela 1 as she proceeds to live Pamela 2's life with Robert, three children and a house in the suburbs. Pamela is so excited to see Robert for the first time in many years (and to have a willing sexual partner) that she unknowingly rekindles a long-burnt-out sexual flame in Pamela 2's marriage. Soon Pamela 1 becomes more comfortable with her role as wife and mother and comes to realize that Pamela 2 did not fully abandon her passion for journalism. She has been working as a freelance writer for a woman's magazine but is forced to write about beauty and fashion, rather than hard-hitting topics. Pamela 1 is also shocked that Pamela 2's husband and family minimize her career. Her idealistic perception of domestic bliss is even further debunked when she learns that Pamela 2 and Robert have both been having affairs.

The Family Man begins with a scene between recent college graduates Jack (Nicholas Cage) and Kate (Téa Leoni) in the airport. Jack is about to board a plane to London to take a prestigious one-year finance position. Although his and Kate's 'plan' is for him to take advantage of this opportunity, Kate cites a bad feeling about the decision and urges him to choose their relationship over

Figure 19   Jack (Nicholas Cage) in *The Family Man* (Ratner, 2000).

his career. Jack chooses to board the plane instead, and the film fast forwards to thirteen years later. Here we see Jack as a single thirty-something who has chosen a career over love and family. Jack's life looks quite different than Pamela's life. He is a successful mergers and acquisitions executive who owns a Ferrari, designer suits, and a penthouse apartment in an exclusive building. Other than the occasional one-night stand, however, he is focused exclusively on work and his business acuity is so cutthroat that he is completely apathetic in the face of his employees' desire to be at home with their kids, rather than in the office, on Christmas Day.

During a late-night stop in a convenience store on Christmas Eve, Jack prevents a robbery from taking place. The robber (Don Cheadle) reveals himself to be a representative of some higher power who sees Jack's efforts to stop the crime as evidence of his capacity for goodness and altruism. As a reward for this good deed, Jack is given an opportunity to see what his life would have been like had he pursued this better side of himself and prioritized his relationship with Kate.

The next day (Christmas morning) Jack wakes up in bed in a New Jersey house with Kate and their two children. Upon glimpsing his alternate life, Jack initially attempts to return to his 'real' life but finds that, in this version of reality, his former self does not exist. He does his best to adjust to his new reality and, although he finds his new situation generic and underwhelming, he is able to successfully 'fake it' with friends and family. While Jack does not abandon hope that this alternate, seemingly less successful version of himself can achieve greater success, he is able to adjust to his new lifestyle. He eventually comes to realize that his love for Kate never faded, and that being a husband and a father appeals to him. However, as soon as Jack comes to this conclusion, he is transported back to his old life but with a new perspective. He gets in touch with Kate, who in this version of her life is on her way to Paris to take a promotion with her law firm, and tries to convince her that they should give their relationship another chance. He chases after her in the airport and convinces her to take a later flight. The film ends with Jack and Kate sitting in an airport lounge talking amiably, with the future undetermined but hopeful.

Me Myself I and *The Family Man* have similar underlying themes. They portray characters who are given a glimpse of what their lives would have been had they made different choices about romantic relationships. Unlike in *Sliding Doors*, we do not see these characters' alternative family selves glimpsing their single lives; they both only offer the perspective of the single selves glimpsing into the married lives. In *Me Myself I* Pamela 2 crosses over into Pamela 1's world, but the film does not show what Pamela 2 does while filling the shoes of an award-winning journalist – we only see that she is eager to return to her life with her husband and children. This emphasis on marriage versus single life suggests that regardless of whether one is happy or miserable as a single person, being married and having children is more fulfilling. While both films ultimately reach the same general conclusion about the benefit of family and love over solitude and professional success, one cannot help but be struck by the gendered nuances therein.

Me Myself I's portrait of depressed single Pamela is comedic and sympathetic, however, the film does not hesitate from implying that her situation is in need of a remedy. After filling Pamela 2's shoes, she returns to her single life with a renewed sense of confidence and takes a few simple steps to improve her previously unhealthy lifestyle: she redecorates her apartment, stocks her fridge, and buys herself flowers. But the film, true to romance form, reveals that due to Pamela 2's handiwork, she has piqued the interest of a man in whom she was interested before the crossover. And, his children from a previous marriage are even more appealing to Pamela 1 now that she has had her trial run as a parent. In short, the glimpse that we get of Pamela's revitalized single self is brief, and thus the film fails to effectively portray what lessons she has learned from the crossover. Its quick movement toward a romantic ending sees Pamela's 'problem' solved, but not without some residual questions about what a satisfied single Pamela might look like.

On the other hand, Jack's single life is seen as *too* satisfying. As far as he is concerned, money can buy him contentment, and being single does not exclude him from any of life's pleasures. Unlike the narrative of *Me Myself I*, the viewer is given no visible evidence of Jack's unhappiness, but is meant to intuit that he must be unsatisfied because he has no lasting relationships. In other words, the underlying causes for the two characters' lessons are strikingly different. The film seeks to correct Jack's superficial notion that greed and narcissism are more satisfying than love, by taking away his success and his money and giving him a family. The fact that *The Family Man*'s opening scenes take place on Christmas Eve, and the film was released during the Christmas season makes obvious its implicit homage to *It's a Wonderful Life*. As opposed to the goal of the classic film, which is to convince the poor, altruistic George Bailey that he is a great person worthy of living, the goal of *The Family Man* is to take away what George Bailey desperately wants – wealth and success – to teach Jack that none of these things are more important than love.

The implications of 'past' love are taken to an even more intertextual level in the nostalgia narrative, which sees a temporally situated fantasy of life in the past represented by a fiction film. These final case studies of temporality in the postfeminist romance cycle, *Sleepless in Seattle* and *Sex and the City*, coalesce many of the issues that we have discussed in this chapter thus far. They represent how seductive the past can be when it is channeled through Hollywood fiction films, and how the oscillation between fiction and reality, past and present, constructs an ongoing circular loop that solicits the participation of its viewers.

The Nostalgia Narrative

Now those were the days when people knew how to be in love.

Annie (Meg Ryan) in *Sleepless in Seattle*

The extreme nostalgia in *Sex and the City* and *Sleepless in Seattle* reveals how much women's roles and courtship rituals have changed over the course of recent history (in the case of these two texts – since the World War II and post-war period). These two texts also imply that inherent in women's postfeminist identity is an impulse to reconcile the past, present, and future simultaneously. However, nostalgia here is completely disconnected from a genuine recollection of, or longing for, the actual, lived historical past (and its accompanying socio-political ramifications). Rather, it is predicated on a desire for the seemingly purer, tidily packaged vision of romantic relationships represented in fictional texts produced in, and/or depicting, past historical periods.

The language of nostalgia in these two texts allows women (both inside and outside of the text) to fulfill their desire to 'have it both ways,' – to long for the unapologetic traditionalism of romance of a prefeminist past while still remaining in the more progressive present – without any negative repercussions. Nostalgia also establishes a collective 'we' among women in and outside of these texts, creating a communal language that they can use, both individually and collectively, to navigate the complicated postfeminist cultural and political terrain and perhaps, more importantly, to communicate with one another. There is some question as to whether its ability to link women with other women within a sort of community that effectively excludes men gives postfeminist nostalgia the potential to take on an empowering political dimension, or if the constraint of its fictional conduit negates this promise.[10]

Sex and the City and *The Way We Were*

Since the beginning of its run on HBO in 1998, and through its afterlife in syndication on TBS and in two feature films, *Sex and the City* has been regularly discussed as a quintessential postfeminist text. This is a result not just of its popularity among women in their twenties and thirties, but also because the program demonstrated a dramatic shift in the way television represented female characters and addressed female spectators. While producing the same kind of active fan base as previous shows created for a female audience throughout television history – such as daytime soap operas and nighttime dramas, as well as previous hit sit-coms like *The Mary Tyler Moore Show* (1970–7) and *Murphy Brown* (1988–98) – *Sex and the City* addresses the specific types of problems and challenges that face young, professional, unmarried women. The fact that the series was created with a considerable budget, was shot on film and on location in New York City, and was shown uninterrupted by commercials, allow for it to assume a more cinematic tone than some of these earlier women's programs.

Sex and the City clearly foregrounds the 'I,' as the show revolves around the subjectivity of Carrie (Sarah Jessica Parker), its central female character and narrator. Although *Sex* also focuses on the relationships of the other three characters, the viewer is most closely aligned with Carrie's point of view and subjective thought process. Carrie maintains a voiceover throughout every episode, not only speaking her own thoughts but also assuming to have knowledge of the thoughts of her friends. In fact, the theme of every show is mirrored by, and often aptly summarized in, the column that Carrie writes in that episode.

What is particularly interesting about *Sex*'s emphasis on subjectivity is its reflection of postfeminism as self-involved or 'me' feminism, as only revolved around a woman's individual choice, as opposed to women's collective choices. Despite the fact that the show is set in expansive Manhattan, its closed textual environment fails to present the female characters as part of a larger community or even as really needing anyone other than those who happen to enter their space. As a result, *Sex*'s four main characters have been read by the media as representations of all possible variations on femininity and female roles. Carrie is cute, agreeable, and playful; Miranda (Cynthia Nixon) is cynical and judgmental; Charlotte (Kristin Davis) is traditional, demure, and naive; and Samantha (Kim Cattrall) is bold and adventurous.

It is the skillful construction of these female characters and their universally identifiable qualities that fosters a sense of community among female spectators who recognize themselves in one or more of them. Recalling the blurred boundary between fact and fiction discussed in Chapter 2, the show's creator and producer Darren Star claimed that all of the scenarios depicted in the show are based on the real-life experiences of female friends and staff writers, and therefore the plots have a distinctly recognizable quality about them.[11] However, this female-to-female identification is channeled through fictional characters, rather than taking place among a real community of women.

The show's ability to blur the lines between reality and fiction was nowhere more evident than in the August 28, 2000 cover story of *TIME* magazine, 'Who needs a husband?', which featured a picture of the *Sex and the City* cast. Two articles accompanied the cover story, one of which discussed the difficult but empowering decision that many women make to forgo marriage and live a single life well into their late thirties and forties, and often permanently. The second of the two articles, entitled 'Waiting for Prince Charming', discussed the relevance of *Sex* as a 'pop-culture icon.'[12] The latter article's author, James Poniewozik, attempted to understand the manner in which *Sex and the City* tapped into the way in which women really think in its avoidance of 'p.c. feminism and love-conquers-all romanticism.' The show's realistic depiction of female interaction was at the core of many of the articles written about it. One critic in the *Los Angeles Times* wrote, 'It is arguably the first show to feature characters who talk the way real women do,'[13] and a *New Yorker* critic stated 'It's thrilling because you finally feel like you're watching real people talk about their real lives.'[14]

In order to prove the show's ability to reflect women's experiences accurately, the *New York Times* article sent a reporter to venture into the suburbs of Atlanta to uncover *Sex*'s popularity in a geographical location far removed from the show's Manhattan setting. It was revealed that *Sex*'s realistic dialogue and portrayal of female camaraderie was universally understood among women, regardless of the difference in geography. One Atlanta woman remarked, 'I feel like they really are saying what we're all thinking,' and another says, 'I love that on the show they talk about men the way that men talk about women. It turns the tables and I like to think of how I can do that in my own life.'[15]

The identification forged between *Sex and the City*'s female audience and the scenarios depicted in the show are mirrored in the episode 'Ex and the City,' which is the final episode of the series' second season. Carrie, Miranda, Charlotte, and Samantha are sitting in a café commiserating about the upcoming marriage of Carrie's ex-boyfriend, Mr. Big. As the women meet for cocktails, Carrie is avoiding the engagement party, which is being held six blocks away at The Plaza Hotel. She cannot accept the fact that Mr. Big, a consummate bachelor who had avoided making a commitment to her, has now chosen to marry a much younger woman with whom he had a whirlwind

Figure 20   Carrie (Sara Jessica Parker) in *Sex and the City* (1998–2004).

courtship. In an attempt to help Carrie with her predicament, Miranda offers Carrie a one-word statement – 'Hubble.' Carrie immediately takes this in and in a moment of understanding confirms Miranda's statement by replying, 'Oh my God, Hubble! It is! It is soooo Hubble!' As the scene soon explains, Hubble is the character played by Robert Redford in *The Way We Were*, who, as Miranda explains it to Samantha, 'is deeply in love with Katie but he can't be with her because she is complicated and has wild, curly hair.'

Carrie claims that just as Hubble never understood Katie, Mr. Big never truly understood her. This provides her with a sense of peace and gives her the courage she needs to attend the engagement party. In the scene immediately following, Carrie goes to The Plaza Hotel (also the site of the final scene of *The Way We Were*) to attend the last minutes of the party. Confronted by Mr. Big outside of the hotel, Carrie proceeds to reenact the final scene of *The Way We Were* when she recites the lines: 'Your girl is beautiful, Hubble.' Mr. Big replies, 'I don't get it' to which Carrie responds, summing up the crux of their relationship problems, by saying, 'No, and you never did.'

The implication of this exchange between Carrie and Big is that he cannot 'get' her because he does not understand the coded language that she is speaking. He does not recognize that she is quoting literally and figuratively

a famous romance text, nor does he recognize the implication of her reenact-
ment of *The Way We Were* and how it relates to their current predicament.
However, the text assumes that the spectator of this episode is fully aware of
the context of Carrie's reference, not just because *The Way We Were* has been
introduced in the preceding scene but because there is an assumption that *Sex
and the City*'s female community of spectators are already familiar with the
plot and pivotal moments of the classic film. Therefore the nostalgia for *The
Way We Were* presented in this scene serves to forge a bond and a level of
understanding between women both within and outside of *Sex and the City*'s
textual environment. Carrie's ability to circumvent Mr. Big's continued power
over her emotions by speaking this communal language, to which she knows
he has no access, creates a sense of victory, both for her and *Sex*'s female
audience.

This episode highlights the manner in which many postfeminist romance
texts, such as those that I examined in Chapter 2, show women to be divided
from men along the lines of a shared, collective language. It also demonstrates
the large degree to which film and television play a role in the formulation of
this language. When Carrie and her friends discuss *The Way We Were*, they
are not only talking about the plot of the film but also their collective memory
of watching the text, despite the fact that they did not necessarily engage in
this activity together. It is implied that the audience of women watching *Sex
and the City* are being cued to take part in the same type of recollection and
therefore they have two degrees of textual identification – that in response
to *Sex and the City,* and another in response to *The Way We Were*. Like the
discussion of the theme song from *The Way We Were* that began this chapter,
Sex and the City's nostalgia renders this recollection as a pleasurable space
that unites a 'we,' which, in this case, not only consists of *Sex*'s contemporary
female spectators, but also of the women of the 1970s (*The Way We Were*'s
period of production) and the women of the 1940s and 1950s (the period
depicted in the film). The pleasure of breaking down these boundaries between
past and present, fiction and reality, and characters and spectators is seen to an
even greater extent in *Sleepless in Seattle*.

Sleepless in Seattle and *An Affair to Remember*

One of many cinematic reexaminations of the 1939 film *Love Affair*, faith-
fully remade twice in Leo McCarey's *An Affair to Remember* and Glenn
Gordon Caron's 1994's *Love Affair*, 1993's *Sleepless in Seattle* is the consummate nostalgia text. Its place within this long lineage of remakes highlights
its self-referential tone, and is evidence of the postfeminist romance cycle's
aforementioned tendency to revisit and recycle the same traditional romance
narrative over and over again. At its core, *Sleepless* is a film about the state of

heterosexual romantic relationships in the 1990s, and presents its female protagonists, Annie (Meg Ryan) and Becky (Rosie O'Donnell), as actively seeking
their destined love matches. They wonder aloud if there is such a thing as
destiny or if their consistent spectatorship of classic romance films has merely
led them to believe that it exists. In the process of engaging with the reality
of their own historical time in which true romance is lacking, the film and its
characters turn to *An Affair to Remember* as a representation of the past and
a purer vision of what romance could and should be.

An Affair to Remember is regularly cited as one of the most popular romance
texts in American film history and was ranked number five on the American
Film Institute's '100 Years, 100 Passions' list. The plot features Nickie (Cary
Grant) and Terry (Deborah Kerr), who meet on a cruise ship. Despite the fact
that they are both involved with other people (both conspicuously absent),
they fall in love. As the boat docks at their destination – New York Harbor
– they decide to end their respective relationships, and to reunite on the top
of the Empire State Building on Valentine's Day. When the day finally comes,
Terry is so overcome with anticipation on her way to meet Nickie that she
focuses her attention upward to the top of the Empire State Building, and
does not see an oncoming taxicab, which hits her. The accident paralyzes her
from the waist down. Nickie interprets her absence as a betrayal and with his
sense of pride devastated, he returns to his life without contacting Terry to see
what became of her. Terry is ashamed of her disability and also refrains from
contacting Nickie, never knowing if he, in fact, showed up for their reunion.
Eventually, through a convoluted turn of events, Nickie realizes what has happened, rushes to Terry's apartment, and the two reconcile in a very emotional,
cathartic concluding scene.

Affair fits perfectly into Steve Neale's characterization of romance as an
inherently temporal form. In his article, 'Melodrama and tears,' Neale argues
that romance films engage in a particularly complex interaction with their
spectators, granting them privileged knowledge of the couple's destiny to be
together. The inability of the characters to communicate their true feelings to
each other causes the spectator to have a profound investment in the eventual
resolution of the couple, and in turn, the film. The structure of the melodrama
text, as Neale points out, is based around the failure of points of view – either
'moral or ideological opinion or position of judgment' or 'function of access
to narrative "facts"' – to match or correspond.[16] Therefore, the film is based
around the prolongation of the time that it takes for the characters' knowledge
to align with the knowledge of the spectator. However, Neale argues, this
alignment often comes too late, causing the spectator to experience a sense of
loss, often leading to tears.

For Neale the tears do not necessarily only accompany a spectator's feeling
of loss in response to a missed opportunity for fulfillment but also indicate

a desire for the future fulfillment of what has been lost in the present. He contends:

> if they are over at this time, in this particular film, the wish and its fantasy are not themselves lost, destroyed forever; they are shown as capable of fulfillment; they can hence be re-engaged, re-articulated, perhaps finally fulfilled in the next film, the next melodrama (or the next episode of a soap opera).[17]

As Neale aptly sums up, the temporality inherent within the individual romance text is not contained within its diegetic confines but is dependent on the spectator for its effect. The extra-textual reach of this interaction is also apparent in the ongoing desire produced by the romance narrative itself, which the individual text lacks the ability to fulfill on its own.

Sleepless in Seattle appropriates the anticipation and desire generated by *Affair*, both in its homage to the film's plot structure and in its reverence for the desire generated by the temporality of its romance. In fact, the desire for the romance narrative is sustained for *Sleepless*'s entire plot, as the two lovers do not actually meet until the last scene of the film. The film is about Sam (Tom Hanks), a recent widower with a young son, Jonah (Ross Malinger) and Annie, a journalist who is engaged to Walter (Bill Pullman), the sweet but dull associate publisher of the newspaper for which she works. The main impetus for action within the plot of the film is Jonah's phone call to a radio show, expressing his concern for his grieving widower father, and his desire to see him start a new relationship. The response to the sensitivity portrayed by Sam in his discussion with the radio psychologist assumes epic proportions, resulting in thousands of letters from women interested in knowing him.

This phone call to the radio show also captures the attention of Annie, who becomes obsessed with Sam and the possibility that he could be her soul mate. Becky encourages her to pretend to write a newspaper story about Sam and the radio show so that she can investigate him under professional pretenses. After receiving a letter from Annie (which she initially threw away but Becky later sent), Jonah becomes convinced that she is the right person for Sam and, in the face of his father's hesitancy, goes to New York on Valentine's Day to meet Annie at the top of the Empire State Building per her request. Sam chases after Jonah, eventually meets up with Annie, and the two immediately recognize the 'magic' between them as soul mates.

Sleepless distinguishes itself from the 1994 *Love Affair* remake not only by refusing to directly imitate the story or use any variation of the *Love Affair* title, but also by suggesting that to be truly contemporary, it must be self-conscious about its own participation in a broader lineage of films and the larger role that such films play in social and historical discourses. The film is not just about romance but about women watching women watch romance and the ramifications of this watching on the romantic 'psyches' of both men and women. In fact, the film assumes that everyone is connected through his or her spectatorship of media texts.

Like the nostalgia depicted in *Sex and the City*, the deeply felt connection between the female characters in *Sleepless* and *An Affair to Remember* has less to do with their experience of the plot of the film than with their experience as spectators watching the film, and the emotional catharsis this spectatorship grants them. Whether *Affair* has been watched once in the past and needs to be recalled from memory, or has been watched over and over again on a daily or weekly basis, all the women in *Sleepless* are familiar with the film. And, like the discussion of *The Way We Were* in *Sex and the City,* this is not only the basis for a sense of solidarity among the women in the film who claim that 'men never get the movie,' but also a foundation for solidarity with the female spectators of *Sleepless*, who not only identify with their onscreen counterparts, but also with their counterparts' identification of another set of onscreen counterparts in *Affair*. Just as Carrie's reference to *The Way We Were* excluded Mr. Big, *Sleepless*'s romance discourse also excludes men. However, in this case they are outsiders by choice, as they consistently belittle the female characters' preoccupation with romance. In fact, as a mocking response to his sister's tear-filled recollection of a scene from *An Affair to Remember*, Sam and his brother-in-law describe their relationship with the classic 'male' action film, *The Dirty Dozen*, and they go out of their way to make clear that their

Figure 21   Annie (Meg Ryan) and Becky (Rosie O'Donnell) in *Sleepless in Seattle* (Ephron, 1993).

recollections are dependent entirely on plot and action, rather than any real emotional response.

This distinction is important as it serves to highlight *Sleepless*'s implicit proposition that media spectatorship plays an important role in informing one's relationship to broader historical discourses. While we have seen how the postfeminist romance film should always be read as implicitly – if not explicitly – engaging women's relationship to larger political, social, and ideological issues, *Sleepless in Seattle*'s transparently discusses such matters, making overt mention of the state of contemporary male-female relations, the changing nature of femininity and masculinity, and the influence of feminism. While women dominate *Sleepless*'s narrative, their investment in the historical time of the past – in *An Affair* – affects their ability to maintain a powerful sense of agency in their own historical present. The male characters in the film are able to distinguish between the past and the present, action and emotion; they thus are granted a seemingly more objective, and perhaps more authoritative, position in the film. As we have seen before, the film creates a set of oppositions placing men on the side of reality and objectivity and women on the side of fantasy and subjectivity.

Several scenes demonstrate the frequency with which the male characters in *Sleepless* spout generalizations about gender positioning in the 1990s: 'Every man in America saw *Fatal Attraction* and it scared the hell out of them,' 'Only desperate women are forced to call into radio talk shows in their search for a husband,' and 'A woman over the age of forty is more likely to be killed by a terrorist than find a husband.' These comments are delivered as comedic asides, which seemingly diffuse their potency. However, they also construct an idea of women that falls in line with the regressive mentality combated by Susan Faludi's *Backlash*, which was the first to identify and discuss postfeminism, and is obviously the unnamed book being referenced in the film. All of the contentions that men make about 'women' are, on some level, a dismissal of the female dependence on fantasy and ideas about life that are overly associated with the past.

For *Sleepless*'s female characters, this logical account of contemporary reality is seen to be of very little interest. Annie and Becky are successful journalists, which assumes that they are highly educated and intelligent, yet, while they are well-versed in their knowledge of romance film and television, they hesitate to counter any of the male-designated logic with an intelligent argument. Even when Annie tries her best to deflate the 'terrorist statistic' by making vague mention of *Backlash*, her argument quickly loses steam. The only topic about which all of the women in the film speak with passion is romance, particularly as it is portrayed in *An Affair*. In fact, the world of *An Affair*, meaning not just the film itself, but the mode of spectatorship that the film elicits, is represented as a welcome and necessary refuge for women. While the men doggedly try to sustain the distinction between *Affair*'s past textual and historical space and the space of the contemporary present, the women invite the collapse of boundaries and find pleasure in moving in and out of these metaphorical spaces. However, it seems that the more they attempt to bring their conception of romance as depicted in *An Affair* into the world of the present, the more it is deflated by the logic of men, and hence the more they need to return to the text as a safe haven.

Both *Sex and the City* and *Sleepless in Seattle* celebrate a fluid idea of spectatorship that allows these female viewers to transcend historical time and assume different subject positions, an act that they share with the other characters discussed in this chapter. As we have seen in all of the examples, the frequent recurrence of a time travel device that pits the past against the present has a great deal to tell us about postfeminist culture. As Jackie Stacey and Lynne Pearce point out in the introduction to the anthology *Romance Revisited*, 'As so many books and films have shown, desire for "another" . . . is often symptomatic of discontent with ourselves and our way of life, and a recognition of this can sometimes provide the catalyst for transformation and change.'[18] We can read these texts as a manifestation of this desire – whether it is the desire for another person, another life, or another time – and that this desire is symptomatic of a larger discontent within the texts' historical present. By presenting the past and the present at the same time, these texts reflect women's negotiation of traditional and contemporary ideas of romance in their own lives. They reinforce a sense of solidarity and community among women who have contradiction and confusion in common. This breakdown of distinctions gets at the blurred boundaries of postfeminism. Sarah Gamble speaks to this issue in her entry on postfeminism in the *Routledge Critical Dictionary of Feminism and Postfeminism*:

> The source of such confusion, for postfeminism as much as for postmodernism, is at least partially due to the semantic uncertainty generated by the prefix. Turning again to the *Concise Oxford Dictionary*, 'post' is defined as 'after in time or order', but not as denoting rejection. Yet many feminists argue strongly that postfeminism constitutes precisely that – a betrayal of a history of feminist struggle, and rejection of all it has gained . . . but it is possible to argue that the prefix 'post' does not necessarily always direct us back to where we've come. Instead, its trajectory is bewilderingly uncertain, since while it can certainly be interpreted as suggestive of a relapse *back* to a former set of ideological beliefs, it can also be read as indicating the *continuation* of the originating term's aims and ideologies, albeit on a different level.[19]

While, as Gamble states, the trajectory of postfeminism is bewilderingly uncertain, as long as this uncertain temporality remains satisfying and women continue to find pleasure in the simultaneous embrace and disavowal of time, contemporary fiction texts will continue to foreground these concerns as a way of representing the ambivalence that pervades this era.

NOTES

1. Mary Ann Doane, *The Desire to Desire: The Woman's Film of the 1940s* (Bloomington: Indiana University Press, 1987), p. 106.
2. Ibid. p. 96.
3. Ibid. p. 107.
4. Yvonne Tasker and Diane Negra, 'Introduction: Feminist politics and postfeminist culture', in Y. Tasker and D. Negra (eds), *Interrogating Postfeminism: Gender and the Politics of Popular Culture* (Durham, NC: Duke University Press, 2007), p. 10.
5. Denise Riley, *Am I That Name?* (Minneapolis: University of Minnesota Press, 1988), p. 96.
6. Ibid. p. 2.
7. Ibid. p. 14.
8. David Bordwell, 'Film futures,' *SubStance*, 97, 31: 1 (2002), 91.
9. The seven conventions of forking-path narratives are: (1) forking paths are linear; (2) the fork is signposted; (3) forking paths intersect sooner or later; (4) forking-path tales are unified by traditional cohesion devices; (5) forking paths will often run parallel; (6) all paths are not equal; the last one taken presupposes the others; and (7) all paths are not equal; the last one taken, or completed, is the least hypothetical one.
10. It is clear that my discussion of the postfeminist nostalgia romance text departs from previous definitions of nostalgia in film and television scholarship, specifically Frederic Jameson's definition of the nostalgia film in his essay 'Post-modernism and consumer society.' Jameson defines two types of nostalgia films: first, 'films about the past and/or about specific generational moments of that past,' as in *American Graffiti* and second, films such as *Raiders of the Lost Ark* which: 'reinventing the feel and shape of characteristic art objects of an older period, seek to reawaken a sense of the past associated with those objects.' While nostalgia romance texts like *Sleepless in Seattle* and *Sex and the City* aim to elicit an emotional response by conjuring an idea of the past, they depart from Jameson's definition in two ways. First, these texts are not set in the past but in the contemporary era of their own production. This setting within the contemporary postfeminist period of the 1990s is instrumental in providing the motivation for the characters' want and/or need to reflect on the past. Second, the nostalgia romance text is not nostalgic for a past historical time per se, but for the 'idea' of that historical time as it is represented in another fictional text, and is reverential to the classic text's narrative and/or its values. In other words, in these film and television texts, what comes to be known as the past is even further removed from a concrete sense of history. Having been channeled through Hollywood fiction, the memories are more subjective and 'water-colored' than usual. Frederic Jameson, 'Post-modernism and consumer society,' in John Belton (ed.), *Movies and Mass Culture* (New Brunswick, NJ: Rutgers University Press, 1996), pp. 190–2.
11. Tim Cornwell, 'Is it just dirty talk for girls?', *TIME*, 15 January 1999.
12. James Poniewozik, 'Waiting for Prince Charming', *TIME*, 28 July 2000, 50–1.

13. Mimi Avins, 'Let's talk about "sex": they sure do', *Los Angeles Times*, 5 June 1999.
14. Nancy Franklin, 'Sex and the single girl', *The New Yorker*, 6 July 1998, 74.
15. Nancy Hass, '*Sex* sells, the city and elsewhere', *The New York Times*, 11 July 1999.
16. Steve Neale, 'Melodrama and tears', *Screen*, 27: 6 (1986), 8.
17. Ibid. p. 21.
18. Jackie Stacey and Lynne Pearce, 'The heart of the matter: feminists revisit romance,' in Jackie Stacey and Lynne Pearce (eds), *Romance Revisited* (New York: New York University Press, 1995), p. 13.
19. Sarah Gamble, 'Postfeminism', in Sarah Gamble (ed.), *The Routledge Critical Dictionary of Feminism and Postfeminism* (New York: Routledge, 1999), p. 44.

4. SEXY VS. FUNNY: SEXUALITY IN THE POSTFEMINIST CYCLE

> If you spell sex in marketing materials, it doesn't sell. If you spell fun, it sells. Sex inside a comedy candy-coats sex and allows the audience to feel comfortable. Laughter covers up insecurity. Sex sells, but not serious sex. Films can be sexy, but they can't portray the sexual intimacy most people crave. In the movies, you have to make safe sex palatable to a younger audience. The portrayal has to be violent or funny.
>
> Producer Peter Guber, *The Hollywood Reporter*[1]

For those who presume that Hollywood's ideological inner workings operate at an unconscious level, Peter Guber's comments regarding sexuality in the above quote, while disturbing, are refreshingly transparent. Sexuality, he contends, has a particular place in contemporary Hollywood films. It must be presented in one of two styles, either comedic or violent, in order to put the audience at ease. However, sex portrayed in a 'realistic' manner cannot be represented in mainstream films because it does not sell, particularly, as Guber goes on to say, to a very important segment of the population – men.[2] This chapter reflects on the implications of Guber's sentiments by examining the discourses in and around female sexuality in the postfeminist romance cycle. In the post-Code era, sexuality is both highly visible and increasingly invisible, depending on the media form that one is considering. On one end of the cultural spectrum we have what Ariel Levy has identified as 'raunch' culture, wherein women and young girls' sexual identity revolves around being seen as a sexual object. On the other end, we see the growing conservative trend toward purity balls wherein young girls make an official pledge to their fathers to remain virgins until they get married. Tied up in all of these contradictory messages are questions about the relationship between sexual exploration (or lack thereof) and romantic love. The postfeminist romance film reflects the complexity of these various perspectives, introducing multiple overlapping sets of tensions to which Guber's opening comments allude: between dramatic and comedic narrative forms, fun and serious female protagonists, and between adventurous sexual desire and a malleable, naive, and demure resistance to sexuality.

The case studies that follow examine these either/or dynamics with a focus on two of the clearest manifestations of postfeminist culture's frequent recapitulation of a false conflict between sexuality and romance. First, we will look at the comedies *When Harry Met Sally*, *Pretty Woman*, *13 Going on 30* and the television show *New Girl* (2011–), which feature female protagonists who are endearing as a direct result of their close resemblance to prepubescent girls. And then we will turn to romantic dramas, including *Fatal Attraction*, *Unfaithful* and *In the Cut* that see their protagonists' pursuit of sexuality outside of the confines of romance as dangerous and often tragic. These are two distinct subgenres that have a point of commonality: romantic fulfillment is part of a female protagonist's personal development but her sexual fulfillment is viewed as peripheral at best and aberrant at worst.

By examining these two strikingly different representations of adult women, and the contexts in which they arise, we can better understand the stakes inherent in the perennially contentious public discourse on the need to regulate female sexuality, and the degree to which romantic discourses play a role therein. The chapter ends with a brief examination of two films, *Friends with Benefits* and *No Strings Attached*, and the television show *Girls* that find middle ground between these two binaries that oppose the cute prepubescent girl and the dangerous woman. These media texts show signs of incremental change in this arena even amidst public debates surrounding women's reproductive rights that remain entrenched in sexual dichotomies.

Sexuality vs. Romance in Film History

Theorist Brian Henderson's aforementioned seminal 1977 article 'Romantic comedy today: semi-tough or impossible?' is a good place to begin this discussion of tension between sexuality and romance in the postfeminist romance film. Henderson argues that cultural transformations of the 1970s and the loosening of industrial restraints like the Production Code posed a significant challenge to the romantic comedy form. Citing a dialogue sequence from Michael Ritchie's 1977 *Semi-Tough* wherein the female protagonist Barbara (Jill Clayburgh) asks the male protagonist Billy (Burt Reynolds), 'How come we never fucked?' he concludes, 'It is arguable that romantic comedy depends on the suppression of this question and that with its surfacing romantic comedy becomes impossible.'[3] Henderson's point is that by resisting the classical romantic comedy golden rule (and industry imperative) by emphasizing, rather than repressing, sexuality, *Semi-Tough* (and, we might assume, other romance films from the 1970s) represents a fundamental and potentially irrevocable shift in the genre. Whether we accept Henderson's contention or not, he does point to a brief instance in American film history during which representations of romance and sexuality were as complex as the real adult behavior that they reflected. But interestingly, feminism plays only an implicit rather than explicit role in Henderson's argument. This is surprising for many reasons, not the least of which is that a female, not a male, character initiates the 'fucking' discussion.

Indeed, *Semi-Tough*, and the scholarly characterization of its significance, further illustrates Chapter 1's discussion of 1970s American cinema's different approach to sexual mores. These changes reflect the degree to which sexuality, specifically its association with heterosexual romantic love, was a prominent part of the era's political discourse.[4] Steven Seidman has argued that there were two major 'fronts' in the sexuality debate in the second-wave feminist movement, remnants of which remain today. While liberal feminists – the older, more traditional group including Betty Friedan – had profoundly different views than younger radical feminists – such as Andrea Dworkin and Kate Millet – both groups frowned upon feminist politics becoming aligned with sexual liberation.[5] Whereas Friedan argued that, 'sex in the America of the feminine mystique is becoming a strangely joyless national compulsion, if not a contemptuous mockery,' the radical feminists' contested the sexual revolution on the grounds that it promoted the same phallocentric sexual framework that feminism was fighting against.[6] As Seidman summarizes, 'radical feminists framed sex as a site of gender politics. What is defined as sex, who does what to whom, how and when, is said to reflect primarily gender power relations.'[7]

Contemporaneous to these politically motivated debates on the intersections of female autonomy, romance, and sexuality was the late Helen Gurley Brown's 1964 book, *Sex and the Single Girl*. Gurley Brown's decidedly non-political, consumer-oriented approach to these issues is regularly pointed to as the precursor to postfeminist ideals. She celebrated the freedom that the sexual revolution granted women, promoting the single woman's pursuit of her own sexual needs, and arguing that personal satisfaction and pleasure could be found through sexual exploration outside of marriage or a committed relationship. This philosophy was further promoted in follow-up books and in the pages of *Cosmopolitan* magazine, of which she remained the editor-in-chief until 1997. Gurley Brown's association of female sexual empowerment with cosmetic and fashion accouterments was interpreted by other second-wavers as pushing women into a cycle of consumerism that was just as enslaving as domesticity and marriage. As she herself noted in 1972, 'There is a catch to achieving single bliss. You have to work like a son of a bitch.'[8]

Gurley Brown's philosophy of sexual empowerment clearly illustrates Hilary Ann Radner's contention that during second-wave feminism individual sexual needs and desires were co-opted by consumer culture. Radner suggests that Gurley Brown initiated a new type of discourse of femininity, which 'marks out an arena of reproduction that is primarily narcissistic – in which the woman reproduces, not another, or for another, but herself for herself.'[9] This discourse indeed becomes dominant in the postfeminist period but, as I will argue later, gets projected onto a much different type of body than that of which Gurley Brown speaks.

Given the cacophony of voices during the 1970s that arose on this issue of female sexuality, and the growing conservatism of the media industry and the socio-political landscape in the 1980s, it is hardly surprising that, with a few exceptions, representations of the woman as sexual desiring subject rarely amount to more than brief glimpses, most of which are eventually counter-manded through narrative means. As we know, sexual representation has always been at the heart of the cultural battles fought on the terrain of the movie industry, including those surrounding the MPAA ratings system con-temporaneous to these feminist political debates.[10] In *Screening Sex*, Linda Williams refers to the hints of 'carnal knowledge' seen in films from the 1960s and 1970s as coming 'to American screens at the end of the Code in some of the same ways in which it comes to the child: in deferred, partial ways, never at the right time, and almost never as a clear revelation,' offering 'a dynamic of a deferred knowledge that either comes too late or a shocking knowledge that comes too soon.'[11]

The way in which sexuality or, carnal knowledge, comes to be represented in the 1980s and 1990s – what is shown, not shown, and the tone of this representation – reveals a great deal about the evolution of the romance genre form and about how contemporary culture treats the very knowledge of which Williams speaks. Even though the current MPAA system is less restrictive than the Production Code, contemporary Hollywood films still marginalize open displays of sexuality. It is diverted, for example, into a different category of direct-to-video films labeled by Nina Martin and Linda Ruth Williams as 'erotic thrillers.'[12] As Linda Williams has argued, in mainstream films, 'the pos-sibly different rhythms and temporalities of a woman's pleasure were simply not acknowledged.'[13] This tendency became even further solidified with the MPAA's introduction of the PG-13 rating in 1984, which informed parents 'some images may not be appropriate for children under the age of 13.'[14] Rather than being either safe for almost all audience members (PG) or a decid-edly adult audience (R), the PG-13 rating combines elements of both – creating a hybrid form in which most representations of sexuality are made palatable to a thirteen-year-old mentality.

Until the mid-1980s, there were many R-rated romantic comedy films that represented both romance and sexuality simultaneously, such as *10* (Edwards, 1979), *Class* (Carlino, 1983), and *About Last Night* (Zwick, 1986), among many others. But toward the end of the decade, and into the 1990s and 2000s, filmmakers took advantage of the PG-13 rating to explore adult female sexuality in distinctly different ways. Adam Markowitz has discussed how 'the once abundant Hollywood Sex Scene is now officially an endangered species' and that this increasing trend in the 1990s was a product of studios' targeting of 'teenage boys, those walking hormone piñatas, as their most reliable customers.' While 'badass heroes, explosions, and tight-shirted ladies' are welcome, 'romantic subplots? *Boooring*. And forget about substantial nudity; teens might want to see it, but the MPAA doesn't want them to – not until they are 17.'[15] Just as Guber's earlier quote suggests, in comedic films, sex became an off-screen activity or played entirely for laughs. Alternatively, it was diverted to serious dramatic films that portray it in a completely opposite context: the forbidden 'fucking,' manifested in an affair or a casual encounter, portrayed as the joyless, counterproductive and often dangerous compulsion described by Friedan, Dworkin and Millet. In other words, second-wave feminists' debates are reflected in these different permutations of female sexuality found in the postfeminist romance film.

Yet another type of representation, Gurley Brown's idea of 'female subject as object', is prominent as well, particularly in media texts that deal with teenage girls. One of the inevitable by-products of contemporary culture's growing unease with adult female sexuality is the increasing proclivity toward taking younger and younger women as objects, marginalizing older women's sexual desires with labels such as 'Cougar' or 'MILF (Mother I would Like to Fuck).' Because the sexualization of young girls is bound up with the changing representation of adult female sexuality, it is worthwhile to explore briefly the terrain of this latter accompanying trend, which has been the subject of much recent critical discussion.

NOT A GIRL . . . NOT YET A WOMAN

Throughout the 1990s and 2000s, American popular culture has seen the collapse of the crucial distinction between female adolescence and adulthood, affecting how we talk about both young and adult women's sexuality. The line from the 2001 Britney Spears song that serves as this section's subheading is an apt example. It is told from the position of a young girl who says that she feels like she is caught in between two worlds and wants a moment that is her own while trying to figure out how to gracefully, and comfortably, move from girlhood to womanhood. However, the song illustrates that no such place exists. What has disappeared is the temporal space in between adolescence and maturity that might serve as a sort of transitional refuge in which young girls figure out how to become women. There is a great irony underlying the fact that Spears articulated this anxiety: the video for her 1998 breakout single 'Baby One More Time,' which features her dressed up like a sexy schoolgirl, is one of the most infamous examples of the objectification of young women.

Kathleen Rowe Karlyn has written eloquently about this issue in her case study of the 1999 Oscar-winning film *American Beauty* (Mendes, 1999). Karlyn links the growing presence of the early 1990s 'girl culture/girl power' movement to the 'crisis in masculinity' and the crisis in the family caused by feminism. She aptly surmises, 'There is no doubt that American culture eroticizes little girls who act like women, and women who act like girls.'[16] The trend about which she speaks is growing more and more pervasive as time passes. For instance, two popular teen television series, The CW's *Gossip Girl* (2007–12) and MTV's *Skins* (2011), provoked the ire of the conservative-leaning Parent's Television Council due to their sexually provocative depictions of teens who are bold in their pursuit of sexual interaction and decidedly less interested in the rituals surrounding dating and courtship. The television show *Glee* (2009–present), which is a frequent target of the Parents' Television Council's attacks, was also the subject of controversy when two of its female stars appeared in a sexually charged photo shoot for the November 2010 issue of *GQ* magazine. It is clear that the *Leave it to Beaver*-era nostalgia-infused ideas of sock hops and soda shops and even the 1980s-era teen romance rituals perpetuated by John Hughes's films are long gone, much to the discomfort of neo-conservative watchdog groups.

In 2004, the *New York Times Magazine* registered on this trend in a cover story entitled 'What ever happened to teen romance?' The article traces the degree to which America's youth have abandoned dating or romance in favor of a culture of sexual exploration or 'hooking up' that is divorced from its traditional associations with emotional attachment, resembling what we might usually consider or want to assume to be adult behavior. Author Benoit Denizet-Lewis interviews many male and female teens from different socio-economic backgrounds, but her focus is on the potential for this trend of sexual experimentation to do emotional harm to the girls.[17] However, with the exception of one female interview subject who claims to have been emotionally hurt because of 'hook-up' culture, most of her teen women claim that they have no problem distinguishing between the two. But the 'expert' consulted on the subject, Dr. Drew Morton, the cohost of *Loveline* and of *Celebrity Rehab*, voices his suspicions about this new supposedly 'empowered' perspective. He reinforces the age-old contention that young women cannot possibly enjoy these interactions: 'The fact is, girls don't enjoy hook-ups nearly as much as boys no matter what they say at the time. They're only doing it because that's what the boys want.'[18]

Whether or not these young women do genuinely enjoy no-strings-attached sexual experiences is difficult if not impossible to answer due to the many layers of cultural constructions and expectations that factor into the question.[19] When turning our attention purely to the visual representations, however, it is perfectly clear that while these texts emphasize, if not fetishize, sexualized images of young women, narratively they downplay the potential satisfaction that they might gain from sex, suggesting that their interests lie solely in romance and emotional connection. This reveals the ways in which contemporary culture disconnects emotions or romantic connections on the one hand and sexual expression on the other.

According to Ariel Levy, this trend has led to the rise of a 'raunch culture' in which young women are not taught how to distinguish between authentic sexual agency and a sexuality that is designed to be seen by others. She argues that our cardio-striptease, 'Girls Gone Wild' era has led young women to think of sexual empowerment as akin to 'performing sexuality,' that is, as purely enacted for the gaze of men, leading them farther and farther away from authentic feelings of sexual pleasure. This, as she explains, could not be further removed from what second-wave feminism had in mind for women. She sarcastically laments the degree to which postfeminism has rendered a feminist outlook outdated:

> If you still suffer from the (hopelessly passé) conviction that valuing a woman on the sole basis of her hotness is, if not disgusting and degrading, then at least dehumanizing, if you still cling to the (pathetically deluded) hope that a more abundant enjoyment of the 'sex stuff' could come from a reexamination of old assumptions, then you are clearly stuck in the past (and you'd better get a clue, but quick).[20]

Levy's identification of the ways in which postfeminist culture has embraced 'hotness' and sexuality as markers of empowerment recalls Radner's discussion of Helen Gurley Brown's conflation of consumerism, sexuality and autonomy forty years earlier, and Charlotte Brundson's argument that early postfeminist films such as *Working Girl* and *Pretty Woman* required that the female characters can only be agents of desire if they are desirable at the same time.[21] As all of these authors argue, the idea that one needs to revel in their own sexual objectification in order to feel like a sexual subject is highly problematic for women. The fact that this is part of contemporary America's sexual climate, the one in which young girls come of age, only raises the stakes even further.

That contemporary culture increasingly sees girls' sexual awakening stripped of authentic emotional or psychological empowerment, and reduced to a facade of performance can be linked to the limited screen representations of healthy and active adult female sexuality seen since the mid-1980s. To return to Peter Guber's comments that open this chapter, the sex that sells is not that which presents the 'intimacy that most people crave' which would be between two consenting adults of an age where the responsibilities of permanent emotional connection would exist. Rather, what sells is images that seem designed to placate cultural anxiety about sexually empowered adult women: images of young girls who are too young to exert their authority in the social and political sphere.

So what then has become of the adult woman since 1977's *Semi-Tough*'s Barbara Bookman? As we will see in the following clusters of case studies, there are two very different places in which she can be found: First, in comedic films and media texts wherein her sexuality is made chaste so as to be palatable to a broad family audience. And second, she is seen in R-rated dramatic films, wherein her active pursuit of sexual fulfillment is intertwined with a plot that turns dark and murderous. Demonstrating the dichotomous nature of these representations illuminates the innumerable perspectives on sexuality that fall in between these positions that Hollywood might explore in more depth and with more frequency.

This section's subheading – a play on the aforementioned Britney Spears song – could very well serve as the theme song for the bulk of comedic romance texts of the postfeminist period. It recalls the other side of the dynamic about which Kathleen Rowe Karlyn speaks: the eroticization of women who act like little girls. However, arguably, these women are not eroticized at all. It is their de-eroticization that makes them so endearing. Whether it be through naiveté, irresponsibility, a failure to acknowledge and act on true sexual desire, or an 'aw shucks' view of men as protectors and keepers of security and family, the traditional romantic comedy female protagonist is rendered adorable and endearing. Even in cases where this character's sexual past is acknowledged, the text always represents her as the kind of woman that men want to marry, not the kind that, to return to Brian Henderson's piece, they want to 'fuck.' This is not to say that 'fucking' is absent in the larger universe in which these films take place, but by presenting this world through the subjectivity of the 'cute' female protagonist, female sexual agency is evaded.

This trend toward cuteness finds its genesis in film and television texts beginning in the late 1980s. *When Harry Met Sally*'s Sally (Meg Ryan) might be seen as the original prototype for the 'cute' girl-woman figure. Beginning with the first post-college segment of the film, she is portrayed as neurotic and uptight about everything including sex, which is made clear by what Harry deems her improper reading of the film *Casablanca*. As they arrive at a diner on their road trip from Chicago to New York, Sally informs Harry that she believes that Elsa (Ingrid Bergman) wants to leave on the plane with her husband, Victor (Paul

Henreid), as opposed to staying with her lover, Rick (Humphrey Bogart). To which Harry replies that the only motivating factor for interpreting the film in this way is that Sally must not have had great sex yet. Indeed, the extent of Sally's sex life portrayed in the movie includes her insistence that she has indeed had 'plenty of great sex' with her college boyfriend, Sheldon, and then her recounting of her 'sex fantasy' where a mystery man 'rips her clothes off' (in which only her fashion choices change as she ages into a mature woman), and, of course, her iconic orgasm performance.

While pre-marriage and post-divorce Harry's (Billy Crystal) sexual behavior – sleeping with women who he does not necessarily like and then sharing the details with both Sally and his best male friend, Jess (Bruno Kirby) – is not seen to be particularly fulfilling, his sexuality is rendered as seamlessly integral to his identity. However, for Sally, issues of sexuality are made to be cute or kooky in some way. In his study of Meg Ryan's romantic comedy stardom, Peter William Evans quite aptly contends that Ryan 'epitomizes the genre's safe-sex alternative,' and that she is the 'very essence of loyalty, trustworthiness, and all things natural, she is the approachable safe harbor for all those negotiating the Scylla and Charybdis of modern sexuality.'[22]

The contemporary romantic comedy's promotion of the safe harbor qualities of the cute female protagonist archetype of which Evans speaks become quite clear when reading the explicit performativity involved in the deli fake orgasm scene (the theatrical gesture that, as Linda Williams argues, the 'repressed, obsessive character' of Sally would 'never do')[23] alongside the only real 'sex scene' in the film between Sally and Harry. It is important to note that the scene comes on the heels of Sally's devastation over discovering that her ex-boyfriend is engaged to another, younger woman after a whirlwind courtship. Her highly emotional response to the news is attributed not to jealousy or regret over her breakup with Joe, but to the fact that she is an unmarried thirty-something woman. In other words, the tears which eventually lead to Sally wiping her nose on Harry's sweater, which eventually leads to the pair's first kiss, are a result of her feelings of inadequacy about her romantic life and the fact that she is getting older. As the kiss becomes more intense, there is an immediate cut (omitting the actual sex scene) to the two, post-coital, with Harry looking uncomfortable and Sally looking pleased. After a brief exchange in which she wanders buoyantly into the kitchen to fetch water, and the two discuss her indexed video collection, they fall asleep together. Then, in keeping with his history of discomfort with the intimacy of the morning after a sexual encounter, Harry gets dressed, arranges a date with Sally for that evening and then quickly kisses her on the forehead and leaves.

It is clear from both characters' facial expressions that the unseen sex scene was a dramatically different experience for both – Harry initially is obviously uncomfortable with its potential to transform the friendship, while Sally clearly sees it as the consummation of a long-standing intimacy that may lead to something romantic. By editing out anything but a kiss, the scene allows for Sally and Harry's characterizations up until that point to remain intact. He is still the philanderer and she is still the cute neurotic who believes in sexuality being contained within the confines of romantic feelings.

Julia Roberts's Vivian in *Pretty Woman*, is also made to be endearing as a direct result of her naive, girlish qualities, despite the fact that the real life version of her character would most likely not bear any resemblance to this depiction. As a consequence, Vivian is portrayed as perhaps the only prostitute who approaches sex as though it were a game of Seven Minutes in Heaven complete with the adolescent mix of giddiness and dread. She proclaims that most people 'shock the hell out of her,' has picnics on the floor of Edward's (Richard Gere) hotel room, has to be taught how to sit down at a dining room table, and flosses regularly so as to not 'neglect her gums.' Her attempts at seduction are rendered cute or humorous, and the mention of drugs and pimps is candy-coated. While, as Hilary Radner has argued, Vivian's worth comes from her character being a 'paragon of sexual knowledge rather than chastity,' it is clear that the film omits the types of sexual interactions that would play out between a prostitute and her john, and merely manages to reinforce the fact that true, or 'real' sexuality is only revealed when two people are in love.[24] The end result of this is that sex can be transformative, shown by how Edward is portrayed gradually as less of a pill and more like the girlish vision of the knight on the white horse that Vivian desires.

Jess, the lead character from the Fox television show *New Girl*, is a more recent incarnation of this girl-woman character. *New Girl* premiered in the 2011 television season and is a creation of writer and executive producer Elizabeth Meriwether, who also wrote the screenplay for *No Strings Attached*, which I will discuss later in the chapter. Actress Zooey Deschanel, who has appeared largely in independent films, plays Jess, a retro-clothes-wearing, quirky schoolteacher who comes to live with three twenty-something guys in a Los Angeles loft. The show focuses on the life lessons learned and general mishaps of this group of four, and revolves around the ways in which Jess is both strange and endearing. The show's first season was a big success, establishing itself as the number one new series in the 18–34 demographic.[25] However, amidst this popularity, the show was the object of criticism for the degree to which Jess's character resembles a young girl rather than a mature and self-possessed twenty-something woman.

A March 2012 *Entertainment Weekly* article addressed this controversy, specifically claims that Jess is an antifeminist character. The piece refers to a 2011 blog post written by comedian Julie Klausner that responds to the phenomenon of 'women who act like girls' or, as she puts it later in the post: 'manic pixie Muppet babies.'[26] Klausner writes:

Figure 22   Jess (Zooey Deschanel) in *New Girl* (2011–).

we're singing the praises of Skittles Sours instead of emulating, say, Kathleen Turner? Barbara Stanwyck? Any female lead from the pre-awkward era who stuck out her tits and didn't talk like Rocky from the *Bullwinkle* cartoons? . . . the larger issue is that it is a lot easier for men – or even guys or bros – to demean us, if we're girls. It's much harder to bring down a woman, or to call her a moron, when she's not in pigtails and Ring Pops.[27]

Creator Meriwether responded to these critiques claiming that she never intended for Jess to be 'cute,' and that she finds evidence of reverse sexism in the backlash. She says, 'It was weird for me, as a feminist who's actively trying to create interesting roles for women, to hear that attack, that Jess is like a little girl.'[28] In fact, these critiques did seem to register with Meriwether more than similar claims did with *Ally McBeal* creator David E. Kelly, who took his wildly successful show, a hallmark of postfeminist media culture, in an increasingly more fantastical direction throughout its run. *New Girl*, on the other hand, saw a marked tonal shift in the middle of the first season, down-playing Jess's quirkiness and even introducing a female character that leveled Klausner-type critiques at Jess within the context of the show's narrative. Being that Meriwether is a member of a clique known as 'The Fempire' that includes some of Hollywood's most sought-after women writers, it is not surprising that she is tuned into the reception of her work, particularly the manner in which it reflects women.[29] But, as Klausner's commentary demonstrates, these depictions have become such a part of the contemporary cultural landscape that even a contentious writer like Meriwether is not always conscious that she is advancing them. To be sure, the depiction of girly women such as Jess elicits conflicted audience responses that can draw on pleasurable recollection of and nostalgia for one's youth while simultaneously upholding this trend toward 'pigtails and Ring Pops.' The 2004 film *13 Going on 30* provides one of the clearest and most literal representations of this paradigm.

WHAT WE HAVE LOST: *13 GOING ON 30*

Diane Negra and Yvonne Tasker have argued that contemporary romantic comedies such as *13 Going on 30* have been instrumental in this trend of 'girling' grown women by presenting female protagonists whose traits are associated with adolescence.[30] The ages foregrounded in the title of the film are ideal from a marketing standpoint, as the film's narrative is clearly meant to appeal to women from both age groups, and presumably any age in between. The plot of the film is similar to that of 1988's *Big* (Marshall, 1988), which was turned into another remake of sorts in 2009's *17 Again* (Steers). But now, the main character has changed from male to female. The film begins in 1987 on the day of our young protagonist Jenna's thirteenth birthday. When Jenna is rejected at her birthday party by the 'six-chicks' – the popular group of girls of which she is dying to be a part, as well as the cool jock on whom she has a crush – she cries alone in a closet. She says aloud that she wishes that she could be 'thirty, flirty, and fabulous' (the title of a *Poise* magazine article she had read earlier in the day) as some 'wishing dust' – a gift from her geeky best friend, Matt – falls on her.

In the next scene, we see Jenna (here played by Jennifer Garner) wake up almost two decades later in her thirty-year-old body, confused and disoriented. She finds that she is the editor of *Poise*, she lives in a huge Manhattan apartment with a sizable shoe collection, and she dates a very good-looking, famous professional hockey player. While on the surface this appears to be the adult life about which Jenna has fantasized, she soon realizes that her thirty-year-old self is not an admirable human being – she rarely speaks to her parents, has been cheating on her boyfriend with a married coworker's husband, and selling company secrets to the competition. The film slowly reveals the various ways in thirty-year-old Jenna is different from thirteen-year-old Jenna, presenting her adolescent characteristics in stark contrast to the jaded and cynical characteristics of her adult self.

When Jenna is assigned a redesign project in order save *Poise* from going out of business, her layouts resemble the pages of a high school yearbook – pictures of a high school prom, football games, and fresh-faced young men and women embracing. In her presentation, she claims that 'we need to find what we've forgotten, what we've left behind – what's good,' – a sentiment that is met with thunderous applause from her coworkers. Jenna's presentation is positioned against the jaded and cynical 'heroin chic'-inspired presentation made by her backstabbing best friend, Tom-Tom (Judy Greer; former leader of the six-chicks). The film longs for Jenna to reclaim her softer side – that which rejects the negativity inherent in 'unhealthy' women with dark circles under their eyes, and embraces the innocence and hope represented by the 1980s of her youth.

The most important component of Jenna's journey as a thirty-year-old is her opportunity to undo her rejection of the romantic overtures of her afore-mentioned best friend, Matt. When Jenna wakes up in 2004, the first thing she does is locate the adult version of Matt. He is embodied by the strikingly hand-some and masculine actor Mark Ruffalo but still retains the same modesty and amiableness as his thirteen-year-old self. Their adult relationship is represented as identical to their childhood relationship: they eat Razzles, swing on swing sets, and maintain a largely unconsummated flirtation. However, when they do kiss, it is portrayed as magical and transformative. The film renders Matt as Jenna's soul mate because his affection for her is based in their adolescent relationship. He sees her through the eyes of an earnest and easily wounded thirteen-year-old boy. Conversely, Jenna's professional hockey-player boy-friend, Alex (Samuel Ball), is represented as undesirable and laughable, largely because he walks scantily clad around her apartment, calls her sexually sug-gestive names like 'sweet bottom,' and seems to have no interest in establishing any sort of emotional connection before having sex.

The contrast between Matt and Alex is nowhere more evident than in the scene when, in an attempt to calm the nerves of a suddenly frigid Jenna, Alex performs an over-the-top erotic strip dance for her to the tune of Vanilla Ice's 'Ice, Ice Baby.' Jenna, lured to his apartment under the pretense of playing board games, is mortified by the dance and covers her eyes in disgust, particu-larly when he begins to disrobe and engage in some vigorous pelvic thrusting. It is made clear that Alex does not succeed in luring Jenna to bed, as in the next scene she complains to her thirteen-year-old neighbor that Alex did not have any decent board games. This scene is an excellent, if somewhat exag-gerated, example of how sexuality in romantic comedies is represented as if it were being navigated through the eyes, and for the eyes of, a thirteen-year-old girl. In this striptease scene, Alex is made comedic and de-sexualized due to his exaggerated characteristics and exhibitionism. This characterization not only ensures the PG-13 audience's comfort level but also guarantees that they are cheering for Jenna to couple with Matt.

This scene can obviously resonate with the thirteen-year-old audience members who most likely share Jenna's disgust and mortification at the male striptease. But what is particularly compelling is how the film, with its clear homage to the 1980s through music and cultural references, may also elicit

Figure 23   Jenna (Jennifer Garner) in *13 Going on 30* (Winick, 2004).

nostalgic feelings among its adult spectators who recall with fondness this pre-sexual period. The film adopts a reflective stance that we have seen in other postfeminist films that seems to ask the adult female audience members to yearn for these less complicated times when playing a good game of Monopoly or Parcheesi provided ample entertainment for an entire evening.

In this regard, it is necessary to look at what the film communicates about adult sexuality in the midst of all of this cuteness. It becomes clear that Jenna's alternate adult self – the one whose shoes she fills – is not just jaded and cut-throat in her professional life but in her personal life as well. As we will see in the next section, it is not uncommon for postfeminist films to conflate a woman's professional success with her destructive sexual appetite but rarely are the two opposing poles, naive youth and dishonest adulthood, contrasted so acutely. It is also telling that the film renders Jenna's advances toward an engaged Matt in an entirely different light than the philandering of her alter-nate self. Perhaps because the film's closed system presents no real options for Jenna other than Alex and Matt, Matt is presented as Jenna's destined love match and thus, anything that she does in the name of this pure, unadulterated love, is acceptable. However, her advances toward Matt go unrequited, and her glimpse into the future ends disappointingly with him marrying his fiancé.

Ultimately, however, the film sees Jenna able to return to the past wiser and more willing to commit to 'what's good.' The first choice that she makes upon returning to her thirteen-year-old body is to kiss Matt and optimize her chance for an adult romantic life spent with this childhood friend. The film's conclud-ing scene flashes forward down this path, and we see a married Jenna and Matt settling into their new home. The film is therefore unambiguous in its celebration of the rosy ideals that dominate our childhood while casting a harsh light on what happens when we lose track of such ideals.

Jenna and the other female protagonists that we have discussed in this section, are funny, engaging, and possess a whole host of other characteristics that are designed to resonate with female spectators. By featuring a protagonist who is both girl and woman at the same time, these texts can appeal to a wide range of audiences and makes them a safe and more lucrative investment for Hollywood studios. But this risk aversion does go hand in hand with the avoidance of the many nuances that make up adult women's lives. Many of these nuances are explored in a strikingly different manner in sexual thriller films.

THE DANGERS OF A GIRL LIKE ALEX IN *FATAL ATTRACTION* AND *UNFAITHFUL*

Sexual thriller films exist at the opposite side of the sexual spectrum as girl-driven comedies. *Fatal Attraction*, *Unfaithful*, and *In the Cut* feature adult women who act like adults and the films represent sex openly, not shunted off-screen or made cute. Sexuality is represented in its own milieu, and unrelated to the optimism and naiveté associated with romantic comedies. In fact, romantic love is either nowhere to be found in these films or it is associated with a dull and mundane (and sexless) marriage.

To understand the context in which the sexual thriller film emerged, we must return to the conservatism in culture and the film industry in the mid-1980s. *Backlash*, one of the first books to identify American culture's turn toward postfeminism names the controversial Adrian Lyne film *Fatal Attraction* as an embodiment of this new position. Author Susan Faludi argues, 'Hollywood joined the backlash a few years later than the media . . . the film industry had a chance to absorb the "trends" the '80s media flashed at independent women – and reflect them back at American moviegoers at twice their size.'[31] And as Suzanne Leonard puts it in her monograph on the film:

> Though the lasting implications of this discussion were not wholly clear in the late 1980s, in fact the film demonstrated an uncanny ability to cleave women, and, more broadly, to diagnose competing cultural investments in notions of 'work' and 'family.' Such distinctions proved prescient, as this divide would become, in the years following the film's release, highly paradigmatic of the postfeminist era.[32]

Fatal Attraction was the first in what became a veritable subgenre of postfeminist films that emphasize strong female sexuality, yet equate it in some way with instability. These films exist in a tonally and aesthetically different universe than their romantic comedy counterparts. As Barbara Creed argues, 'Narratives such as these do not explore the lover's dream of unity and wholeness; instead, they argue that such a union is not possible, and that romantic love is a myth that masks the true nature of desire.'[33] Monica Pearl has argued that sexual thrillers represent anxiety over the AIDS crisis through scenarios in which characters can be killed through an act of sex. This is demonstrated in films such as *Body of Evidence* (Edel, 1993) and *Basic Instinct* (Verhoeven, 1992). In the case of an adultery film such as *Damage* (Malle, 1992), there is an implicit suggestion that a liaison that is extra-marital, or extra-anything, will lead to a 'lethal infection' which will destroy the agent that brings the contagion into the family realm, ultimately destroying the family unit itself.[34]

Maria Lauret also interprets the 'cluster of metaphors, visual puns, and connotations' that revolve around sexual intercourse in films from this period as indicative of a fear surrounding the transmission of AIDS, and the general dangers of living in contemporary society.[35] While the fear of AIDS transmission was largely associated with homosexuality, there was also a significant degree to which these threats were correlated with women's increasing sexual experimentation. The havoc brought on by the important social and political movements of the 1960s and 1970s was negotiated in these films that are highly sexual in content, and in which female sexuality is both fetishized and feared.[36] As Suzanne Leonard writes in reference to *Fatal Attraction*, the film 'maps out a dynamic that is central to the postsexual-revolutionary period and in turn to a postfeminist age, since it suggests that the gains to be gotten from a widespread relaxation of sexual mores have nevertheless occasioned a widespread cultural implosion.'[37]

An investigation of sexually charged films produced since the 1980s is tantamount to conducting an auteur study of a few select filmmakers, namely directors Adrian Lyne and Paul Verhoven, and screenwriter Joe Eszterhas. These three men produced a series of films that defined the emergence of a sub-genre in the 1980s and 1990s, including: *Flashdance* (1983), *Jagged Edge* (1985), *9½ Weeks* (1986), *Fatal Attraction* (1987), *Betrayed* (1988), *Basic Instinct* (1992), *Indecent Proposal* (1993), *Sliver* (1993), *Showgirls* (1995), *Jade* (1995), *Lolita* (1997), and *Unfaithful* (2002). With the exception of *Flashdance* and *Indecent Proposal*, in which women are depicted as visual commodities to be consumed by men, all of these films, to varying degrees, align female sexuality with violence. Lyne's films are well known for their ability to tap into cultural attitudes toward male and female relationships at particular historical moments. Therefore, it is fascinating to examine how little changes in his treatment of female sexuality between *Fatal Attraction*, made in 1987, and *Unfaithful*, made fifteen years later. Both films tell essentially the same story – a spouse whose adultery leads to violence – but despite the fact that the gender of the cheating spouse changes from one film to the other, it is still the hypersexual woman who bears the brunt of the responsibility for the havoc that these sexual acts inflict on the domestic arrangement.

One of the major underlying questions raised by both *Fatal Attraction* and *Unfaithful* is why someone would cheat if they have a relatively happy marriage. *Fatal Attraction* establishes Dan and Beth's home as a happy one, despite their disagreements on whether or not they should move from their cramped Manhattan apartment to a house in upstate New York. Their daughter is precocious and seemingly wise beyond her years. The only thing that seems to be missing from this happy household is sex. Upon returning home after the cocktail party when Dan and Alex first exchange glances, Dan is eager to make love to his wife but she compels him to take the dog for a walk and when he returns home, finds Ellen, their daughter, in their bed. Later in the film, when Dan is admiring Beth in the mirror as she prepares for a dinner party, they are again interrupted by their guests ringing the buzzer. The film suggests that marriage is not an environment that fosters highly passionate sexual moments, and that sometimes even routine sex is impossible.

Dan and Beth's mundane, domestic life is, of course, presented in contrast to Alex's life as a single woman, which, prior to and during the weekend affair, includes spontaneous sex in the kitchen sink and in an elevator. However, while seemingly appealing at first, Alex's solitary lifestyle quickly reveals itself as not only much lonelier than the domestic life shared by Beth and Dan, but as grounds for troubled and dangerous behavior. As Suzanne Leonard argues, 'According to the film's logic, singlehood ushers in unhappiness and loneliness, whereas the contented image of Beth counters the presentation of Alex as a woman who refuses to face the punishing effects of her own choices.'[38] The mise-en-scène of the film is instrumental in establishing the contrast between the domestic environments of Beth and Dan and that of Alex. While Dan and Beth have a home filled with warm colors, wall hangings, and plush furniture, Alex's place is almost entirely white and sparsely decorated. This contrast is magnified when Dan and Beth make the move to the suburbs and their home becomes even further appointed with the accouterments of domestic bliss – there is a warm fire consistently burning in the fireplace, a big back yard, and Beth is seen to play the traditional domestic role of homemaker as she paints the walls and makes their house a home. As Leonard states, 'Such visual and thematic glorifications of Beth frame her life as comfortable and happy, and endorse feminine identities that adhere to traditional gender standards.'[39]

Many feminist theorists such as Barbara Creed and Deborah Jermyn have read Alex's character within the context of Julia Kristeva's theories of the abject. The abject, as Deborah Jermyn characterizes it, is 'all those things which threaten society's established boundaries.'[40] Alex challenges traditional notions of appropriate femininity (that is, she does not know her place), and as Jermyn argues, like her female counterparts in other contemporary sexual thriller films such as *Basic Instinct*, *The Crush* (Shapiro, 1993), *The Hand That Rocks the Cradle* (Hanson, 1992), *Jade* and *Single White Female* (Schroeder, 1992), she threatens the stability of the domestic environment and the happiness of the other 'good' woman. Jermyn argues that, as opposed to viewing these different representations of women and femininity exclusively as manifestations of male anxiety over women's changing roles in society, it is possible to think of them as 'the embodiment of a female dilemma, an exploration and momentary enjoyment of conflicting roles and behavior, rather than solely a reflection of male fears.'[41] Alex is seen to cross over into the domestic space quite easily – she sits and converses comfortably with Beth in the Gallagher living room, and she takes on a somewhat maternal air toward Ellen on their trip to the amusement park. And, equally, by the end of the film, Beth has abandoned her calm and pleasant demeanor for a tough and angry one. She is the one who commits the ultimate violence in the film by shooting Alex in defense of her home and family.

Jermyn's argument for the 'blurrier than meets the eye' opposition between Alex and Beth introduces a nuanced interpretation of the film that leaves open alternative readings of these characters. However, it is difficult to interpret the movement of Alex's initial sexual rebellion into a psychotic break as having the potential to elicit the same empathy from a female audience, as do Beth's actions, which serve to reinforce a moral code. Since, as Lyne states, 'everyone knows a girl like Alex,' there is plenty of reason to be scared about unwittingly choosing the wrong candidate for extramarital fun. This is a sentiment that is reflected by the widower Sam, Tom Hanks's character in *Sleepless in Seattle*, when he asks his young son who is encouraging him to date again, 'Didn't you see *Fatal Attraction*? Well I did. And it scared the hell out of me. It scared the hell out of every man in America!'

Although adapted from the 1969 Claude Chabrol film *La Femme Infidèle*, Lyne's *Unfaithful*, made in 2002, has a great deal in common with *Fatal Attraction*. What is most notable for our analysis is the fact that, in keeping with Jermyn's 'blurrier than meets the eye' argument with regard to *Fatal Attraction*, the figures of Beth and Alex are merged into one female character. Connie (Diane Lane) is both warm, domestic mother and sexual aggressor/home wrecker. Her family life with Edward (Richard Gere), with a precocious young child and dog (always underfoot), has become tedious, uncommunicative, and lacking in sexual spark. All efforts made by Connie and Edward to retain their sexual intimacy are interrupted or squashed by the tediousness of their domestic life. When Connie goes into the city one day to run errands, she finds herself in the middle of a wind storm. Desperately trying to hail a taxi so that she can catch a train home, she loses her footing and accidentally bumps into Paul Martel (Olivier Martinez), an attractive book dealer, on a Soho street. After she and Paul retrieve their dropped items, he invites her up to his apartment so that she can tend to the wound on her knee caused by the fall. At first Connie is hesitant, but she eventually agrees, and continues up to Paul's apartment even after noticing an available taxi passing by.

After two innocent but sexually charged visits to Paul's apartment, Connie eventually returns to begin an affair with him, which consists of daytime visits while her son is at school and Edward is at work. Eventually, Edward begins to suspect Connie's infidelity and has her followed by a private detective. After the detective confirms the affair, Edward pays a visit to Paul and, in a fit of rage, bludgeons him to death and buries him in a landfill. When Connie learns of Edward's crime, she must decide whether to turn him in to the police and completely transform their way of life, or live with the knowledge of both of their heinous misdeeds.

What *Unfaithful* emphasizes more explicitly than *Fatal Attraction* is that life is about the choices that we make rather than about fate controlling our lives. As Paul states, 'There are no mistakes, there is what you do and don't do.' Inclement weather forces Connie to bump into Paul (just as a rainstorm forces Dan and Alex under the same umbrella and into the shelter of a restaurant for their first dinner), However, Connie's choice to ignore the taxi and follow Paul into his apartment is what leads her down the path of infidelity. The film's conclusion underscores the idea of paths not taken when it replays this scene again but shows Connie choosing to get into the taxi this time. It also presents a striking contrast between the types of transgressions that take place in the city versus the sexless and boring domestic life represented by the suburbs.

Unfaithful follows the plot line of the original Chabrol film in having Connie pursue the affair with Paul primarily out of boredom and with Edward eventually killing Paul. There are compelling links between this plot line and that of *Fatal Attraction*. Both films explore the concept of choices and how they can ultimately affect your life and the lives of those close to you, but in both films these choices are sexual in nature, and women bear the brunt of their ramifications. While *Fatal Attraction* can be interpreted as a cautionary tale for men who cheat on their wives, the primary punishment is inflicted on the women – both Beth and Alex suffer violent fates (at the end of the film it is implied that Dan will resume his role as husband and father). This is also true in *Unfaithful*. Although it is Edward who kills Paul, the responsibility for the murder ultimately rests on Connie's shoulders and her act of infidelity.

Connie's foray into this forbidden realm of sexual expression is also seen as preventing her from fulfilling her domestic roles as wife and mother. The more involved she becomes with Paul, the more she neglects her responsibilities. She is unable to make dinner for her family without burning it and she forgets to pick up her son from school on time. She also risks her own life (and the groceries in the back seat) when she makes a sudden turn on the freeway toward

Figure 24   Connie (Diane Lane) in *Unfaithful* (Lyne, 2002).

New York City, nearly getting into a car accident. One woman, it seems, cannot simultaneously engage in a sexually torrid affair and fulfill her domestic duties successfully. Connie represents the extreme example of cultural warnings against a woman prioritizing her sexuality over her role as a housewife and a mother – this results in disastrous consequences for her and her way of life (not to mention Paul, the ultimate victim of her indiscretions).

Sex and Disarticulation in *In the Cut*

In the Cut serves as an interesting complement to the discussion of these Lyne films. On the surface, the film has the distinguished 'art house milieu' pedigree of which Peter Guber speaks. It was adapted from a novel by Susanna Moore, directed by New Zealand auteur Jane Campion, and made within an independent context by Pathé Productions. Campion is, of course, a highly regarded director whose films typically feature complicated female characters that resist the typical feminine archetypes of Hollywood filmmaking. *In the Cut*, an international coproduction, does share characteristics with Campion's other films – specifically *The Piano* (1993) and *Holy Smoke* (1999) – in its exploration of the complexities of female sexual agency. However, the film ultimately has more in common with commercially driven, sexually explicit films such as *Basic Instinct*, *Fatal Attraction*, and *Unfaithful*. One can only wonder if this is a result of it being her first and only film set in the United States. While Campion's work traditionally explores the blurred lines between sexuality, love, and violence, *In the Cut* takes a decidedly more dour turn than her previous efforts.

In the Cut was unpopular with American audiences, earning less than $5 million in its US theatrical release.[42] Presumably, one of the reasons for this lackluster box office performance is the compelling, yet ultimately flawed, against-type casting of Meg Ryan as Frannie. As previously mentioned, Ryan, along with Sandra Bullock and Julia Roberts, is one of romantic comedy's golden girls and, as discussed earlier with regard to her performance as Sally in *When Harry Met Sally*, she typically portrays the archetypal 'cute' romantic comedy female protagonist. Because Ryan has been pigeon-holed into this type of role, one of the undeniable issues surrounding the reception of *In the Cut* is whether or not audiences would be willing to believe, let alone identify with, Ryan as a sullen school teacher. While one cannot fault Ryan or Campion for attempting to bridge the romantic comedy and sexual thriller divide, the film's lack of popularity is indicative in part of audiences' unwillingness to take this same leap.

The film follows Frannie, a New York City English teacher, who finds herself in the middle of an increasingly violent drama after a girl is murdered and decapitated in her neighborhood. After learning that Frannie was in the same bar as the victim the day of the murder, the police seek her out for questioning. She fails to tell the investigating detective, Malloy (Mark Ruffalo, again, in a dramatically different role than that of *13 Going on 30*), that she in fact saw the victim performing oral sex on a man only identifiable through his tattoo, and she maintains her silence even after she notices that Malloy has the same tattoo as the suspected murderer. Despite (or perhaps, because of) the danger involved, Frannie pursues a sexual relationship with Malloy. The affair has enough violent undertones to prolong Frannie's suspicions about Malloy's guilt, which is augmented by his brusque and dodgy demeanor.

As the film progresses, Frannie becomes increasingly enmeshed in this world of danger and violence – she escapes an attack from a man who may or may not be the killer, is stalked by an ex-boyfriend, and maintains an inappropriately close relationship with one of her male students, who is obsessed with the serial killer John Wayne Gacy. Her half-sister becomes the latest victim of the murderer's violent crimes, and Frannie narrowly escapes victimization herself when she learns that Malloy's partner Rodriguez (who also shares the same tattoo) is the perpetrator. The ending is one of the few elements that changes in the adaptation from the book to the film. Whereas in the film Frannie escapes her own killing, and safely returns to her apartment and her relationship with Malloy, in the book Frannie actually narrates her own decapitation at the hands of Rodriguez.

In stark contrast to the New York City represented in the romantic comedy world of *13 Going on 30*, or even *Fatal Attraction* and *Unfaithful*, with their upper-middle-class Manhattan locations, expensive restaurants and clubs, large and well-decorated apartments, and well-groomed, articulate and well-

Figure 25   Frannie (Meg Ryan) in *In the Cut* (Campion, 2003).

educated characters, *In the Cut* represents New York as a dirty, graffiti-filled, and highly dangerous place. The hyper-stylized cinematography of Dion Beebe emphasizes the aura of dislocation and sense of danger, particularly with the use of shaky, hand-held cameras, and the positioning of Frannie as the object of an unidentified and disembodied voyeuristic gaze. The world view of *In the Cut* is one of immobility and meaningless, unsatisfying, and aggressive personal interactions.

Like Campion's *The Piano* and *Holy Smoke*, *In the Cut* emphasizes the female protagonist's efforts to locate a sense of self through language. In *The Piano*, Ada (Holly Hunter) uses her piano to speak and, in *Holy Smoke*, Ruth (Kate Winslet) appropriates the language of religious fanaticism as a substitute for her own voice and then, as a result of the intervention of PJ (Harvey Keitel), is compelled to find a true sense of self. In *In the Cut*, Frannie's passion is words. She posts phrases and poems around her apartment and continually probes one of her African-American students for new and interesting uses of slang. However, as Frannie says, just as most slang is either sexual or violent, almost all of the interaction and communication in the film takes on sexual or violent connotations. Despite the fact that she is a scholar of words, Frannie, like Ada and Ruth, has difficulty articulating her desires within the boundaries of traditional language and strives to find other avenues of expression. As Sue Thornham argues, Frannie 'provides, in fact, very few of her own words. Murmuring to herself, her voice sometimes repeats, fascinated, the language of the street, but is more often heard quoting fragments of poetry (Dante, Keats) from the Poetry in Transit program.'[43] She is only able to express her desire through her sexual relationship with the equally verbally challenged Malloy. The perverse satisfaction that she gains from their encounters is only heightened as she becomes more and more convinced that he is the murderer.

Romantic iconography has no place in this world, as all of the relationships in the film – even the ones that are only referred to – are lacking in genuine affection. Like the aforementioned sexual thriller films that are akin to *In the Cut*, the sexual encounters between Frannie and Malloy are designed to be titillating. Frannie's sexual exploration is undercut not necessarily because of the explicitness of its representation but because she seems to derive no real pleasure from her encounters with Malloy. The potential for empowerment in Frannie's use of sexuality as a form of communication or language is diminished as the film continues to associate sex with the looming threat of violence. As Thornham states, 'her attempted assertion of sexual control renders her vulnerable to a far more powerful and pervasive male sadistic fantasy.'[44]

Thornham suggests that *In the Cut* is a romance film for the *Sex and the City* generation in that it negotiates the same problems as the latter text, specifically the relationship between sex and romance, but offers a dramatically different resolution. While in *Sex and the City* 'a feminized New York is reaffirmed as the place in which romance can be re-authored by women to serve a female narcissistic pleasure,' *In the Cut* uses its 'its multiple and often shockingly disparate references and registers' to perform 'disturbingly but triumphantly, the strategy that [Adrienne] Rich calls "re-vision" – looking back, . . . seeing with fresh eyes,' entering some old (and not so old) texts 'from a new critical direction.'[45] When analyzing *In the Cut* in the context of Campion's work overall, it is tempting to read the film in the way that Thornham suggests: as a text that interrogates romantic structures in the postfeminist period and recasts the gender dynamics within them. However, there are even more levels to be found when reading the film within the context of the other sexual thrillers that I have discussed in this chapter. The sexual-thriller female protagonists explore their sexual desires outside of typical gender normative boundaries but their pursuit of satisfaction is inevitably deemed to be misguided or dangerous by the conclusion of the film.

As a final meditation on the degree to which the comedy and drama texts that we have analyzed thus far offer a strikingly paradoxical mise-en-scène of pleasure and desire for contemporary female audiences, one needs to look no further than their marketing materials, which serve as a visual shorthand for the type of sex (or lack thereof) that they 'spell.'

The promotional poster for *13 Going on 30*, with its colorful, pastel type features Garner in a long shot in the right side of the frame, dressed in a frilly polka-dotted dress with a petite pink flowery purse in her hand and red high heels. She looks directly at the viewer, blowing a bubble-gum bubble with a befuddled expression on her face. The tag line reads: 'a comedy for the kid in

Figure 26   Promotional poster for *13 Going on 30* (Winick, 2004). © Columbia Tri-Star Pictures, 2004.

all of us.' In contrast, the image on the cover of the *In the Cut* DVD is black, with a white and red type, featuring Ryan and Ruffalo in moody, shadowy brown and flesh colored hues. Both figures are positioned in a medium shot, with Ruffalo in profile grabbing the side of Ryan's face seductively. It resembles the *13 Going on 30* poster in that our female protagonist looks directly at the viewer. However Ryan's expression is one of fear and hesitation. Appropriately, the tag line reads: 'Everything you know about desire is dead wrong.' To return once again to Peter Guber's statements that began this chapter, these marketing materials signal to the audience the kinds of representations of sexuality and romance that are going to see: either comedic, cute, and filled with bright colors and happy endings, or violent, filled with dissatisfying relationships, murder, and stark urban landscapes. These two different types of postfeminist romance texts come with their respective systems of representation and their own systems of pleasure. What they do not present is both of these perspectives at the same time. It is instructive then to look briefly at two 2011 films, *No Strings Attached* and *Friends with Benefits*, and the 2012 television show *Girls*, that bridge the gap between these either/or imperatives.

Figure 27   Promotional poster for *In the Cut* (Campion, 2003). © Pathé Productions, 2003.

SEX AND ROMANCE: WHERE ARE WE GOING?

No Strings Attached and *Friends with Benefits* are both mainstream Hollywood romantic comedies with casts populated by Hollywood's most desirable young stars. Both films share roughly the same plot that revolves around whether a professionally accomplished man and woman – Emma (Natalie Portman) and Adam (Ashton Kutcher) in *No Strings* and Jamie (Mila Kunis) and Dylan (Justin Timberlake) in *Friends* – can engage in a sexual relationship without developing romantic feelings for each other. The films were developed and released during the same time period – *No Strings* opened on January 21, 2011 and *Friends* followed 6 months later on July 22, 2011. This was both a stroke of bad luck and a testament to the generational outlook captured by both films. Both performed decently at the box office but its earlier release date gave *No Strings* the edge, with a domestic return of just under $71 million, compared with the better-reviewed *Friends with Benefits*'s roughly $56 million.[46]

These films' plots ask the diametrically opposite question from what *When Harry Met Sally* asked twenty-two years earlier. Instead of exploring whether a man and a woman can be friends without having sex, *No Strings* and *Friends* explore whether two friends can have sex without falling in love. As we might expect, the answer to this question is no. However, despite the conventionality of their happy endings, the films manage to circumvent many of the pitfalls that accompany the depiction of female sexual desire that we have examined thus far and point to some future directions for the postfeminist romance cycle.

In both films, the female characters desire sex as much as the male characters, and while the films are comedies, the depiction of sexual intercourse is not rendered comedic but as an act of intimacy that, at least at the beginning, is disconnected from feelings of romantic love. Both women are professionally successful – Emma is a doctor and Jamie is a corporate headhunter – and while they have their quirks and goofy moments, they are portrayed as serious-minded adults who maintain control over their careers and their personal lives. Emma and Jamie have issues with intimacy that stem from their respective childhoods that they must overcome in order to let themselves fall in love, but neither film portrays this as a potentially dangerous or lethal disability. In fact, Adam and Dylan have their emotional and intimacy problems (both related to their fathers) that pose equal barriers to the happy ending.

The characters' sexual interactions and the satisfaction that they gain from these encounters is shown explicitly, with montage sequences featuring the many places where, and the frequency with which, they have sex. The equita-bility of the sexual dynamic recalls films from the 1970s that we have examined in previous chapters. In fact, *Friends with Benefits* features a scene in which Jamie watches *Bob and Ted and Carol and Alice* with her hippie mother Lorna (Patricia Clarkson). The free love ideals explored in this real film shown within the film are contrasted with the unnamed fictional romantic comedy that the characters also watch in the film (featuring actors Jason Segal and Rashida Jones) that makes comedic use of many of the romance structure's clichés that I discussed in the Introduction. That *Friends with Benefits* posits these two types of films as influences on its own hybrid approach to romance and sexuality is a testament to its attempt to offer a similarly nuanced perspective.

If we return again to marketing materials, we can see that this symmetry is present even in the representation of the characters on the promotional posters. *No Strings Attached*'s tagline 'Friendship has its benefits' is a play on the phrase 'friends with benefits' which is the more frequently used descriptor among younger generations for sex without romantic connection. It is also one of the few obvious cues to the fact that both films had this title while in development.[47] *Friends with Benefits*, which was able to keep the title after Paramount withdrew its protest, has no tagline, but it does list its Facebook page, which is an acknowledgment of the effectiveness of the social networking site as a marketing tool for the film's desired 18–40 demographic. Both images see the actors given almost equal visual weight, which mirrors the comparable

Figure 28   Promotional poster for *Friends with Benefits* (Gluck, 2011). © Screen
Gems, 2011.

agency each has within the narrative. The characters' poses are flirtatious but
not explicitly sexual, although the *No Strings Attached* poster does suggest a
post-coital moment. Unlike the posters for *13 Going on 30* and *In the Cut*, the
women's faces portray neither befuddled nor fearful expressions but convey
confidence and pleasure.

The 2011 release dates of *Friends with Benefits* and *No Strings Attached*
predated the resuscitated public debate in and around female sexuality that
took the country by storm in early 2012. This controversy revolved around
the increasing threats to Planned Parenthood's funding and religious institu-
tions' objections to the 2010 Affordable Care Act's requirement that they
provide birth control to their employees. These debates hit their peak when
Sandra Fluke, a Georgetown University law student, testified in front of
a Congressional committee in February 2012. Fluke argued that her birth
control should be covered by her student health plan, despite the fact that
Georgetown is a Jesuit university. Conservative commentators, led by radio
host Rush Limbaugh, responded to her testimony with rhetoric that fell right
in line with the dichotomous ideas surrounding sexuality on which we have
focused throughout the chapter. Limbaugh called Fluke a 'slut' and a 'prosti-

Figure 29   Promotional poster for *No Strings Attached* (Reitman, 2011). © DW
Studios, LLC, Cold Spring Pictures LLC and Spyglass Entertainment
Funding, LLC. All rights reserved.

tute' and that in wanting access to contraception, she 'wants to be paid to have
sex. She's having so much sex, she can't afford the contraception.'[48] A political firestorm erupted in response to Limbaugh's comments. Facebook groups
were formed, and petitions were signed to urge Limbaugh's sponsors to pull
their advertising from his show. And, a lively public discussion about what
Democrats called 'the conservative war on women' began.[49]

The HBO television show *Girls* premiered a little over a month after the
Fluke controversy. The show tapped into this conversation about women's
sexuality and provoked commentary from all sides of the political spectrum
in ways that were reminiscent of, but subtly different from, that elicited by
Sex and the City fourteen years earlier. *Girls* is raw while *Sex* was flashy, the
characters are fledgling while *Sex*'s were upwardly mobile. As the vulture.com
critic Emma Straub put it, 'It's a sign of how devoted writer-director Lena
Dunham is to real talk that *Girls* opens with food hanging out of her mouth
. . . Yes, this is glossy HBO, but Hannah eats more in this scene than Carrie
Bradshaw and her buddies did in an entire season.'[50] The show drew criticism
on social media for its nepotistic casting, as well as for its lack of diversity but

predominantly for its frank depiction of sexuality, the tone of which is a far cry from the well-lit, meticulously choreographed sexual situations seen in its predecessor.

The conversation about sex in *Girls*'s first season focused predominantly on the relationship between its central female protagonist, Hannah (played by the show's creator, writer and sometimes director, Lena Dunham), and her lover turned boyfriend, Adam (Adam Sackler). These sex scenes feature full female nudity on Dunham's part, and include masturbation, role-playing, and in one episode, Adam urinating on Hannah in the shower. Adam is an eccentric and enigmatic figure with whom Hannah desperately wants to be in a monogamous relationship, and thus the emotional and sexual power dynamics between the two are uneven. Even when Adam agrees to be Hannah's boyfriend toward the end of the first season, his character's unpredictability keeps her guessing as to his true feelings and motivations.

Hannah and Adam's character dynamics infuse their sexual interactions with a tone that is a combination of disturbing, funny, and uncomfortable. The show's depiction of sexuality fits somewhere in between the either/or dynamics of romantic comedy and romantic drama, with Hannah being insecure, quirky, self-aware and funny but against the backdrop of erotic sexual scenarios that resembles independent or art-house cinema of Jane Campion, Todd Solondz, Catherine Breillat, and Dunham's own *Tiny Furniture* (2010). This combination of traits remains fairly uncommon on television where even explicit sex scenes tend to err more toward soft rather than hard-core pornography.

Elaine Blair responds to concerns about *Girls*'s 'controversial' representations in her illuminating June 2012 *The New York Review of Books* piece:

> Hannah's predicament is common enough in life, but it's not one you see often, if ever, on film. Indeed, romantic comedy (and in television variations) devotes its energies to obscuring the possible gaps between things like companionability, attraction, and intense sexual arousal. Hannah's is also a situation that would be impossible to depict without a graphic sex scene, and offers a very clear example of what sex scenes are good for. If all you want to do is convey an erotic tension between two people, you can leave out explicit depictions of sex acts. But if you are interested in the psychological implications of what happens between people during sex, you need to show something of the sex.[51]

Indeed, as Blair argues, if the presentation of the effects that sexual interaction has on its participants, both male and female, is to approach some semblance of reality, the media must not shy away from depicting sex in all of its complexity. What Dunham's *Girls* suggests is that for many women the pursuit of a satisfying relationship consists of some combination of girlish idealism, disturbing and satisfying sexual scenarios and emotional connectedness. This blend of elements, as Blair attests, sets 'the viewer free from having to keep score on either the man's or the woman's behalf.'[52]

Girls, *Friends with Benefits* and *No Strings Attached* suggest that the contemporary media can still provoke discussions about sexuality in ways that do not resort to convention or shorthand. New generations of female artists such as Elizabeth Meriwether and Lena Dunham are pushing such matters into the forefront of their creative work, absorbing and reflecting a changing and often virulent contemporary socio-political climate to offer a different glimpse into how feminist discourses, women's sexuality, and romantic relationships can be realigned. In the following chapter, we will look at how two female artists of a different generation are contributing to the landscape of the postfeminist romance in their own distinctive ways.

NOTES

1. Anne Thompson, 'Sex sells on the big screen . . . unless it's serious', *The Hollywood Reporter*, 20 March 2005. See http://www.hollywoodreporter.com/thr/columns/risky_business_display.jsp?vnu_content_id=1000845904.
2. Ibid.
3. Brian Henderson, 'Romantic comedy today: semi-tough or impossible?', *Film Quarterly*, 31: 4 (1978), 21.
4. For a concise and comprehensive examination of the representation of feminist discourses and sexuality in 1970s television, see Elena Levine, *Wallowing in Sex: the New Sexual Culture of 1970s American Television* (Durham, NC: Duke University Press, 2007).
5. Steven Seidman, *Romantic Longings: Love in America, 1830–1980* (New York: Routledge, 1991), p. 137.
6. Betty Freidan, *The Feminine Mystique* (New York: Dell, 1964), p. 261.
7. Seidman, *Romantic Longings*, p. 138.
8. Helen Gurley Brown, *Sex and the New Single Girl* (New York: Bernard Geis Associates, 1972), p. 21.
9. Hilary Ann Radner, *Shopping Around: Feminine Culture and the Pursuit of Pleasure* (New York: Routledge, 1995), p. xi.
10. As Stephen Prince highlights, most of the major controversies of this period were a result of the provocative mix of sex and violence in R-rated films. The MPAA was under tremendous pressure to change its rating system to more accurately reflect this content. The PG-13 rating was developed in 1984 in response to the public's distaste for the excessive depiction of violence in PG-rated films, such as *Indiana Jones and the Temple of Doom*, a sequel to the more family friendly *Raiders of the Lost Ark*. However its designation as containing material that 'may be inappropriate for young children' was also applied to films with sexual content as well. The development of the NC-17 rating in 1990, which was meant to demarcate films containing strong sexual content within a more adult and often more artistic context, did nothing to alleviate the complexities of how and to what degree sexuality should be represented in mainstream films. In fact, directors edited out as much sexual gratuity as possible in order to avoid receiving the NC-17 rating, which was deemed box office poison. From the late 1980s to the contemporary period, sexual representation in American film is still largely fought on the battleground of PG-13

versus R. Stephen Prince, *A New Pot of Gold: Hollywood Under the Electronic Rainbow, 1980–1989* (Berkeley: University of California Press, 2000), pp. 365–9.

11. Linda Williams, *Screening Sex* (Raleigh: Duke University Press, 2008), p. 72.
12. See Linda Ruth Williams, *The Erotic Thriller in Contemporary Cinema*, (Bloomington: Indiana University Press, 2005), and Nina Martin, *Sexy Thrills: Undressing the Erotic Thriller* (Urbana: University of Illinois Press, 2007).
13. Williams, *Screening Sex*, p. 156
14. From 1984 to 1986, the PG-13 rating read 'parents are strongly cautioned to give special guidance for children under the age of 13. Some material may be inappropriate for children.' And, then from 1986–90 it was changed to 'parents strongly cautioned: Some material may be inappropriate for children under 13.'
15. Adam Markowitz, 'Where's the love?', *Entertainment Weekly*, 22 March 2013, 38.
16. Kathleen Rowe Karlyn, 'Too close for comfort: *American Beauty* and the incest motif', *Cinema Journal*, 44: 1 (Fall 2004), 73.
17. Benoit Denizet-Lewis, 'Teen Romance?', *New York Times*, 30 May 2004.
18. Ibid.
19. As demonstrated by a broad range of recent books on the topic, including Gigi Durham's *The Lolita Effect* (New York: Overlook, 2009), Jean Kilbourne's *So Sexy So Soon: the New Sexualized Childhood and What Parents Can Do to Protect Their Kids* (New York: Ballantine Books, 2009), and Sharon Lamb and Lyn Mikel Brown's *Packaging Girlhood: Rescuing Our Daughters from Marketers' Schemes* (New York: St. Martin's Griffin, 2007), this has become a significant cultural issue that many people are striving to address and remedy.
20. Ariel Levy, *Female Chauvinist Pigs: Women and the Rise of Raunch Culture* (New York: Free Press, 2005), p. 92.
21. Charlotte Brundson, *Screen Tastes: Soap Opera to Satellite Dishes* (New York: Routledge, 1997), p. 94.
22. Peter William Evans, 'Meg Ryan, megastar', in Peter William Evans and Celestino Deleyto (eds), *Terms of Endearment: Hollywood Romantic Comedy of the 1980s and 1990s* (Edinburgh: Edinburgh University Press, 1998), p. 193.
23. Williams, *Screening Sex*, p. 156.
24. Hilary Ann Radner, 'Free enterprise and the marriage plot', in Jim Collins, Hilary Radner and Ava Preacher Collins (eds), *Film Theory Goes to the Movies* (New York: Routledge, 1993), p. 62.
25. Melissa Maerz, 'New Girl gets a new attitude', *Entertainment Weekly*, 23 March 2012, 44.
26. See http://julieklausner.tumblr.com/post/6331886267/dont-fear-the-dowager-a-valentine-to-maturity-an.
27. See http://julieklausner.tumblr.com/post/6331886267/dont-fear-the-dowager-a-valentine-to-maturity-an.
28. Maerz, 'New Girl'.
29. Other members of the 'Fempire' clique include: Diablo Cody, screenwriter of *Juno* (Reitman, 2007) and *Young Adult* (Reitman, 2011), Lorene Scafaria, screenwriter of *Nick and Norah's Infinite Playlist* (Sollett, 2008) and *Seeking a Friend for the End of the World* (2012), which she also directed, and Dana Fox, screenwriter of *What Happens in Vegas* (Vaughan, 2008) and *Couples Retreat* (Billingsly, 2009). See http://www.nytimes.com/2009/03/22/fashion/22fempire.html?pagewanted=all.
30. Yvonne Tasker and Diane Negra, 'Introduction: Feminist politics and postfeminist culture,' in *Interrogating Postfeminism: Gender and the Politics of Popular Culture* (Durham, NC: Duke University Press, 2007), p. 9.
31. Susan Faludi, *Backlash: The War Against American Women* (New York: Anchor, 1992), pp. 112–13.

32. Suzanne Leonard, *Fatal Attraction*, (Malden: Wiley Blackwell, 2009), p. 3.
33. Barbara Creed, 'Abject desire and *Basic Instinct*: a tale of cynical romance', in Lynne Pearce and Gina Wisker (eds), *Fatal Attractions: Rescripting Romance in Contemporary Literature and Film* (London: Pluto Press, 1998), p. 174.
34. Monica B. Pearl, 'Symptoms of AIDS in contemporary film: mortal anxiety in an age of sexual panic', in Michele Aaron (ed.), *The Body's Perilous Pleasures: Dangerous Desires and Contemporary Culture* (Edinburgh: Edinburgh University Press, 1999), p. 221.
35. Maura Lauret, 'Hollywood romance in the AIDS era: *Ghost* and *When Harry Met Sally*', in Lynne Pearce and Gina Wisker (eds), *Fatal Attractions: Rescripting Romance in Contemporary Literature and Film* (London: Pluto Press, 1998), p. 22.
36. Steve Neale argues that the growing awareness of AIDS and the increasingly conservative political climate of the 1980s contributed to the romantic comedy's retreat from the sexual explicitness seen in the nervous romance films of the 1960s and 1970s, creating a new trend of 'new' romance films, that show 'markedly – and knowingly – "old-fashioned"' attributes. Steve Neale, 'The big romance or something wild? Romantic comedy today', *Screen*, 33: 3 (Autumn 1992), 287. Monica Pearl concurs, arguing that a seemingly conventional romantic comedy film such as *Prelude to a Kiss* (René, 1992) reflects a broader social anxiety about AIDS. The film's depiction of a younger woman whose soul is trapped in an elderly man's body, mirrors the effect of the AIDS crisis as it depicts the protagonist as having to deal with the premature sudden aging and deterioration of his wife's body. She claims, 'It is difficult . . . not to see the movie as a parable of the way that AIDS descends tragically and confusingly on couples in love.' Pearl, 'Symptoms of AIDS', p. 216.
37. Leonard, *Fatal Attraction*, p. 94.
38. Ibid. p. 68.
39. Ibid. p. 69.
40. Deborah Jermyn, 'Rereading the bitches from hell: a feminist appropriation of the female psychopath', *Screen*, 37: 3 (Autumn 1998), 254.
41. Ibid. p. 255.
42. See http://boxofficemojo.com/movies/?id=inthecut.htm.
43. Sue Thornham, 'Starting to feel like a chick: re-visioning romance in *In the Cut*', *Feminist Media Studies*, 7: 1 (2007), 40–1.
44. Ibid. p. 43.
45. Ibid. p. 44.
46. See http://boxofficemojo.com/movies/?id=friendswithbenefits10.htm.
47. See http://www.variety.com/article/VR1118018733.
48. See http://www.washingtonpost.com/blogs/the-buzz/post/rush-limbaugh-calls-georgetown-student-sandra-fluke-a-slut-for-advocating-contraception/2012/03/02/gIQAvjfSmR_blog.html.
49. Ibid.
50. See http://www.vulture.com/2012/04/girls-recap-season-1-episode-1.html.
51. Elaine Blair, 'The loves of Lena Dunham', *The New York Review of Books*, 7 June 2012.
52. Ibid.

5. INDEPENDENCE VS. DEPENDENCE: ECONOMICS IN THE POSTFEMINIST CYCLE

A father-daughter shopping scene figures prominently in the 2000 Nancy Meyers film *What Women Want*. Nick (Mel Gibson), who has been recently endowed with a gift to hear women's thoughts, takes the teenage Alex (Ashley Johnson) to a brightly lit store filled with colorful clothes in order to embark on what is deemed the second most important shopping experience of a woman's life: finding the perfect prom dress. Shopping here is a form of bonding between the father and daughter whose relationship has been strained until Nick's 'gift' enables him to hear his daughter's negative opinion of him. The film suggests that their estrangement can be easily overcome through one satisfying shopping experience, and indeed this sequence consequently proves to be a turning point in their relationship.

The sequence is a montage without dialogue set to the song 'What a Girl Wants' by Christina Aguilera, and features Alex trying on a variety of different dresses and outfits, looking for the one that will be most likely to secure her the best, and presumably most romantic evening. Alex and Nick exchange a series of playful glances in a shot-reverse-shot structure typical of the intensified continuity system that sees him approving or disapproving each outfit choice. Nick soon becomes bored, and in response to one of the better dress choices, holds up a sign that reads, 'How much?' This is a humorous and playful response to his daughter's obvious indifference to the costs of her perfect prom experience. It might also be read as an unintentional Brechtian device used to call attention to the degree to which Alex and the (presumably female) viewer's pleasure is intertwined with excessive spending and consumption.

Figure 30   Nick (Mel Gibson) in *What Women Want* (Meyers, 2000).

From the lyrics of the popular song[1] which imply that colorful clothes bought on someone else's dime is what a girl wants, to the film's substantial production budget of $70 million that enabled the song's licensing, to the design of this scene and its appealing colorful aesthetics, it is clear that both diegetic and extra-diegetic money are inextricably intertwined with the narrative satisfaction of Alex, the 'girl' in the film, as well as the more general 'girl' identified by the song. That this scene is staged and shot by Nancy Meyers, who is one of the most successful and profitable female directors working in Hollywood, raises interesting questions about how the conventions of big-budget filmmaking shapes her films' presentation of female independence, familial relationships, and ideas about heterosexual romance.

If we consider this scene in contrast to a shopping scene in director Nicole Holofcener's independent feature *Walking and Talking*, made for a modest budget of $1 million four years earlier, the connotations of *What Women Want*'s shopping scene are brought into even clearer view. In *Walking and Talking*, two lifelong best friends, Laura and Amelia (played by Anne Heche and Catherine Keener), embark on what is deemed the most important shopping experience of a woman's life – looking for her wedding dress. The dressing room in which the scene takes place is devoid of color, with a mirror in the center and only a rack of white dresses surrounding the two women. Laura struggles to get a dress on, and is distracted from the act as a result of her involvement in Amelia's description of a first date the night before. The conversation soon turns from an exchange about the euphoric feelings that are part and parcel of a new sexual relationship to Laura and her fiancé's staid and

Figure 31   Amelia (Catherine Keener) and Laura (Anne Heche) in *Walking and Talking* (Holofcener, 1996).

routine sex life. In the midst of this exchange, they turn, almost as an after-thought, to look at the dress that Laura is trying on. They agree that its lacy, billowing traditional silhouette is not in keeping with Laura's more simple style, and they reject it and move on to the next one without much fanfare. With no diegetic music, very little editing, and the almost laughable disregard for the commodity around which the excursion is based, this scene is about the two women's friendship. They happen to be shopping, but this is not a shopping scene. If anything, the mythology surrounding the event that they are shopping for – a wedding – is demystified.

Contrasting these two scenes is illuminating for multiple reasons. They not only feature the act of shopping but also allude to the process of the makeo-ver, both of which are prominent tropes in postfeminist media culture. But more importantly, they highlight two very different perspectives on their female characters' attitude toward what culture deems the two great roman-tic moments of her life – Alex's prom night and Laura's wedding. The scene from *What Women Want* implies that commodities are intertwined with, and produce, pleasurable feelings, whereas that from *Walking and Talking* reveals that the preparation for what is culturally constructed as the happiest day of a woman's life can be downright mundane.

Using Meyers's *It's Complicated* and Holofcener's *Friends with Money* respectively, this chapter examines two very different types of postfeminist romance films from two of the most successful women filmmakers of the past thirty years. Each filmmaker puts her own imprint on the cycle that is quite different from her counterpart, adopting narratological and formal elements from the industrial context in which she works. Meyers's films adhere closely to Hollywood conventions but are unconventional in their representation of female protagonists whose professional success is celebrated and foregrounded in the narrative. The mise-en-scène of luxury that is the result of this success is pleasurable to look at but raises questions about its elevated importance in relationship to the protagonist's autonomy and pursuit of romantic love. Holofcener's films are also preoccupied with the myopic personal and professional problems of wealthy characters. In contrast to Meyers, she subscribes to independent cinema's more spare, episodic approach to storytelling, which depicts both wealth and romance narrative conventions as awkward and anticlimactic. In fact, some might say that they stretch the boundaries of what we should call a romance film.

Meyers and Holofcener have obvious differences but looking at their work side by side reveals the broad spectrum of films that make up the postfeminist romance landscape. In this chapter's case studies we see that these writer-directors represent the complexities of desire, economics, and love, and how ideas of independence and dependence are far from clear-cut, for either the woman inside the text or the women who make them. Analyzing the different formulas each filmmaker posits for wading through these complications, and the different models of pleasure therein, serves as an illuminating meditation on how women artists may offer some variations on, or alternatives to, representing postfeminist culture's most pressing concerns.

In order to see how we can read both of these filmmakers and their work as falling on different sides of the cycle's landscape, it is informative to examine the institutional settings that serve as the context for their careers, their discussion of their own place within the industry and how their films have been read and interpreted by mainstream film critics. Doing so illustrates how economics, industrial geography, the filmmakers' sensibilities, and popular reception play into the construction of desire and pleasure in and around their films.

About Needing, Fearing and Surrendering to Love: Nancy Meyers and *It's Complicated*

Nancy Meyers has spent her career in Hollywood, first as a writer, and now as a writer-director, and is one of only a handful of women who is given the opportunity to helm multimillion-dollar Hollywood films with A-list casts. While female directors have always been a rarity in Hollywood, those with name and 'brand' recognition are even rarer. Hilary Radner has argued that Nancy Meyers is one of the few auteurs of what she calls 'neo-feminist' cinema,[2] which 'facilitates the marketing of her films within Conglomerate Hollywood.'[3] Meyers's ability to brand herself in association with female-centered and female-oriented romance genre films positions her on the other side of the spectrum from a Hollywood director like Kathryn Bigelow whose 'brand' revolves around the fact that she is a woman who makes 'men's' films, much to the ongoing fascination of critics. In other words, more than their male counterparts, female directors in Hollywood tend to need to be branded vis-à-vis gender in order to make themselves and their films marketable. As Judith Mayne has brilliantly argued, this has been the case even since the 1920s, with Dorothy Arzner, the only major female director of the classical Hollywood studio system. Arzner's work and her public persona have precipitated the same type of discourse in and around gender and the gendered slant of her films as these contemporary female directors and their work.[4]

Meyers's success as a contemporary auteur has a lot to do with her close adherence to the tradition of the romantic and screwball comedy tradition, and in keeping with these forms, she navigates any and all social and political issues through the lens of romance. She makes this position clear in an interview prior to the release of her 2003 smash hit, *Something's Gotta Give*:

> this is a movie about people falling in love late in life. I wouldn't be comfortable writing it in any way other than as a romantic comedy. I think it's how I write, so to me there was no choice in should it be a drama or should it be a romantic comedy. I think as a drama it'd probably have very few people going to see it.

And then when asked to discuss the intersection between the romantic comedy form, and the representation of gender, she continues:

> I don't know that a man couldn't write a movie on the subject. I don't think he would write one like this one because this movie is very much from Diane [Keaton]'s character's point of view as well as from Jack [Nicholson]'s, and I would imagine if a man were writing it the woman would be more of a secondary character who came into his life, and he actually comes into her life.[5]

As Meyers's remarks make evident, by relying on the narrative structure of the romantic comedy, she is successfully able to make her imprint on the genre, and differentiate her output from other films and filmmakers with whom she might be associated. More specifically, she is both a woman over fifty and tells stories that foreground the perspectives of women, many of whom are also over fifty. This female perspective in the writing and screenwriting stage has become increasingly more common as many postfeminist romance films are based on female-penned novels. However, this rarely translates into opportunities for women to direct. Men direct the majority of the films in the postfeminist cycle.

Because Meyers, like the late Nora Ephron, is a rarity in that she is a woman writing and directing films (from her own scripts) that foreground female characters, and presumably aims to appeal to a female audience, her output can safely fall into the definition of the derogatory category of 'chick flicks.' (This is a designation that I will revisit in my discussion of Nicole Holofcener.) However, unlike Ephron, whose output was instrumental to the genesis of the adolescent girl-woman archetype that I discussed in Chapter 4, Meyers's female protagonists' quirkiness is accompanied by a host of other equally important qualities: intelligence, worldliness, confidence, and professional success. Indeed, she is one of the only mainstream romance filmmakers to represent female characters whose professional lives are central rather than peripheral to the plots of her films and whose success is an integral component of defining their sense of self, rather than as something that is causing them to be distressed or to be deemed sad or lonely. In fact, the films implicitly if not explicitly critique a culture in which women's professional success is perceived as threatening to men.

In this way, Meyers's films are distinctive in that they gesture towards a realization and embodiment of second-wave feminist ideals in which a woman can unapologetically value her career and successfully balance this with other aspects of her life. However, the language of this independence is spoken with a vocabulary of desire made possible by the commodities that an upper-middle-class status makes available. This makes her romance films examples not just of intensified continuity, but intensified mise-en-scène. In fact, through Meyers' lens, the Hollywood romance is intensified to such a degree that its basis in real life and real emotions can be called into question. The complex way in which these elements of dependence and independence coexist in and outside of her work make her a fascinating figure through whom the intertwined nature of industry, economics, politics, gender and genre is revealed.

NANCY MEYERS IN CONTEXT

Meyers career began in the 1980s as a writer collaborating with her now ex-husband Charles Shyer. Together they cowrote many female-centric films starring big Hollywood actresses, most of which Shyer directed, including *Private Benjamin* (1980; cowritten and directed by Howard Zieff) with Goldie Hawn, *Irreconcilable Differences* (1984) with Shelley Long, *Baby Boom* (1987) and *Father of the Bride* (1991) with Diane Keaton, and the misguided revamp of classical screwball comedy, *I Love Trouble* with Julia Roberts (1994). Meyers' first foray into directing was with *The Parent Trap* in 1998, a remake of the 1961 film for which she got co-screenplay credit along with Shyer. She then went on to make *What Women Want*, which is the only film that she has directed for which she did not receive story or script credit. It went on to be the most successful film ever to be directed by a woman at that time, with a domestic gross of just over $182 million.[6] *Something's Gotta Give* with Jack Nicholson and Diane Keaton was made in 2003 with an $80 million budget which went on to a domestic gross of just over $124 million.[7] 2006's *The Holiday* with Cameron Diaz and Kate Winslet, with an $85 million budget, was slightly less successful, with a domestic gross of just over $63 million.[8] And *It's Complicated*, her most recent film as of writing this, earned a worldwide gross of over $112 million against a budget of $85 million.[9]

Budgets and grosses have not played a significant role in my analyses of films up until this point but are essential to this chapter's argument in order to highlight what is perhaps fairly obvious but nonetheless important to reiterate: Meyers is working with sizeable budgets made possible by the Hollywood industry. Even her less popular films have generated substantial worldwide revenues. What this money buys is not just the big-name actors and actresses that star in her films, but significant budgets for the types of grandeur that Hollywood films are known for: popular music soundtracks and expensive production design and costumes, among other things. More often than not, when there is a conversation about contemporary big-budget filmmaking, it is in reference to more male-driven genres such as the science-fiction and action film and/or in the context of specific directors such as George Lucas and James Cameron who specialize in the flashy special effects and CGI (computer-generated imagery) that these genres typically involve. But just as economics play a big part in how these fictional worlds are built, made more mesmerizing, and consequently more memorable, they are also a fundamental component of women's genre filmmaking. And, no one is better than Meyers at building memorable and awe-inspiring visual environments. Like most women's filmmakers and genre films, Meyers and her films are, as Hilary Radner has argued, 'ignored or condemned by critics and scholars' when they should be examined for their reflection of how sizable budgets create a consistent mise-en-scène of luxury.[10] Radner argues that Meyers's films show 'an autonomous self that seeks its own fulfillment as its primary goal, ultimately challenging the notion of a natural order associated with the traditional romance,'[11] I, by contrast, will argue that the mise-en-scène of luxury is not just fundamental to Meyers's visual style, but that her films portray romance as a fulfilling and desirable commodity in itself.

To be sure, this lifestyle fetishism makes Meyers's films what they are, but is never really what they are about. The fact that all of the interior spaces of her films look like they come straight out of the pages of a home décor magazine (and in fact, as I will discuss later, they later become featured in such publications) and the food and table settings like they have been arranged by a food stylist goes without comment. While certainly the professional success of Meyers's female protagonists might afford them such a lifestyle, its opulence is rarely acknowledged by anyone within the world of the film and is merely passed off as normal. As Radner aptly sums up, for Meyers 'cinema is not merely a shop window; the goods that it displays are crucial to its art.'[12] Indeed, the goods that fill Meyers's mise-en-scène provide the landscape for, and become intertwined with, the requisite romance narrative structure. Her films are embodiments of what Eva Illouz has identified as the intersection of two processes, which arguably have become more and more prominent in the contemporary era: first, the 'romanticization of commodities,' in which they acquire 'a romantic aura' and the 'commodification of romance' which 'concerns the ways in which romantic practices increasingly interlocked with and became defined as the consumption of leisure goods and leisure technologies offered by the nascent mass market.'[13] Diane Negra has labeled the postfeminist manifestation of this trend as 'the hyper-aestheticization of everyday life'[14] in which an 'identification with a level of luxury consumption far out of proportion to one's actual financial circumstances is emerging as a hallmark of contemporary existence.'[15]

Meyers's entire oeuvre supports Illouz and Negra's points here as it depicts romance (and relational affect more generally) as one of the many commodities in its broader hyper-aestheticized mise-en-scène. As *New York Times* film critic Manohla Dargis observes in her review of *The Holiday*, 'The men and women in a Nancy Meyers film don't just fall in love; they talk about falling in love, about falling out of love, about needing, fearing and surrendering to love.'[16] In other words, romance does not just have meaning as the narrative framework for Meyers's films, as her aforementioned interview comments on romantic comedy attest, but is elevated to such a level of excess and meaning so hyper-aestheticized that it becomes performative. There is no better example of this confluence of factors than the memorable sequence from *Something's Gotta Give* in which a heartbroken Erica sobs uncontrollably and unpredictably while she writes her play amid the backdrop of her exquisitely adorned Oceanside Hamptons house, accompanied by the sounds of Edith Piaf. Thinking back to Nick's 'How much?' sign in the *What Women Want* shopping sequence, it becomes clear that this could be asked of all of Meyers films. In the case of *Something's Gotta Give*, one might ponder: how much does that house, that décor, and those clothes cost? But also, how much crying, how many tissues and how much intertextuality does it take to get to the requisite resolution of 'the problem' stage of this particular romance narrative?

The habitual product placement and intertextuality in Meyers's films makes them perfect examples of the slippage between reality and fantasy that I discussed in Chapter 2. Almost all of her films feature some example of a cycle in which life imitates art, and then vice versa. This manifests itself in two ways. First, like Erica's self-referential playwriting career in *Something's Gotta Give*, most of Meyers's female characters work in creative fields that contribute to the culture in which fantasy and reality are interchangeable. For instance, in *The Parent Trap*, Elizabeth (Natasha Richardson) is a wedding-dress designer. *What Women Want*'s Darcy (Helen Hunt) is an advertising executive who expertly sells women commodities by appealing to their 'real' selves. In *The Holiday*, Iris (Kate Winslet) writes a wedding column for a newspaper, and Amanda (Cameron Diaz) produces movie trailers. And, as I will go on to discuss in terms of *It's Complicated*, Jane (Meryl Streep) owns a Dean and Deluca-like gourmet food store and restaurant in which food is not just a form of sustenance but is elevated to a fetish object.

The second way in which the reality-fantasy slippage can be seen in Meyers work is in her films' endings. As Dargis's comments about *The Holiday* attest, the endings do not just feature the formation of a heterosexual couple but hyper-aestheticize this connection to such an extent that they call attention to their own fiction-based fantasy. To put it another way, we might say that they are announcing themselves to be participants in an ongoing discourse of love as it is seen in the movies, rather than attempting to realistically represent genuine emotional attachment. For instance, the end of *What Women Want* sees Darcy appropriating but reversing the language of fairy tales by declaring herself the prince that needs to rescue Nick. In *Something's Gotta Give*, Harry (Jack Nicholson) takes a cue from Erica's play about their relationship and flies to Paris to declare his love for her, with the resolution occurring on a bridge with snow falling, to which Harry (recognizing the performative nature of it all) states, 'Anything else?' And, Amanda runs (in high heels) back to declare her love for Graham (Jude Law) after she hears the trailer of her life play out in her head. After making this decision, the trailer welcomes her back to 'real love.'

Radner rightly contends that Meyers's happy endings may appear to 'support the romantic paradigm' but cannot overcome their contradictions. I would further contend that Meyers's ability to camouflage the contradictions that underlie all of her films – between her representations of strong, seemingly independent women and their reliance on the language of love and commodity consumption to speak this independence – is exactly what has led her to be the single most successful contemporary romance filmmaker. Her success lays bare the paradoxical nature of what it takes to give mainstream audiences 'what they want' (a reference to her own film by that title and the aforementioned Christina Aguilera song). These elements are most transparent in *It's Complicated*, which arguably is Meyers's least tightly constructed film to date. Because the film's romantic narrative momentum wilts under the weight of its own complexity (in keeping with its title), the connections between the independent protagonist, the mise-en-scène of luxury and heterosexual romance are more conspicuous than in her previous films. Consequently, we can see the underlying machinations that make her films so intoxicatingly pleasurable.

LOVE, DIVORCE AND RENOVATION IN *IT'S COMPLICATED*

It's Complicated is centered on divorcee Jane Adler (Meryl Streep), a mother of three grown children, the oldest of whom – Lauren (Caitlin Fitzgerald) – is planning a wedding, the second oldest – Luke (Hunter Parrish) – is celebrating his college graduation, and the youngest – Gaby (Zoe Kazan) – is moving away from home for the first time. The beginning of the film emphasizes Jane's recognition of a quickly moving life cycle where she is more observer than participant. It is clear that most of Jane's life has been dedicated to serving the needs of others, both literally (we see her pouring coffee for her customers in her restaurant) and figuratively.

The film's arc centers on Jane beginning to take center stage in her own life again and fulfilling her own long-neglected needs in several ways. She engages in a romantic and sexual relationship, first with her lawyer ex-husband, Jake (Alec Baldwin), and then her architect, Adam (Steve Martin), and second, she builds a huge addition on her home, which will give her the 'kitchen she always wanted.' We see Jane hesitantly wade her way into an affair with Jake, which is initially energizing but eventually becomes too uncomfortably deceitful as it forces them to betray not just Jake's wife, Agness (Lake Bell), but their mutual children as well. However, the affair does boost her sexual confidence, making her more receptive to the overtures of Adam, who is deemed the more appropriate love interest both because of his humility and willingness to court Jane, but also, as I will argue, because he is the character associated with providing Jane with what she most wants: the long-awaited addition to her house.

As in Meyers's earlier films, the life choices of Jane and the films' characters are navigated through the vocabulary of consumption. Indeed, Meyers has said: 'What the characters wear and how they live and decorate really say something about them.'[17] I would take this one step further and say that these elements not only say something about *It's Complicated*'s characters but do much of the talking. This becomes most obvious when the film's love triangle loses steam about three quarters of the way through the film and Jane stops the affair with Jake in favor of a relationship with Adam. While there are convoluted plot twists that follow that see Adam learn the complex truth about Jane and Jake and stop seeing Jane, the last quarter of the film comes to rely almost entirely on the language of consumption to sustain itself. Even its subdued conclusion that only promises rather than delivers a happy ending between Adam and Jane is spoken through the mutually beneficial consumptive processes that have defined their relationship. The film's reliance on the conflation of romance and the language of commodity fetishism is made perfectly clear in its opening scenes.

The opening credits play with Spanish guitar music over alternating static frame shots and sweeping camera movements of a blue sky, palm trees, rooftops of Spanish-style homes, the ocean, and then the oceanfront community of Santa Barbara. Eventually, the camera leads us to an outdoor cocktail party at a house overlooking the water where waiters deliver champagne, outdoor musicians entertain the guests, and all of the attendees look like they stepped out of a Brooks Brothers catalog. We then focus on Jane and her ex-husband Jake dedicating a toast to their hosts – Sally (Nora Dunn) and Ted (Bruce Altman) – whose thirtieth wedding anniversary the party is celebrating. Through this opening dialogue sequence it becomes clear that these two couples were once close, and celebrated their fifteenth year anniversary together on a trip to Spain. But according to the film's chronology, five years after this anniversary Jane and Jake split up because he had an affair with Agness (Lake Bell), his current, much younger wife. Jane and Jake have had a fraught relationship ever since. In the midst of this conversation, during which Jane is finishing Jake's sentences, we cut to an image of Agness moving toward the group. Through a series of shot-reverse-shots, the viewer is invited to gaze along with Jane in slow motion at Agness's perfect, scantily clad body, which is a striking contrast to the fully clothed bodies of the mostly fifty-something party attendees. After sharing some stilted yet courteous conversation with the couple, Jane departs the party but takes a moment to look back at Jake and Agness cuddling while they gaze at the ocean.

Adhering to an intensified continuity style, this scene's dialogue and visual cues introduce the basic aesthetic and narrative framework in which the film operates. First, it makes clear that initially Jane is an onlooker rather than a real player in the world around her, which mostly consists of couples. The fact that Jane is gazing at, rather than participating in, this milieu is most literally represented in the way that she gawks at Agness, her ex-husband's preferred love interest, and then looks with disdain at their seemingly loving embrace from afar. The scene also makes clear that every moment in the life of Meyers characters, whether large or small, foregrounds what they are eating, buying and wearing. This is evident in the party itself, which presents another example of hyper-aestheticization, with the ocean as backdrop, live music, flowing cocktails, and beautiful people. It looks exactly like what a party in the movies should look like.

The connection between consumption and important life stages is also made clear in subsequent scenes where we see Jane offering to come down to help her youngest daughter set up her new home by taking her to 'that big Bed, Bath and Beyond to get kitchen stuff' and when she finds that the only way that she can help with her son's graduation party is by handing over her credit card. Later, we see Lauren and fiancé Harley (John Krasinski) dining at the luxury hotel (also the site of a midday tryst between Jane and Jake) before their meeting with a wedding planner, during which they will look at wedding flowers and cakes. According to Lauren, the worst thing that can happen to their relationship is that Harley 'goes into a coma' while they are planning what looks to be a very expensive affair. In other words, in order for the event to be a satisfying experience, he must be a full and active participant in picking out every single object that will make it fit the culturally constructed vision of the perfect wedding. Even the discussion of important life events from the past, such as a past anniversary, is imbued with extravagant spending on international travel. We hear about a vacation that the two couples took to Spain, and later we find out that Adam learned of his wife's infidelity on a biking trip through Tuscany.

This opening scene also plants the seeds of the film's dynamic of 'appropriate' and 'inappropriate' lifestyle consumption that moves the plot, and the love triangle, forward. First, the fact that Agness's younger, fit body is held up as the most desirable gets dissected more and more as the film progresses. Initially, Jane's response to Agness's enviable physique is to go see a plastic surgeon for a consultation on how he might go about fixing her drooping eyelid. But after the doctor informs her what the procedure involves and the recovery time, she quickly scurries out of the office and into the elevator, only to run into Jake and Agness who are coming out of a fertility clinic on a lower floor of the same building. As they enter the elevator, Jane examines Agness again, although this time she looks skeptically at the tiger tattoo on Agness's back.

In this sequence of scenes, we see Jane wisely accept her own aging body for what it is and refuse to alter it through an improper act of consumption: plastic surgery. Meyers quite skillfully contrasts this with Agness, whose tiger tattoo sees her quite willing to manipulate her body, and Jake, who later tells Jane that he has to go to the fertility clinic every other day to donate sperm in order to impregnate Agness. He estimates that he will be seventy-nine when the planned baby will graduate college. In other words, the couple's attempt to manipulate their bodies through an in vitro pregnancy brought on by Jake's age (we are told that Agness had no trouble conceiving with a previous partner) is clearly deemed laughable if not entirely inappropriate. This is made clear in a later scene inside the fertility clinic where the camera scans the waiting room to reveal only fifty- to sixty-something men sitting alongside their twenty-something female partners.

The film does not wholly vilify Agness. Jane acknowledges that she has a stressful, high-powered job as the head of a marketing department that might contribute to her cold demeanor. But Jake refers to her as 'crazy' and 'so amped up on hormone injections' that he needs an exorcist. To this end, while Agness's younger and culturally preferred body is initially idealized, it eventually becomes associated with extreme behavior and a harsh and sterile mise-en-scène. What we see of her and Jake's home is contemporary with sleek lines and modern architecture, and she is often clothed in minimalist dark tones. While Jane is a professional chef who elicits appreciative accolades for her cuisine throughout the film, we are told that Agness does not cook and the family menu is dictated by her young son's limited palate. Clearly, while Agness is deemed a participant in the materialistic world in which the film takes place, her consumption is positioned in stark contrast to the warmer, wiser, giving, natural consumption represented by Jane and her domestic and professional spaces.

Jane is a perfect example of what Diane Negra has called the postfeminist domestic body, which 'is relaxed, integrated, bountiful, connected to nature and to others.'[18] After the two begin their affair, Jake even mentions that he appreciates the fact that Jane has 'gone native' by discontinuing bikini waxes, but this serves as a broader metaphor for what he calls her 'loose' approach to sex in contrast to the sex with Agness that is scheduled around her ovulation cycle.[19] Meyers's efforts to make Jane's body the preferred and more desirable body functions similarly to the way that Erica's body is eventually deemed sexually attractive to Harry in *Something's Gotta Give*. Sadie Wearing has described this as the rehabilitation of 'the middle-aged female body into heterosexual visibility and hence activity.'[20]

There are many ways in which the film positions Jane as the more narratively visible body and preferred love object, but the bulk of the visual and verbal language that serves to explain this is based in the mise-en-scène that defines her consumption. The examples are almost too numerous to list, but the most noteworthy is the addition that Jane plans to put on her house. This choice leads to her meeting Adam, her architect and potential love interest. Jane's empty-nester status has brought on her desire to 'get a real kitchen,' which is deemed not only positive but necessary, despite the fact that her house – and her kitchen, particularly – is already visually comparable to that seen in a designer's showcase, with high end appliances and marble countertops not to mention overflowing fruit baskets and freshly baked pastries on display.

In 'Something's Gotta Give: Nancy Meyers, feminist auteur (2003),' Radner discusses how an *Architectural Digest* article that featured Erica's Oceanside Hamptons home in *Something's Gotta Give* is an example of the 'film's dependence upon an aesthetic defined by the visual vernacular of tasteful (and expensive) consumerism.'[21] *It's Complicated* works within this same mode and similar accompanying stories appeared in the pages of *Elle Décor* and *Traditional Home*. The headline for the latter's accompanying story highlights how Jane's home décor (designed in collaboration with production designer Jon Hutman, and set decorator Beth Rubino with whom Meyers also worked on *Something's Gotta Give*) is intertwined with the romance triangle: 'Take a serene Santa Barbara setting with to-die-for interiors, add a triangle mixing love, divorce, and renovation, and you have all the elements of an unusual romantic comedy.'[22] The article speaks of how the décor works not just with the plot of the film, to depict 'casual elegance and not just a fancy way of life' but also takes Streep's coloring into account:

> From cashmere throws and chair upholstery to a bowl of fruit on the dining table, the color orange (think of the orange/brown color of an Hermès box) is used as an accent throughout the film. The decor had to accent Streep's fair complexion as well, so Meyers used creams and beiges that would capture the beauty of her skin.[23]

While all filmmakers are attentive to constructing the appropriate settings in which their action will take place, it is clear that Meyers and her team are encouraging the types of visual links between lifestyle, wealth and desire that are made by this *Traditional Home* writer. In fact, there are numerous bloggers who have devoted posts to coveting this house, including Lindsay Blake's iamnotastalker.com, a site dedicated to investigating movie and television sets, in which she states that she is 'so obsessed with the *It's Complicated* house – it is exactly the type of place I'd love to own myself someday.'[24]

What is interesting about the discourse in and around this house versus the luxurious homes in other Meyers films is that the plot of *It's Complicated* revolves around Jane's desire to change the house and improve it beyond its already impressive state. As previously noted, this act of consumption is seen as perfectly appropriate and not at all excessive because it is aligned with her new empty-nester life stage. She is now permitted to buy things for herself instead of only buying them for others. And, since, as previously mentioned, this effort to update and expand her living space leads her to meet Adam, it becomes one of the most precise and efficient ways that the language of romance and consumption can be spoken simultaneously.

The first time we see Jane and Adam meet, she is clearly oblivious to the fact that Adam is attracted to her. In fact, she does not even remember the fact that they have met before (prior to the film's time frame). However, once she takes a look at the addition blueprints that he has drawn up, she suddenly takes notice of him, and their discussion about the house doubles as the language of courtship and flirtation. Jane responds to the plans with enthusiastic oohs and aahs at his ability to turn her forty-seven e-mails about house details into 'something beautiful.' When she requests that he remove the second 'his' sink from the master bathroom, leaving only a 'hers,' because her current second sink 'makes her feel bad,' he replies: 'You don't think in the future you might want a his?' Later, we see Adam give her a guided tour of the layout of the house where he chivalrously opens imaginary doors and pulls out the chairs from an imaginary table to give her a feel for it. The house here is not just an object that demonstrates Jane's economic status or represents her life stage but has now become intertwined with her romantic trajectory as well.

Figure 32   Jane (Meryl Streep) and Adam (Steve Martin) in *It's Complicated* (Meyers, 2009).

Jane's appreciation of what Adam can do for her both professionally and romantically is matched by Adam's affection for how Jane's professional prowess as a chef can translate into the personal sphere. Indeed, just as Jane's present emotional state is mostly spoken through the vocabulary of home improvement, her emotional past is recounted through the vocabulary of culinary production and consumption. She recounts her personal history to Adam as she is serving him a *croque monsieur* and ice cream from scratch during their first shared dinner. Moreover, the stories that she tells him are of her training as a chef in Paris, and later, the different dishes that she was making when she acquired the scars on her hands and arms. Just as Adam endears himself to Jane by involving her in, and literally walking her through, his planning process for her addition, the scene where Jane teaches Adam how to make chocolate croissants serves as foreplay, leading to their first real kiss.

Jake also talks at great length about Jane's cooking abilities throughout the film. What brings on the downfall of their affair is when he fails to show up for a romantic dinner for which she has prepared his favorite meal. His lack of appreciation for the lovingly made meal of roast chicken, mashed potatoes, sautéed string beans, and double fudge chocolate cake is symptomatic of his lack of sustained appreciation for her. With Jake, Jane is forced into the uncomfortable role of home wrecker; with Adam she is building a bigger home with a better kitchen that will foster the mutual enjoyment of the production and consumption that they both represent to each other.

Certainly, the characterization and casting of Steve Martin as affable and heartbroken Adam versus Alec Baldwin as cocky and smarmy Jake almost predetermines the film's 'happy' ending. However, the concluding scene that sees Adam choose not to hand over Jane's house job to his partner like he has planned, and instead show up on the first day of building, does strike one as (literally) watered down. It is a rainy day, and Jane walks anxiously out of her house toward the group of workers to see if Adam is among them. Once we see that he is, he asks Jane if she knows that it is good luck to start building in the rain. After Jane invites him and his crew inside, he asks her if she has any of those chocolate croissants that he has such fond memories of. She replies, 'you like those, huh?' The film then fades out on a conversation between the two about whether she should go into town to procure the croissants from her store.

One could argue that this more understated dénouement is a more realistic alternative to Meyers's usual endings in that it resists presenting an easy resolution to Adam and Jane's problems. However, we might also view it as more performative than her prior work because Adam and Jane's relationship remains intertwined with the commodities that have provided the language of their courtship. We believe in the promise of an actual affective bond between the two characters and want them to have their happy ending. However, their resolution does not contain language that speaks of their mutual attraction but that which speaks of the addition and food. In this way, *It's Complicated* is complicated. On one hand, it is an incredibly satisfying, well-acted romance film, with the central conflicts resolved and a promise of a happy ending between Jane and a man who respects and admires her success. On the other hand, the film transparently satisfies another kind of desire, which is that of commodity fetishism enabled by the film's significant production budget. To have love alongside a beautiful home and fantastic food without having to consider the costs of such an arrangement is the pleasurable fantasy that Meyers's films offer. But one does wonder whether the desire generated by this intensified mise-en-scène of wealth exceeds that generated by the characters' emotional connection.

Does it change the parameters of the cycle when the romance between people is overshadowed by a romance between people and 'things?' In even pointing to these types of questions, Meyers's film traverses well-worn postfeminist terrain wherein consumerism is intertwined with both female autonomy and love. That it is an accomplished yet unapologetic female protagonist, and in this case a female protagonist over forty, that is powerful enough to have this wealth and this multitude of choices at her disposal makes Meyers's films stand out from their peers. These big-budget Hollywood qualities also make for a fascinating comparison with independent postfeminist romance films that deal with the same sets of issues but within a different mode of production.

THEY DO NOT LIVE IN THESE MOVIES: ECONOMICS AND LOVE IN
NICOLE HOLOFCENER'S *FRIENDS WITH MONEY*

During the same period in which Hollywood saw few women in positions of power, the 1990s and early 2000s saw a surge in the number of independent female filmmakers such as Alison Anders, Nancy Savoca, Mary Harron, Rebecca Miller and Nicole Holofcener, among others, who seized opportunities to make, and get distribution for, films which revealed a different approach to representing the female experience. In his 2005 book *American Independent Cinema*, Geoff King remarks on the connections between independent filmmaking as a mode of production that is often explicitly, if not, implicitly, resistant to the standard Hollywood narrative conventions, and cites women's roles in such an arena:

> To eschew plot-centric forms in the cinema is, in many cases, to choose or suffer operation on the limited resources available in the independent sphere, to be relegated to what some would consider a secondary position akin to that generally offered to women in society. The corollary should be that women are more likely to be at home in the indie sector, which may be true in some respects as far as sensibility is concerned but is clearly not the case in terms of equal availability of opportunities or resources.[25]

King arguably overstates his point by conflating independent filmmakers' deviation from traditional plot-centric conventions and women's position within society, but he still points to some compelling ways in which the realities of female filmmakers' secondary status in the Hollywood film industry might motivate the pursuit of a different sensibility and approach in the independent sphere. Nicole Holofcener's oeuvre, specifically *Friends with Money*, serves as a fascinating case study to support King's points, and to serve as a point of comparison to Meyers's films.

Holofcener is indeed 'at home' in the indie sector. She has made four modestly successful independent features that focus on women's romantic and platonic relationships but defy many of the conventions that characterize the postfeminist romance cycle. She is both outsider and insider in relationship to the still largely male-dominated contemporary independent cinema tradition and Hollywood's economic infrastructure and plot-centric conventions. Holofcener's ability to make films that call upon, and yet are still distinct from, traits from both modes of production confounds some critics and audiences, but results in a unique take on the romance film that points to some alternative possibilities for the cycle.

The reasons why female filmmakers like Holofcener are rarely discussed at any length in terms of romance filmmaking or the independent cinema are wide-ranging. But certainly one of the factors is the fact that the 'little engine that could' history of the independent cinema tends to be masculinized. Scholar Christina Lane, whose book *Feminist Hollywood: Point Break to Born in Flames* is one of the few to tackle the topic of female independent filmmaking, offers a fascinating take on this issue in her article, 'Just another girl outside the neo-indie':[26]

> a new brand of indie auteurism, grew as a result of the desire for festivals and independent studios to draw attention to their films by promoting the director as a maverick who had seized the reins of low-budget production and, in his own hip, cool way, made the system work for him. And it was nearly always a *him* because the traditional director's 'mystique' of auteurism pervaded the indie festivals and studios' marketing campaigns, excluding women from increasingly commercialized imagery. As the 1990s continued, it became less likely that films would be advertised on the basis of a 'woman director,' meaning that women filmmakers and 'female' genres became less marketable and less marketed, in a reciprocal spiral.[27]

The impact of the 'reciprocal spiral' of which Lane speaks in which women filmmakers become less visible in the mainstream discourse in and around independent cinema is clearly evident in Liese Spencer's review of Holofcener's aforementioned first feature *Walking and Talking* in *Sight and Sound*:

> *Walking and Talking* is a welcome example of that rare hybrid: the independent cinema chick movie. This debut feature from Nicole Holofcener is a quick-witted study of female friendship, which conveys warmth and emotion without resorting either to *Oprah*-like confessional or melodrama.[28]

The category of chick flick returns again in an interview with Kristi Mitsuda for the online magazine, *Reverse Shot* (RS):

> RS: Does it ever bother you when people lump your films into that 'chick flick' category simply because you focus on women?
> NH: You know, I don't know; I don't think they are chick flicks.
> RS: I don't either, which is why I wonder if it bothers you.
> NH: You know, it would bother me if I couldn't get financing because people said, 'Oh, this is a chick flick.' But I get to make them, so you can call them whatever you want [laughs]. So if they need to be labeled, that's okay, as long as I can make them.[29]

Holofcener's comments shed a lot of light on her perception of herself in the context of the industry. She is, by necessity, more concerned with being able to raise the minimal budgets that will enable her to make the films that she wants to make, and less invested in how they are labeled by viewers or marketed by distribution companies. Yet despite the obvious difference between her outsider status within the broader industrial landscape and the insider status of someone like Meyers, critics still seem intent on placing them into the same 'chick flick' category because their films tread on the same thematic terrain. But as Spencer points out, Holofcener's films bear enough of a trace of the independent film tradition in that they fall short of the hyper-aesthetic realm of *Oprah* and melodrama, a category in which Meyers would also presumably be placed.

Neither Holofcener nor Meyers may ever be able to avoid the convenient and unimaginative label of 'chick flick' filmmaker; however it is quite clear upon close inspection that while *Friends with Money* shares the same discursive elements as *It's Complicated*, it explores them through a different aesthetic and narrative lens. By highlighting the connection between the mise-en-scène of wealth and affective relations and infusing elements of the awkward, the de-aesthetizied and the anticlimactic, the film falls in line with what Kathleen Rowe Karlyn has identified as independent romance films' ability to engage with 'the social realities of the present.'[30]

As Spencer observed, *Friends with Money* is indeed a rare hybrid, but one which marries the romance narrative with a biting perspective on the manner in which contemporary culture links affect with consumerism. It fits within what Geoff King has described as independent cinema's use of 'devices designed to deny, block, delay or complicate the anticipated development of narrative'[31] and 'focusing on something closer to the rhythms and textures of ordinary life.'[32] The film's point of distinction then is not its 'various anxieties and dissatisfactions surrounding heterosex' that may lead one to conclude that 'female friendship is the new love' as Celestino Deyleto has argued.[33] Rather, it seems more in line with the way in which Deleyto has described another independent romance film, *Before Sunset*:

> The fantasy of this film does not exclude reality but rather, builds its romantic discourse on the frustrations of the everyday ... realism as a filmic mode has undoubtedly constituted a more fertile field for independent cinema to explore the vicissitudes of modern love.[34]

Certainly this penetrating and some might say narratively awkward representation of romance in the context of the everyday may not provide any false or easy resolutions to the problems and paradoxes that arise from romance. But it clearly still instills the sense that romance can be a satisfying if not potentially fulfilling dimension of a woman's life.

'Even When It's Boring': Holofcener in Context

Nicole Holofcener's career trajectory blurs the same boundaries as her films: she is one part outsider, and one part insider. She grew up in New York City and then moved with her family to Los Angeles when she was twelve years old. She later returned to New York and became a production assistant on Woody Allen's *A Midsummer Night's Sex Comedy* (1982), through the help of her stepfather Charles Joffe – an executive producer of Allen's films since 1969. Holofcener also worked as an apprentice for Allen's editor Susan Morse on *Hannah and Her Sisters* (1996) and received her Master of Fine Arts from Columbia University, where she received positive attention for her short film, *Angry* (1992).[35] She scraped together $1 million in financing in order to make her first feature, *Walking and Talking*, which focuses on the complex friendship between two childhood best friends and their romantic trials and tribulations. *Walking and Talking* was distributed by Miramax, was well received by critics, and earned a respectable $1.2 million at the domestic box office;[36] however, Holofcener struggled to get financing for her next film, *Lovely and Amazing*. She was only able to make the film, released in 2001, after she agreed to shoot it on high-definition video for the miniscule budget of $250,000.[37]

Loving and Amazing focuses on the Marks family and touches upon the mother and three daughters' struggle with issues of self-acceptance revolving around weight, appearance, and professional success. It was eventually picked up for distribution by Lions Gate and saw a domestic gross of over $4 million.[38] *Friends with Money* (2006) was Holofcener's first union film and most successful film to date. Distributed by Sony Pictures Classics, it earned a domestic gross of $13 million against a budget of $6,500,000.[39] *Please Give* had its world premiere at the Sundance Film Festival on January 22, 2009 and went on to earn a domestic gross of $4 million against a $3 million budget.[40]

Here the industrial differences between Holofcener and Meyers are evident. Holofcener's budgets are miniscule in comparison to Meyers's multimillion-dollar productions, and her films give women's relationships with other women as much weight as their romantic relationships. These elements plus the distribution of the narrative across multiple characters make her films decidedly more meandering and less 'plot-centric' than their Hollywood counterparts. As Brenda Blethyn, the actress who plays the Marks matriarch in *Lovely and Amazing* has stated: 'Nicole is only interested in the actual truth of things. Even when the truth is boring.'[41] In other words, Holofcener has been given the label of the 'female Woody Allen' for good reason. Her films have a great deal in common with his loose character-driven narratives and emphasis on dialogue instead of action. Plus, like Allen, Holofcener is not particularly interested in making her characters seem likeable or even identifiable. Manohla Dargis summarizes this perfectly in her review of *Please Give:*

> Few American filmmakers create female characters as realistically funny, attractively imperfect and flat-out annoying as does Ms. Holofcener . . . You may not love them, but you recognize their charms and frailties, their fears and hopes . . . We don't necessarily or only go to the movies to see mirror versions of ourselves: we also want (or think we do) better, kinder, nobler, prettier and thinner images, idealized types and aspirational figures we can take pleasure in or laugh at in all their plastic unreality. The female characters in Ms. Holofcener's films don't live in those movies: they watch them.[42]

When thinking back to *It's Complicated*, Dargis's comments come into even clearer and humorous view, as the idealized types, plastic unreality and parties that look like they belong in the movies are an obvious example of the kind of women's films to which she is referring here. And, *Friends with Money*, like *Please Give*, sees Holofcener featuring characters that may share the same social class as Meyers' characters, but are made acutely aware of the problems that come along with it. *Friends with Money*, to use Claire Perkins description of a subgenre of independent films that she calls '"smart films," relies on classical narrative strategies' but these elements are also 'mobilized as a means of critiquing bourgeois taste and culture.'[43] Furthermore, as Michael Newman has argued, *Friends with Money*'s representation of characters 'in their full specificity and distinctness' is representative of independent cinema's assertion of 'the uniqueness of identity positions, while the Hollywood emphasis on transcendent human connectedness is called into question, if not demolished.'[44]

The film focuses on four women, Olivia (Jennifer Aniston), an aimless pothead high school teacher-turned-maid, Christine (Catherine Keener), an unhappily married screenwriter, Jane (Frances McDormand), a depressed clothing designer going through a mid-life crisis, and Franny (Joan Cusack), a wealthy, altruistic stay-at-home mother. The film shows the intertwined lives of these friends and their significant others. It is bookended by two gatherings – the first, the celebration of Jane's forty-third birthday and the last, a gathering at an ALS (Amyotrophic Lateral Sclerosis) fundraising dinner. The film is about the ways in which women support each other, but also emphasizes how, behind closed doors, friends spend a fair amount of time expressing concern about, and passing judgment on, each other's life choices.

Holofcener's presentation of this dynamic is characteristic of her subtle style, as these scenes fall short of cattiness, but feel acerbic enough to be recognizable to anyone who has walked away from a social event and had an opinion about the people with whom they interacted. The caring yet critical lens through which the friends judge each other is familiar and humorous not just because it may mirror spectators' real-life relationships but also because we might think of it as loosely mirroring the relationship between spectators and Holofcener's films. As the aforementioned critics make clear, watching the 'boring truth' of women who make bad choices that lead to unsatisfying conclusions makes for a viewing experience that is often uncomfortable because of how skillfully it subverts the model of 'plastic unreality' that Hollywood often offers.

The contrast between Holofcener's and Meyers's treatment of the intertwined nature of work, economics, and lifestyle fetishism can be seen in *Friends with Money*'s first scenes. The film opens on a sequence in which a woman cleans a house, doing the kind of labor that we rarely see depicted in film, and even more rarely see depicted as our female protagonist's career choice. We see medium shots of this character photographed primarily from the neck down, cleaning the toilet, pulling hair out of the bath tub drain, and opening drawers to place knick-knacks but do not see her face until about two minutes into the film's running time.[45] Once the viewer gets the big reveal that this maid – Olivia – is played by the biggest star in film – Jennifer Aniston – we see her help herself to the vibrator left in the knick-knack drawer (the act of using it is also left off-screen). And then, after she replaces the vibrator matter-of-factly, she takes her money and leaves. Intercut with Olivia's cleaning scenes is a scene set in Christine and David's (Jason Isaacs) house where an architect is showing them a miniature model of a second-story addition for their home. They are exuberant that the addition will give them a view of the ocean, and readily shrug off the architect's warning that adding a second story in a neighborhood full of single-story homes might upset their neighbors. When they admire the miniature couple on the balcony of the model home, David remarks, 'Look honey, it's us!' At the end of the scene, when Christine goes to get coffee for David and the architect, she clumsily hits her leg on the table and winces in pain. The fact that neither man notices or asks her if she is okay seems insignificant at the time but becomes a recurring trope for the film's depiction of Christine and David's marriage.

I will return to, and elaborate on, these first two sets of scenes later, but first want to briefly address what the two other scenes in this opening sequence show us about the two characters that I will spend less time discussing – Jane and Franny. Jane, whose forty-third birthday celebration marks the beginning of the film, is going through a midlife crisis that consists of her neglecting her hygiene and going off on angry tirades toward anyone whose actions displease her. One of the plot points of the film explores whether Jane's husband (Simon McBurney), whose metrosexual interest in sample sales and designer clothes strikes her friends as erring on the homosexual side, is gay. This question is introduced in their first scene when we see a gender reversal of the usual pre-party clothes deliberations, in which Aaron asks Jane whether or not his shirt looks okay and debates changing into the 'new striped one' which he can 'tuck in' to which Jane lovingly responds, 'you're pathetic.' While the film sees Aaron explore a friendship with an equally metrosexual man (humorously, also named Aaron), it is ultimately confirmed that he is not homosexual and is completely devoted to and emotionally supportive of his wife and child.

What is most compelling about the Jane/Aaron storyline in the context of this discussion is that they (and the other Aaron) own their own retail businesses. Jane is a clothing designer, Aaron a maker of organic bath and beauty products, and the other Aaron, a sock designer. However, with the exception of a quick glimpse of their products here and there and a short scene of all of the female characters trying on Jane's clothes in anticipation of the ALS fundraiser, the film does not dwell in any way on the commodity culture of which they are a part. Nor does it aestheticize the commodities themselves. When Jane's clothing is mentioned, it is for its exquisite construction but also for its astronomical price tag. Jane responds, 'I know it's overpriced, but it has to be' thereby consciously acknowledging the mythology around fashion in which perception is everything. Jane knows that she must work within this system in order to be successful but she is aware of its superficiality. The film makes clear its distance from mainstream consumer culture and its hyper-aestheticization in Hollywood cinema by having Jane's big breakdown take place in an Old Navy store. Brand placement, yes, but the depiction of the store, its employees, and its customers is far from flattering. To this end, while the film calls attention to the disjunction between the superficial projection of value that we place on objects versus their real value, these characters are still firmly situated in an upper-middle-class milieu. As the title of the films tells us, these are 'friends with money' and thus, these problems are only experienced by people of their class status.

A case in point is Franny, the wealthiest of the four characters. The film's opening scenes see her ask her husband, Matt (Greg Germann), why he had to spend $95 on a pair of shoes for their young, growing daughter. Franny's defining characteristic is this recurring sense of guilt over spending her inherited wealth to spoil their kids (which comes up again on a Christmas shopping trip later in the film) rather than do good for people. Franny has the least amount of screen time and does not go through the same type of emotional journey as the other three women. Her characterization seems designed to make it clear that even people with a great deal of wealth have hang-ups and neuroses about the responsibilities that come along with money. However, Holofcener's representation of Franny's and Matt's relationship as more stable and sexually satisfying than the rest of the couples in the film does not do much to dispel the conception that wealthy people might be happier. As Aaron remarks in reference to Franny and Matt: 'I would have a lot of sex if I had that much money, I mean you know, nothing to worry about. No stress.'

Returning to the opening depicting the characters of Olivia and Christine, we see the seeds for the film's most explicit interrogation of the complex and intertwined nature of labor, economics, commodity culture, romance and sexuality, and their ramifications for a woman's sense of autonomy and independence. Christine and Olivia are the only two primary characters who are seen working, and their narratives reveal, in quite different ways, how the type of labor that is often left off-screen (both figuratively and literally) is linked to the seemingly effortless appearance of wealth and a clean and aesthetically pleasing home environment that we have come to expect from Hollywood productions like those of Meyers. We might imagine that, as Dargis states, just as Holofcener's female characters are the type to watch a movie and not be in a movie, the cottage that Olivia cleans is not a house that she could live in, but one that she might see in a movie, and Christine, being a screenwriter, might be the one to provide the script.

As a part of a screenwriting team with her husband, the blurred boundary between Christine's marriage and workplace is mirrored by the conflicts between their fictional characters, whose lines they read aloud to each other across their shared office. The first time we see their collaborative work process it is at first difficult to tell if we are witnessing a real conversation or a conversation from the script that they are writing. Since David reads the lines of the male characters and Christine reads the lines of the female characters, their performances of these roles become confused with reality. But this scene also points to, and reflects on, the type of performativity that is involved in the Hollywood film that they are writing. The male characters enacted by, and presumably written by, David are just as abrasive and uncaring as he is. Holofcener's approach to shooting these sequences, in a tight shot-reverse-shot style, isolating Christine and David in medium shots at their respective desks across the room from one another, emphasizes the distance of their relationship. The physical distance as exemplified by visual style also extends into the bedroom, as their friends continually discuss their lack of a sex life.

It is ironic that while the film emphasizes Christine's growing frustration with the emotional and physical distance she feels from a brutally honest David, their relationship is seen to cause her to disregard the feelings of others as well. This is most clearly represented by the house addition, which is one of the most fascinating points of comparison with *It's Complicated*, as there are a lot of similarities between the value placed on each addition, but notable differences. Christine and David's addition will also serve their desire to see the ocean and allow them to showcase their 'good taste,' but building it will detrimentally affect the lives of their neighbors. They not only disregard this reality but seem to enjoy the act of being seen performing a particular type of commodity fetishism. This is exemplified by Christine's comment, 'I swear to God I feel like as soon as we did it [went with modern decor] everyone else did it.' In other words, just like the happy miniature couple in the model house, being associated with their beautiful home will be enough to make it appear

Figure 33 Christine (Catherine Keener) in *Friends with Money* (Holofcener, 2006).

that they have a beautiful marriage. Like *It's Complicated*, the addition is being used narratively as a stand-in for genuine affect.

Friends with Money eventually highlights the addition's problematic significance in Christine's life. Toward the end of the film, a disgruntled neighbor takes the time to show Christine that she and David's idyllic second-floor view of the ocean will block the views of everyone else in the neighborhood. It is at this point that she comes to the realization that the cost of appearing to have expensive 'good taste,' and of playing the role of a character in the fantasy addition narrative, is preventing her from meaningful relationships with those around her. In other words, the combination of consumption and emotional well-being is seen to backfire. Once Christine recognizes what is problematic about the addition, she is also able to recognize what is lacking in her relationship with David. Christine decides to put an end to the marriage when she has her third clumsy mishap (mirroring that in the first scene), and he neglects to ask her if she is okay again. She comes to realize that he too is more invested in the superficial idea of their marriage than the complex emotional connection and intimacy that it should involve.

Olivia's job as a maid and general approach to life – she is also a habitual marijuana smoker and stalks a married man with whom she had a fleeting affair – is the anchor point for most of the discourse in and around labor and economics in *Friends with Money*. We are made to understand that Olivia was once a dedicated eleventh-grade teacher who worked at a 'fancy' school in Santa Monica, but was so disgusted by the fact that the wealthy students' threw quarters at her old Honda that she quit and took up house cleaning instead. In one of the first group scenes, David asks Olivia 'is that hip now, working as a maid?' This idea of 'choice' and 'hipness' associated with Olivia's career path seems to imply that because she is Caucasian and well-educated there must be some other explanation for why she would stoop so low as to perform manual labor. (This same standard or expectation is not the case, however, with the film's ubiquitous Mexican laborers who aid and support the main characters' lifestyle choices.) As David's comments (and later comments from Olivia's female friends) reveal, unlike a typical contemporary romance film in which a female protagonist is good at her job but bad at love, Olivia is bad at both. In fact, being the only unmarried character in the film, she is the only one who is seen to pursue a romantic relationship. The meandering way in which this romantic trajectory unfolds is one of the most striking points of departure from the typical romance narrative structure. Olivia tries to cross over into the hyper-aestheticized world that she sees in the movies, only to eventually come to terms with the fact that this persona that she is trying on is just that: a performance. The blurring of boundaries between reality and fantasy is recognized as providing an illusory sense of satisfaction.

Olivia's impulse to cross this boundary between her real life and a fantasy life is seen in the vibrator scene at the beginning of the film. It suggests that not only does she feel a certain sense of ownership over the homes of her employers' and their personal items, but these spaces and goods allow her to act out the sexual and commodity-driven fantasy life of a wealthier person. This carries over into her relationship with Mike (Scott Caan), the handsome, narcissistic personal trainer with whom Franny sets her up. Olivia not only brings Mike to her cleaning jobs with her but also has sex with him in the bedrooms of her employers' homes. The boundaries are even further blurred when, after they leave each house, Mike claims half of her salary in some bizarre variant of the john/prostitute/pimp relationship. Mike even goes as far as to give Olivia a French maid's costume for her birthday so that they can fulfill one of his sexual fantasies. We see that this birthday present is more of a gift to Mike than to Olivia, as she is visibly apathetic during the entire escapade. It is the indignity of this experience augmented by her discovery later that evening that Mike is dating another woman that brings Olivia to a realization that allowing her personal life to blur into her professional life, and borrowing someone else's ideas of happiness, are causing her to compromise her own sense of fulfillment. This, of course, is similar to Christine's realization about the addition and her marriage.

One of the film's most humorous commentaries on Olivia's investment in, and eventual disenchantment with, 'buying' commodified fantasies is her obsession with a specific and very expensive Lancôme face cream, aptly named Resolution. Because she cannot afford the cream's $75 price tag, she goes from one department cosmetic store counter to another to strategically procure samples of it, which we see her carefully stack on her bathroom shelf and use throughout the film. However, at the same time that she becomes less and less enchanted with her job, she steals a full jar of the night cream (another dubious act left off-screen) from one of her employer's homes. As she calls each of her clients to let them know about her decision to quit, we see her liberally applying the cream to her feet, now showing a blatant disregard for its value. It is quite revealing how Olivia's suppression of her own needs and desires is linked with her obsession with the Resolution and what it can do for the lines on her face. And, reflecting Christine's character trajectory, as soon as she becomes more in touch with a sense of independence, her investment in the culturally perpetuated ideas of the 'self' promised by this commodity ceases completely.

Olivia's dismissal of the fantasy of the face cream is also intertwined with her openness to the romantic overtures of her cleaning client Marty (Bob Stephenson) who, being cheap, overweight, sloppy, unemployed, and divorced, is about as far from the pre-packaged romantic leading man type as you can get. While Marty turns out not only to be a nice guy but independently wealthy, the brief glimpse that we get into their romantic relationship at the end of the film is anything but perfect. The film's final scene shows the two in bed together with Olivia making some redecoration suggestions. She then turns to Marty and asks, 'You remember when we first met, and you bargained down my price? Why would you do that, when you have a lot of money?' He says, 'I'm sorry, I just, I guess I have some issues. You know how people sort of have problems? I have them.' To which she replies, 'That's okay. I've got problems.' And, in true Holofcener fashion, it is on this line that the film fades out.

There is no guarantee of a happy ending between Olivia and Marty. However, it seems no coincidence that the thrust of this awkward closing conversation revolves around the complications and problems that are intertwined with money and the ill-conceived perceptions that are wrapped up in it. This is an obvious contrast to *It's Complicated*'s chocolate croissant ending, which feels satisfying because if the relationship between Jane and Adam does not work out, she will still have plenty of delicious food to eat and a great addition to enjoy. *Friends with Money*, on the other hand, seems to suggest that neither love nor decorating will bring these characters the satisfaction they crave.

This study of Meyers's *It's Complicated* and Holofcener's *Friends with Money* reveals that women writer-directors bring a range of unique and valuable insights to the postfeminist romance film. While these two filmmakers come at the cycle from different industrial perspectives, their filmographies, and specifically these films, have as many instructive areas of overlap as they do dissimilarities. Clearly, a filmmaker's economic infrastructure and a film's resulting aesthetic attributes affect whether it results in a boring painful romantic reality, or a beautifully designed playful romantic romp but their different sensibilities are an equally important component of their different films. As Manohla Dargis's earlier comments suggest, Meyers's female characters – who can have, if not buy, it all – may be more idealized figures and her films more conventionally pleasurable to watch than Holofcener's, whose characters' attempts to better themselves through commodity culture are fruitless. The two filmmakers' distribution patterns and box office returns certainly support this contention. However, both visions point to future paths for romance films, both of which speak to the importance of female voices in the genre, and to the complex overlap between personal and economic independence, platonic and love relationships, and the considerable pleasure to be found in the consummation of consumer and romantic desire.

Notes

1. This song title also serves as the title of Diane Negra's aforementioned book on the topic of consumerism and postfeminism: *What a Girl Wants?: Fantasizing the Reclamation of Self in Postfeminism* (New York: Routledge, 2009).
2. Radner's definition of neo-feminism is an extension of her aforementioned discussion of Helen Gurley Brown's perspective on women's liberation. In her 2011 book, *Neo-Feminist Cinema: Girly Films, Chick Flicks and Consumer Culture*, she describes neo-feminism as that which 'seeks to provide a means of survival and success for the woman who, without family or other sources of material support, counts her own body and the work that it performs as her principal resource. Though neo-feminism can be said to challenge patriarchal structures, it does so in the name of capitalism, in which allegiance to family, for example, has little significance within an economic field.' *Neo-Feminist Cinema: Girly Films, Chick Flicks and Consumer Culture* (New York: Routledge, 2011), p. 11.
3. Radner, *Neo-Feminist Cinema*, p. 172.
4. See Judith Mayne, *Directed by Dorothy Arzner* (Bloomington: Indiana University Press, 1994).
5. Nancy Meyers, 'Nancy Meyers: late bloomer', interviewed by Fred Topel, in Patrick McGilligan (ed.), *Backstory 4: Interviews with Screenwriters of the 1970s and 1980s* (Berkeley: University of California Press, 2006), p. 265.
6. See http://boxofficemojo.com/movies/?id=whatwomenwant.htm.
7. See http://boxofficemojo.com/movies/?id=somethingsgottagive.htm.
8. See http://boxofficemojo.com/movies/?id=holiday.htm.
9. See http://boxofficemojo.com/movies/?id=itscomplicated.htm.
10. Radner, *Neo-Feminist Cinema*, p. 172.
11. Ibid. p. 180
12. Ibid. p. 179.
13. Eva Illouz, *Constructing the Romantic Utopia: Love and the Cultural Contradictions of Capitalism* (Berkeley: University of California Press, 1997), p. 26.
14. Negra, *What a Girl Wants*, p. 152.
15. Ibid. p. 126.
16. Manohla Dargis, 'Changing address, altering love lives', *The New York Times*, 8 December 2006. See http://movies.nytimes.com/2006/12/08/movies/08holi.html?scp=6&sq=nancy%20meyers&st=cse.
17. See http://www.traditionalhome.com/design_decorating/showhouses/set-design_ss1.html.
18. Negra, *What a Girl Wants*, p. 130.
19. Margaret Tally poses some compelling questions in and around the representation of middle-aged female sexuality in Meyers's *Something's Gotta Give* and other contemporary films. She states: 'There's a fine line . . . between portraying women as sexually free and reducing them to essentially sexual beings. However, in a culture

which has effectively reduced middle-aged women to a kind of invisibility with respect to their sexuality, these newer films at least reopen the question of whether accomplished, professional, middle-aged women can be portrayed as having sexual lives as well, or whether they must renounce their sexuality because they are no longer young.' See Margaret Tally, 'Hollywood and the "older bird" chick flick', in Suzanne Ferriss and Mallory Young (eds), *Chick Flicks: Contemporary Women at the Movies* (New York: Routledge, 2008), p. 129.

20. Sadie Wearing, 'Subjects of rejuvenation: aging in postfeminist culture', in Yvonne Tasker and Diane Negra (eds), *Interrogating Postfeminism: Gender and the Politics of Popular Culture* (Durham, NC: Duke University Press, 2007), p. 302.

21. Radner, *Neo-Feminist Cinema*, p. 179.

22. See http://www.traditionalhome.com/design_decorating/showhouses/set-design_ss1.html.

23. See http://www.traditionalhome.com/design_decorating/showhouses/set-design_ss1.html.

24. See http://www.iamnotastalker.com/2010/09/17/the-its-complicated-house/.

25. Geoff King, *American Independent Cinema* (Bloomington: Indiana University Press, 2005), p. 227.

26. While scholars such as King attest to the fact that the independent sphere was, and still is, far from the idyllic equal opportunity democratic collective that one would hope it would be, its historiography tends to be dominated by the success stories of a few filmmakers. The leading books on the topic place women, people of color, and gay and lesbian filmmakers in their own chapter(s) with the discussion of the broader tendencies within the contemporary independent sphere largely dominated by the stories of Caucasian, heterosexual, middle-class men. As far as women filmmakers are concerned this may very well be because, with the possible exception of Kathryn Bigelow, they have not been as successful in crossing over into the Hollywood mainstream as their male counterparts and therefore are lesser-known and easier to overlook.

27. Christina Lane, 'Just another girl outside of the neo-indie', in Christine Holmlund and Justin Wyatt (eds), *Contemporary American Independent Film: From the Margins to the Mainstream* (New York: Routledge, 2004), p. 201.

28. Liese Spencer, '*Walking and Talking*', in Jim Hiller (ed.), *American Independent Cinema: a Sight and Sound Reader* (London: British Film Institute, 2008), p. 141.

29. See http://www.reverseshot.com/article/nicole_holofcener. This is typical of the types of questions that Holofcener is asked and the types of sentiments she expresses in interviews. A very similar interaction occurred in an interview for *Please Give* in which she responds to Andrew O'Hehir's question about being a chick flick director in the following way, 'I'm not trying to do anything except tell the story that interests me. It just happens that these people are women, or more characters in my movies are women, and it's the same thing when people want to call me a female director. I'm just a director. I can't deny that my audiences are definitely more female, but I think that's partly because people call them women's movies. There was one magazine that called this movie a "bitchy chat-fest chick flick." And it was a positive review! Like, what guy, and what intelligent woman, would ever go see that? It's frustrating.' Andrew O'Hehir, 'The art of making "vagina movies"', *Salon*, 29 April 2010, http://www.salon.com/entertainment/movies/our_picks/index.html?story=/ent/movies/andrew_ohehir/2010/04/29/holofcener.

30. Kathleen Rowe Karlyn, 'Allison Anders *Gas, Food, Lodging*: independent cinema and the new romance', in Peter William Evans and Celestino Deleyto (eds), *Terms*

of Endearment: Hollywood Romantic Comedy of the 1980s and 1990s (Edinburgh: Edinburgh University Press, 1998), p. 171.

31. King, *American Independent Cinema*, p. 63.
32. Ibid. p. 80.
33. Celestino Deleyto, *The Secret Life of Romantic Comedy* (Manchester: Manchester University Press, 2009), p. 154.
34. Ibid. p. 157.
35. Margy Rochlin, 'FILM; just like her family: complicated', *The New York Times*, 23 June 2002, http://www.nytimes.com/2002/06/23/movies/film-just-like-her-family-complicated.html?scp=2&sq=holofcener&st=cse.
36. See http://www.the-numbers.com/movies/1996/0WKTK.php.
37. Patricia Thompson, 'Femme Helmers strive for level playing field', *Variety*, 28 July 2002, http://www.variety.com/article/VR1117870380.html?categoryid=1329&cs=1&query=femme+helmers, referenced in King, *American Independent Cinema*, p. 226.
38. See http://boxofficemojo.com/movies/?id=lovelyandamazing.htm.
39. See http://boxofficemojo.com/movies/?id=friendswithmoney.htm.
40. See http://boxofficemojo.com/movies/?id=lovelyandamazing.htm.
41. Rochlin, 'FILM; just like her family'.
42. Manohla Dargis, 'Holding up a mirror to women, thorns and all', *The New York Times*, 30 April 2010, http://movies.nytimes.com/2010/04/30/movies/30please.html?scp=1&sq=dargis%20please%20give&st=cse.
43. Claire Perkins, *American Smart Cinema* (Edinburgh: Edinburgh University Press, 2012), p. 6.
44. Michael Z. Newman, *Indie: An American Film Culture* (New York: Columbia University Press, 2011), p. 34.
45. The fact that this character, Olivia, is played by Jennifer Aniston leads one to wonder if this early omission is meant to emphasize the usually anonymous work of manual domestic laborers, or if it is because the audience is meant to guess whether or not the actress could possible de-glamorize herself enough to play the role of the maid who is actually seen cleaning.

CONCLUSION:
BEGINNINGS VS. ENDINGS: THE FUTURE
OF THE POSTFEMINIST CYCLE

Like any conceptual framework, the one I have outlined in *American Postfeminist Cinema* is not intended to be exhaustive but rather to serve as a jumping off point for future conversations about both romance and postfeminist media. As my breakdown of the structural and discursive elements of the cycle in the Introduction reveals, there are countless texts that have been produced since the beginning of the 1980s that could fall into the binaries that I outline in my case studies, just as there are certainly many other binaries that dominate postfeminist culture that could generate additional case studies. However, I have also argued that we can learn a great deal more about the postfeminist romance cycle, both past and present, if we continue to eliminate the typically iron-clad binary between comedy and drama and the boundaries between film and other media, and even social discourse. For in the preceding chapters, we have examined how the postfeminist period has seen its most potent and contentious concerns addressed and negotiated through romance's narrative structure in diverse forms, of which film remains central.

While I hope *American Postfeminist Cinema* will inspire new research projects, here I briefly consider what our case studies have shown us about endings, which seems a particularly appropriate task for the end of a book about romance. At many points throughout this study, we have discussed how the momentum of romance, in both life and entertainment, moves toward a resolution and conclusion. And indeed, as discussed in the Introduction, the ending of a narrative has a central place in debates over the differences between comedy and drama. Yet take, for example, 2001's *Bridget Jones's*

Figure 34   The end of *Bridget Jones's Diary* (Maguire, 2001).

Diary that sees Bridget, the female protagonist, finally find happiness with her love interest, Mark Darcy, in the film's final scene. The film fades out on their kiss and the words 'The End' appear on screen, only to be scratched out and replaced by the words 'The Beginning.' As this brief moment shows, the ending in the romance always signals the beginning of something else. Romance is a cycle that always repeats, in a sequel, in another media text, or in the cultural discourse on love. The issues that the film explores, and the frustration or joy it elicits, can and will continue after it is over and circulate into our broader culture. Likewise, many of our case studies have revealed that endings prompt complex responses. Our examination of *Kitty Foyle* showed that even though the film's ending seems predetermined, it still managed to elicit ambivalent feelings of both sadness and happiness from one of its critics. The critical response to *An UnMarried Woman* demonstrated that the film's ambiguous ending was read as a sign of the times, leaving some critics celebrating and others disappointed. And, in *Friends with Money* we saw how a romance film made within the independent sphere of production can have an anticlimactic ending that does not tell the audience anything about a couple or their relationship.

As a brief closing meditation on the debates that are generated by and about the postfeminist romance, I turn to 2011's spring surprise comedy hit, *Bridesmaids*. Paul Feig's film returns us to questions posed in the Introduction. How does the postfeminist romance cycle deliver on the promise, as Lori Gottlieb's earlier question asks, to provide women with ' empowerment and happily ever after?' *Bridesmaids* has generated, and responded to, culturally potent discussions about women's representation in the media, women in comedy, and women's genres. The film was seen as breaking new ground in these areas but with its politically progressive attributes presented and negotiated within the parameters of the postfeminist cycle.

Throughout the book we have discussed how the contemporary romance negotiates contentious social and political issues in an experiential space that falls between the either/or and the both/and, and the beginning and the ending. What *Bridesmaids* demonstrates is that the romance is so elastic that it can even encompass a discourse that, to many critics, is working at cross-purposes with the genre. In fact, recalling *An UnMarried Woman*, the either/or at work in *Bridesmaids* primarily lies in the extra-textual discourse surrounding the film, and not in the film itself. As we will see, critics discuss how the film has the potential to be groundbreaking for women but perceive this potential to be tempered by its dependence on the conventions of the romance genre. And, thus the film and its critical reception offer a compelling final glimpse into the complex refrains in play around women's entertainment in the postfeminist era.

Bridesmaids is cowritten by, and stars, former *Saturday Night Live* cast member Kristen Wiig, and is executive-produced by Judd Apatow. Apatow is, of course, the auteur of the popular bromance cycle which has burgeoned during the last two decades, and includes films such as *The 40-Year-Old Virgin* (Apatow, 2005), *Knocked Up* (Apatow, 2007), and *Superbad* (Mottola, 2007), among many others. The bromance film fits within the postfeminist romance cycle framework analyzed throughout *American Postfeminist Cinema* but deviates in a few key ways from the other male protagonist films analyzed in Chapter 3. The bromance male protagonist is seen to be 'less than' because of his immaturity and inability to fulfill certain social and cultural expectations surrounding masculinity. One of his failings is an overattachment to another man, or a group of men, which serves as a substitute for his pursuit of a heterosexual relationship. And, like *The Family Man*, this lead character is only seen to be successful if he grows up and accepts that heterosexual romance, and the family life to which it may inevitably lead, is the best life path.

Bridesmaids was lauded in the mainstream press as the female version of the bromance film *The Hangover* (Phillips, 2009), a runaway hit which chronicles a Vegas bachelor party gone wrong. Like *The Hangover*, *Bridesmaids* focuses on an upcoming wedding, it features a motley crew of a bridal party, and sees its characters engage in a broad range of physical comedy hijinks. Both *The Hangover* and *Bridesmaids*, and others in the bromance cycle, continue the tradition of what William Paul has called 'animal comedy' in which physical comedy generally receives pride of place over verbal comedy'[1] and 'there is a conflation of the infantile and the adult.'[2] However, unlike the male-dominated cycle of 1970s and 1980s films on which Paul focuses, and the bromance cycle, in which 'female desire is at best a nebulous business,'[3] *Bridesmaids*'s animality is not only embodied by women through physical acts of comedy but these acts are frequently motivated by their libidos.

Bridesmaids' plot focuses on Annie (Wiig), who is struggling and aimless after losing her small bakery business and boyfriend. She has taken a job as a jewelry salesperson and is living in a less than optimal roommate situation in Milwaukee. Her only refuge is her relationship with her lifelong best friend Lillian (Maya Rudolph) who announces early in the film that she is engaged. As the maid of honor, Annie is responsible for planning and executing a number of wedding-related events that will include Lillian's four other bridesmaids. One of these bridesmaids is Helen (Rose Byrne) the wealthy and beautiful wife of Lillian's fiancé's boss who has recently become close to Lillian: a little too close, as far as Annie is concerned.

Annie becomes jealous of Helen and Lillian's burgeoning friendship and begins to compete with Helen, trying to be the best and most supportive bridesmaid. Annie's increasingly erratic behavior at various events eventually causes a rift between her and Lillian, which leads Annie to find solace in an affable police officer named Nathan (Chris O'Dowd). Despite Nathan's best efforts to be a supportive and positive force in Annie's life – in striking contrast to Annie's cocky and smarmy 'fuck buddy' Ted (Jon Hamm, in an uncredited performance) – Annie rejects him after their first night spent together. Eventually, Annie comes to an understanding with Helen and reconciles with Lillian, who goes on to have a seamless, albeit hilariously over-the-top, wedding. And most importantly, for the purposes of this brief discussion, the final scene of the film sees Nathan show up unexpectedly at the end of Lillian's wedding to forgive Annie for rejecting him. They kiss, and then pull off in his police car.

Bridesmaids was critically highly regarded but controversial when it was released because of its portrayal of these comedians engaging in extreme physical comedy, which traditionally has been the domain of men. Critics viewed the film's use of bathroom humor, specifically scatological acts and vomiting, and its frank sexual innuendo, as marking a new phase in the representation of women that deviated significantly from the traditional expectations in and around female behavior. The fact that these 'unfeminine' acts are presented in the context of a narrative revolving around a conventionally feminine institution – a wedding – and associated with more typical wedding-related media texts, such as *27 Dresses*, was seen to be even more adventurous. In other words, the film covers well-traveled postfeminist romance terrain but takes it in an unexpected direction. As Manhola Dargis aptly summarizes in her review,

> In most wedding movies an actress may have the starring part (though not always), but it's only because her character's function is to land a

man rather than to be funny. Too many studio bosses seem to think that a woman's place is in a Vera Wang.[4]

What Dargis is arguing here is reminiscent of my earlier brief discussion of Holofcener's *Walking and Talking*. *Bridesmaids* is a film that takes a wedding as a backdrop but is not really about the wedding, or the image of a female character who is heading down the aisle. In fact, our exposure to Lillian and her fiancé's relationship is limited. But contrary to what Dargis's review implies, *Bridesmaids* is also a film about our female character 'landing a man.' Indeed, the film fits into the postfeminist romance model in many ways that I will outline below.

Bridesmaids embodies Chapter 4's discussion of the dichotomy between real sex and funny sex made palatable in order to appeal to a wider audience. The film's opening scenes see Annie experimenting with a number of sexual positions with Ted. Try and try as she does to take pleasure from the experience, she remains visibly uncomfortable and unsatisfied with Ted's efforts, and asks him to change his tactic to no avail. The film does not sidetrack the representation of Annie as a sexual being who is mostly comfortable being intimate outside of the context of a relationship, but these scenes are rendered wholly comedic and performative. In this first scene she pretends to be sexually excited, just as she pretends the next morning to be perfectly coiffed and fresh-breathed when Ted wakes up. She is trying to be the girl with whom he wants to stay overnight and attend a wedding, instead of the girl who he asks to leave after sex and will not let park in his driveway.

This sexual relationship is positioned in contrast to the scenes of genuine intimacy between Annie and Nathan, which, true to form, are left off-screen. The casting of actress Jill Clayburgh as Annie's mother is particularly notable when considering the representation of Annie as being caught between these two 'types' of intimacy. As we examined in Chapter 1's analysis of *An UnMarried Woman* and Chapter 4's discussion of *Semi-Tough*, Clayburgh's unique star presence led her to be seen as an actress whose characters embodied changing conceptions of femininity and sexuality in the 1970s. Wiig's portrayal of Annie reflects Clayburgh's 'can't quite get it all together'-ness but the connotations of her quirkiness reflect the expectations of a decidedly different cultural landscape.

The type of femininity that Annie feels the need to perform is reflective of that which we have seen throughout our discussion of the postfeminist romance cycle. At the heart of the competition between Annie and Helen is the fact that Annie is the 'real' girl with whom the audience is meant to identify and Helen is the preferred, feminine ideal that the audience is presumably meant to simultaneously idealize and resent. The film eventually resolves this tension by seeing Helen come down to earth and reveal the less than perfect aspects of her life, and by asking Annie for help. Helen's perfectly coiffed facade is debunked through her confessions and the laughably over-the-top wedding events that she plans, but, as we have seen in other postfeminist romance films, her upper-middle-class lifestyle and the wardrobe and surroundings that come along with it are still ultimately deemed desirable.

The film clearly intends for the relationships between the women – both Annie and Lillian, and Annie and Helen – to be the film's true motivating narrative force. It is, as the title suggests, about the bridesmaids. However, since the bridesmaids' job is to give Lillian the wedding that she has always dreamed of, the film also supports the heterosexual romance narrative structure. Annie and Nathan's relationship is secondary to the wedding plot, but coexistent with the film's emphasis on marriage. However, like the wedding scene that precedes it – which includes fireworks and names in lights – the final scene between Annie and Nathan is clearly self-conscious about its function in satisfying the expectations that surround the traditional happy ending resolution. It becomes evident through a series of facial gestures that Helen has facilitated Annie and Nathan's reconciliation but the means through which this has happened are left off-screen. The film also provides no explanation for why Nathan is wearing a suit, given that he has arrived too late to attend the reception. It also seems antithetical to his characterization that he would leave duty in Wisconsin to drive to the wedding in Illinois. Ultimately, the film assumes the audience will overlook these extenuating circumstances because the film satisfies our desire to see Annie earn both friendship and love.

Its adherence to the conventions of the postfeminist romance cycle does not negate the ways in which *Bridesmaids* is breaking new ground with regard to women in comedy, but sees these two elements working together to both

Figure 35   Annie (Kristen Wiig) and Nathan (Chris O'Dowd) in *Bridesmaids* (Feig, 2011).

reinforce and call attention to the prominent role of romance in entertainment about and for women. In her influential piece 'Why *Bridesmaids* matters,' Indiewire blogger Melissa Silverstein has a different perspective on the compatibility of these two elements:

> But women and comedy is stuck in the romantic comedy genre and it's about time that we get a film that could potentially break through as a full blown comedy. As I've said before I wish this film didn't have a wedding theme focus to it because I am sick of wedding flicks but I can see it as a bridge film. What I mean is that a comedy about a wedding and a single woman who has to be her best friend's maid of honor is probably the only type of comedy that could get made at a studio because of the complete discomfort with women being funny. [5]

Silverstein's labeling of *Bridesmaids* as a 'bridge' film that pits progressive ideas of women in comedy against the romantic comedy genre, echoes Dargis's earlier review. Both critics seem invested in the idea that the formulaic attributes of a traditional romantic comedy diminish the film's political potential. They argue that *Bridesmaids* goes far in advancing different ideas about women, but that its focus on wedding culture is limiting. It is interesting that their concerns lie more with the film's wedding-related theme rather than with its romance structure. They seem to be able to overlook *Bridesmaids*'s romance attributes because it deviates from the romantic comedy formula in subtle yet effective ways. Silverstein even goes as far to say that if women do not support *Bridesmaids* then they will be 'stuck with romantic comedies for years to come . . . about women who inherently suck.'

These critics' responses to *Bridesmaids* pose compelling questions about where gender and genre meet and the degree to which female-oriented genre films can align with political discussions around feminism and women's progress. Dargis and Silverstein's comments reflect the general critical consensus about the film, which saw it as innovative and groundbreaking in this regard. But other critics questioned its innovatory potential, not because of how reliant it is on women's genres but because it relies too heavily on male genres. *The New Republic*'s Ruth Franklin sums up, 'I . . . didn't yet know that the right to barf on screen would one day be heralded as a touchstone of women's equality in film.'[6] Franklin's concerns recall and counter Kathleen Rowe's powerful contention that for unruly 'spectacle-making' female comedians, such as Rosanne Arnold (whose career has always been plagued by these questions), 'laughter is a powerful means of self-definition and a weapon for feminist appropriation.'[7]

To consider *Bridesmaids* as potentially both progressive and degrading is yet another example of how an ending is not just an ending but sometimes a cue for considering both the flexibility and constraints of genres and cycles. Franklin poses this problematic in a different way:

> But *Bridesmaids*, in its tulle-trimmed wake, leaves unanswered some serious questions about exactly how far the 'female-driven' film – those movies about women that men don't want to make – can go.[8]

Given that *Bridesmaids* is both a romance film and not a romance film returns us to questions that we asked in our discussion of Nancy Meyers and Nicole Holofcener's films in Chapter 5. Specifically, can Hollywood make a film about women that does not adopt the romance narrative structure? Does the ambivalence that underlies *Bridesmaids*, and its critical reception, point to the possibility of new approaches to romance and the female-oriented films as Silverstein and Franklin suggest? Undoubtedly, these are questions that will fuel future research. As long as romance continues to be the most significant narrative form through which contemporary discourses about women are negotiated, there will be plenty of film and media texts to discuss and discourses to unravel.

NOTES

1. William Paul, *Laughing Screaming: Modern Hollywood Horror and Comedy* (New York: Columbia University Press, 1994), p. 86.
2. Ibid. p. 108.
3. Ibid. p. 101.
4. Manohla Dargis, 'Deflating that big, puffy white gown', *The New York Times*, 12 May 2011.
5. See http://blogs.indiewire.com/womenandhollywood/why_bridesmaids_matters.
6. Ruth Franklin, 'You'll laugh, you'll cry, you'll hurl', *The New Republic*, 18 May 2011. Accessed online at http://www.newrepublic.com/article/the-read/88547/bridesmaids-movie-judd-apatow-kristen-wiig-feminism#.
7. Kathleen Rowe, *The Unruly Woman: Gender and the Genres of Laughter* (Austin: University of Texas Press, 1995), p. 3.
8. Franklin, 'You'll laugh, you'll cry'.

SELECTED BIBLIOGRAPHY

Abbott, Stacey and Deborah Jermyn (eds), *Falling in Love Again: Romantic Comedy in Contemporary Cinema* (New York: I. B. Tauris, 2009).

Adelman, Kim, *The Ultimate Guide to Chick Flicks: the Romance, the Glamour, the Tears, and More!* (New York: Broadway Books, 2005).

Akass, Kim and Janet McCabe (eds), *Reading Sex and the City* (London: I. B. Tauris, 2004).

Allen, Robert C., *Channels of Discourse: Television and Contemporary Criticism* (Chapel Hill: University of North Carolina Press, 1986).

— *To Be Continued . . .: Soap Operas Around the World* (New York: Routledge, 1995).

Altman, Rick, *Film/Genre* (London: BFI Publishing, 1999).

Ang, Ien, *Watching Dallas: Soap Opera and the Melodramatic Imagination* (London: Methuen, 1985).

Assiter, Alison, 'Romance fiction: porn for women?', in Gary Day and Clive Bloom (eds), *Perspectives on Pornography: Sexuality in Film and Literature* (London: Macmillan Press, 1988), pp. 101–9.

Babington, Bruce and Peter William Evans, *Affairs to Remember: the Hollywood Comedy of the Sexes* (Manchester: Manchester University Press, 1989).

Barthes, Roland, *A Lover's Discourse* (New York: Hill and Wang, 1978).

Baumgardner, Jennifer and Amy Richards (eds), *Manifesta: Young Women, Feminism and the Future* (New York: Farrar, Straus & Giroux, 2000).

Behrendt, Greg and Liz Tuccillo, *He's Just Not That Into You: the No-Excuses Truth to Understanding Guys* (New York: Simon Spotlight, 2004).

Bergstrom, Janet, 'Enunciation and sexual difference', *Camera Obscura*, 3–4 (1979), 33–69.

— 'Alternation, segmentation, hypnosis: interview with Raymond Bellour – an excerpt', in Constance Penley (ed.), *Feminism and Film Theory* (New York: Routledge, 1988), pp. 186–95.

Berlant, Lauren Gail, *Intimacy* (Chicago: University of Chicago Press, 2000).

— *The Female Complaint: the Unfinished Business of Sentimentality in American Culture* (Durham, NC: Duke University Press, 2008).

Bernstein, Matthew, '1940 – Movies and the reassessment of America', in Wheeler Winston Dixon (ed.), *American Cinema of the 1940s* (New Brunswick, NJ: Rutgers University Press, 2006), pp. 22–47.

Bordwell, David, 'Film futures', *SubStance*, 97, 31: 1 (2002), 88–104.

— *The Way Hollywood Tells It: Story and Style in Modern Movies* (Berkeley: University of California Press, 2006).

Bordwell, David, Kristen Thompson and Janet Staiger, *The Classical Hollywood Cinema: Film Style and Mode of Production to 1960* (New York: Columbia University Press, 1985).

Bovenschen, Silvia, 'Is there a feminist aesthetic?', *New German Critique*, 10 (Winter 1977), 111–37.

Brooks, Ann, *Postfeminisms: Feminism, Cultural Theory and Cultural Forms* (New York: Routledge, 1997).

Brooks, Peter, *The Melodramatic Imagination* (New York: Columbia, 1985).

Brown, Helen Gurley, *Sex and the New Single Girl* (New York: Bernard Geis Associates, 1972).

Brundson, Charlotte, *Screen Tastes: Soap Opera to Satellite Dishes* (London: Routledge, 1997).

— *The Feminist, the Housewife, and the Soap Opera* (Oxford: Oxford University Press, 2000).

Brundson, Charlotte, Julie D'Acci and Lynn Spigel (eds), *Feminist Television Criticism: a Reader* (Oxford: Oxford University Press, 1997).

Butler, Judith, *Gender Trouble: Feminism and the Subversion of Identity* (New York: Routledge, 1990).

— *Bodies That Matter: on the Discursive Limits of Sex* (New York: Routledge, 1993).

Byars, Jackie, 'Reading feminine discourse in prime-time television in the US', *Communication*, 9 (1987), 287–303.

— 'Gazes/voices/power: expanding psychoanalysis for feminist film and television theory', in E. Diedre Pribram (ed.), *Female Spectators* (London: Verso, 1988), pp. 110–31.

Carson, Diane, Linda Dittmar and Janice Welsch (eds), *Multiple Voices in Feminist Film Criticism* (Minneapolis: University of Minnesota Press, 1994).

Cavell, Stanley, *Pursuits of Happiness: the Hollywood Comedy of Remarriage* (Cambridge, MA: Harvard University Press, 1981).

— *Contesting Tears: the Hollywood Melodrama of the Unknown Woman* (Chicago: University of Chicago Press, 1989).

Clover, Carol, *Men, Women, and Chainsaws: Gender and the Modern Horror Film* (Princeton: Princeton University Press, 1993).

Collins, Jim, *Bring on the Books for Everybody: How Literacy Culture Became Popular Culture* (Durham, NC: Duke University Press, 2010).

Coppock, Vicki, Deena Haydon and Ingrid Richter, *The Illusions of 'Post-Feminism': New Women, Old Myths, Feminist Perspectives on the Past and Present* (London: Taylor & Francis, 1995).

Crittenden, Ann, *The Price of Motherhood: Why the Most Important Job in the World is Still the Least Valued*, 1st edn (New York: Metropolitan Books, 2001).

Crittenden, Danielle, *What Our Mothers Didn't Tell Us: Why Happiness Eludes the Modern Woman* (New York: Touchstone, 1999).

D'Acci, Julie, *Television and the Case of Cagney and Lacey* (Chapel Hill: University of North Carolina Press, 1994).

Davis, Flora, *Moving the Mountain: the Women's Movement in America since 1960* (Champaign-Urbana: University of Illinois Press, 1999).

Davis, Glyn, Kay Dickinson and British Film Institute, *Teen TV: Genre, Consumption, Identity* (London: BFI Publishing, 2004).

deLauretis, Teresa, *Alice Doesn't: Feminism, Semiotics, Cinema* (Bloomington: Indiana University Press, 1984).

— (ed.), *Feminist Studies, Critical Studies* (Milwaukee: University of Wisconsin Press, 1986).

— *Technologies of Gender: Essays on Theory, Film and Fiction* (Bloomington: Indiana University Press, 1987).

— 'Aesthetic and feminist theory: rethinking women's cinema', in E. Diedre Pribram (ed.), *Female Spectators* (London: Verso, 1988), pp. 174–95.

— *Lesbian Sexuality and Perverse Desire* (Bloomington: Indiana University Press, 1994).

Deleyto, Celestino, 'Between friends: love and friendship in contemporary romantic comedy', *Screen*, 44: 2 (Summer 2003), 167–82.

— *The Secret Life of Romantic Comedy* (Manchester: Manchester University Press, 2009).

Dennis, Jeffery P., *Queering Teen Culture: All-American Boys and Same-Sex Desire in Film and Television* (New York: Harrington Park Press, 2006).

Doane, Mary Ann, *The Desire to Desire: the Woman's Film of the 1940s* (Bloomington: Indiana University Press, 1987).

— *Femmes Fatales: Feminism, Film Theory, Psychoanalysis* (New York: Routledge, 1991).

Douglas, Susan J., *Where the Girls Are: Growing Up Female with the Mass Media* (New York: Times Books, 1995).

— *Enlightened Sexism: the Seductive Message That Feminism's Work is Done*, 1st edn (New York: Times Books, 2010).

Dow, Bonnie J., *Prime-Time Feminism: Television, Media Culture and the Women's Movement Since 1970* (Philadelphia: University of Philadelphia Press, 1996).

Doyle, Laura, *The Surrendered Single: a Practical Guide to Attracting and Marrying the Man Who's Right for You* (New York: Fireside, 2002).

Ehrenreich, Barbara, Elizabeth Hess and Gloria Jacobs, *Re-Making Love: the Feminization of Sex* (New York: Anchor Press, 1986).

Else-Mitchell, Rosamund and Naomi Flutter (eds), *Talking Up: Young Woman's Take on Feminism* (North Melbourne: Spinifex Press, 1998).

Erens, Patricia (ed.), *Issues in Feminist Film Criticism* (Bloomington: Indiana University Press, 1990).

Evans, Peter William and Celestino Deleyto, *Terms of Endearment: Hollywood Romantic Comedy of the 1980s and 1990s* (Edinburgh: Edinburgh University Press, 1998).

Faludi, Susan, *Backlash: the War Against American Women* (New York: Anchor, 1992).

Fein, Ellen and Sherrie Schneider, *The Rules: Time-tested Secrets for Capturing the Heart of Mr. Right* (New York: Warner Books, 1995).

Ferriss, Suzanne and Mallory Young (eds), *Chick Lit: the New Woman's Fiction* (New York: Routledge, 2006).

— *Chick Flicks: Contemporary Women at the Movies* (New York: Routledge, 2008).

Feuer, Jane, *Seeing Through the Eighties: Television and Reaganism* (Durham, NC: Duke University Press, 1995).

Freidan, Betty, *The Feminine Mystique* (New York: Dell, 1964).

Freidberg, Anne, *Window Shopping: Cinema and the Post-Modern* (Berkeley: University of California Press, 1993).

French, Marilyn, *The War Against Women* (New York: Matrix, 1992).

Frye, Northrop, *The Secular Scripture: a Study of the Structure of Romance* (Cambridge, MA: Harvard University Press, 1976).

— *Anatomy of Criticism: Four Essays* (Princeton: Princeton University Press, 2000).

Fuchs, Barbara, *Romance* (New York: Routledge, 2004).

Gamble, Sarah, *The Routledge Critical Dictionary of Feminism and Postfeminism* (New York: Routledge, 2000).

Gehring, Wes D., *Romantic vs. Screwball Comedy: Charting the Difference* (Lanham: Scarecrow Press, 2002).

Genz, Stéphanie, *Postfemininities in Popular Culture* (New York: Palgrave Macmillan, 2009).

Genz, Stéphanie and Benjamin A. Brabon, *Postfeminism: Cultural Texts and Theories* (Edinburgh: Edinburgh University Press, 2009).

Gill, Rosalind, *Gender in Media* (Cambridge: Polity Press, 2007).

Gill, Rosalind and Christina Scharff, *New Femininities: Postfeminism, Neoliberalism, and Subjectivity* (New York: Palgrave Macmillan, 2011).

Gledhill, Christine, *Home is Where the Heart is: Studies in Melodrama and the Woman's Film* (London: BFI Publishing, 1987).

— 'Pleasurable negotiations', in E. Diedre Pribram (ed.), *Female Spectators* (London: Verso, 1988), pp. 64–89.

— 'Speculations on the relationship between soap opera and melodrama', *Quarterly Review of Film and Video*, 14 (1992), 103–24.

Glitre, Kathrina, *Hollywood Romantic Comedy: States of the Union, 1934–65* (New York: Palgrave Macmillan, 2006).

Gottlieb, Lori, *Mary Him: the Case for Settling for Mr. Good Enough* (New York: Dutton, 2010).

Grindon, Leger, *The Hollywood Romantic Comedy* (Malden: Wiley Blackwell, 2011).

Gurewitch, Morton, *The Comedy of Romantic Irony* (Lanham: University Press of America, 2002).

Hansen, Karen V. and Illene J. Philipson (eds), *Women, Class, and the Feminist Imagination* (Philadelphia: Temple University Press, 1990).

Harvey, James, *Romantic Comedy in Hollywood* (New York: DaCapo Press, 1998).

Harzewski, Stephanie, *Chicklit and Postfeminism* (Charlottesville: University of Virginia Press, 2011).

Haskell, Molly, *From Reverence to Rape: the Treatment of Women in the Movies* (New York: Penguin, 1974).

Heide, Margaret J., *Television Culture and Women's Lives: Thirtysomething and the Contradictions of Gender* (Philadelphia: University of Pennsylvania Press, 1995).

Henderson, Brian, 'Romantic comedy today: Semi-tough or impossible?', in Barry Keith Grant (ed.), *Film Genre Reader* (Austin: University of Texas Press, 1986), pp. 309–28.

Hewlitt, Sylvia Ann, *Creating a Life: Professional Women and the Quest for Children* (New York: Miramax Books, 2002).

Heywood, Leslie, (ed.), *Third Wave Agenda: Being Feminist, Doing Feminism* (Minneapolis: University of Minnesota Press, 1997).

— *The Women's Movement Today: an Encyclopedia of Third-Wave Feminism*, 2 vols (Westport: Greenwood Press, 2006).

Hollinger, Karen, *In the Company of Women: Contemporary Female Friendship Films* (Minneapolis: University of Minnesota Press, 1998).
— 'From female friends to literary ladies: the contemporary's woman's film', in Steve Neale (ed.), *Genre and Contemporary Hollywood* (London: British Film Institute, 2002), pp. 77–90.
Holmlund, Chris and Justin Wyatt, *Contemporary American Independent Film: From the Margins to the Mainstream* (London: Routledge, 2005).
hooks, bell, *Reel to Reel: Race, Sex and Class at the Movies* (New York: Routledge, 1996).
— *Feminism is for Everybody* (Cambridge, MA: South End Press, 2000).
Illouz, Eva, *Consuming the Romantic Utopia: Love and the Cultural Contradictions of Capitalism* (Berkeley: University of California Press, 1997).
— *Cold Intimacies: the Making of Emotional Capitalism* (Cambridge: Polity Press, 2007).
— *Saving the Modern Soul: Therapy, Emotions, and the Culture of Self-Help* (Berkeley: University of California Press, 2008).
Ingraham, Chrys, *Thinking Straight: the Power, the Promise, and the Paradox of Heterosexuality* (New York: Routledge, 2005).
— *White Weddings: Romancing Heterosexuality in Popular Culture*, 2nd edn (New York: Routledge, 2008).
Jackson, Stevi, 'Love and romance as subjects of feminist knowledge', in Mary Kennedy, Cathy Lubelska and Val Walsh (eds), *Making Connections: Women's Studies, Women's Movements, Women's Lives* (London: Taylor and Francis, 1993), pp. 39–50.
Jacobs, Lea, *The Wages of Sin: Censorship and the Fallen Woman Film 1928–1942* (Madison: University of Wisconsin Press, 1991).
Jameson, Fredric, 'Magical narratives: romance as a genre', *New Literary History*, 7: 1, Critical Challenges: The Bellagio Symposium (Autumn 1975), 135–63.
— *Signatures of the Visible* (New York: Routledge, 1990).
— *Postmodernism, or, the Cultural Logic of Late Capitalism*, Post-Contemporary Interventions (Durham, NC: Duke University Press, 1991).
Jenkins, Henry, *Convergence Culture: Where Old and New Media Collide* (New York: New York University Press, 2006).
Jermyn, Deborah, 'Rereading the bitches from hell: a feminist appropriation of the female psychopath', *Screen*, 37: 3 (Autumn 1998), 251–67.
— *Sex and the City* (Detroit: Wayne State University Press, 2009).
Jordan, Chris, *Movies and the Reagan Presidency: Success and Ethics* (Westport: Praeger, 2003).
Kaler, Anne K. and Rosemary E. Johnson-Kurek, *Romantic Conventions* (Bowling Green: Bowling Green State University Popular Press, 1999).
Kamen, Paula, *Her Way: Young Women Remake the Sexual Revolution* (New York: New York University Press, 2000).
Kaplan, E. Ann (ed.), *Women & Film: Both Sides of the Camera* (New York: Methuen, 1983).
— *Psychoanalysis and Cinema* (New York: Routledge, 1990).
Karlyn, Kathleen Rowe, 'Allison Anders *Gas, Food, Lodging*: independent cinema and the new romance', in Peter William Evans and Celestino Deleyto (eds), *Terms of Endearment: Hollywood Romantic Comedy of the 1980s and 1990s* (Edinburgh: Edinburgh University Press, 1998), pp. 168–87.
— 'Too close for comfort: *American Beauty* and the incest motif', *Cinema Journal*, 44: 1 (Fall 2004), 69–93.
— *Unruly Girls, Unrepentant Mothers: Redefining Feminism on Screen* (Austin: University of Texas Press, 2011).

Kim, L. S., '"Sex and the Single Girl" in postfeminism: the "F" word on television', *Television and New Media*, 2: 4 (November 2001), 319–34.

King, Geoff, *Film Comedy* (London: Wallflower Press, 2002).

— *New Hollywood Cinema: an Introduction* (New York: Columbia University Press, 2002).

— *American Independent Cinema* (Bloomington: Indiana University Press, 2005).

— *Indiewood, USA: Where Hollywood Meets Independent Cinema* (New York: Palgrave Macmillan, 2009).

Klein, Amanda Ann, *American Film Cycles: Reframing Genres, Screening Social Problems & Defining Subcultures* (Austin: University of Texas Press, 2011).

Krutnik, Frank, 'The faint aroma of performing seals: the "nervous" romance and the comedy of the sexes', *Velvet Light Trap*, 26 (1990), 57–72.

— 'Conforming passions? Contemporary romantic comedy', in Steve Neale (ed.), *Genre and Contemporary Hollywood* (London: British Film Institute, 2002), pp. 130–47.

Kuhn, Annette, *Women's Pictures: Feminism and Cinema* (London: Routledge, 1982).

Lane, Christina, *Feminist Hollywood: From Born in Flames to Point Break, Contemporary Film and Television Series* (Detroit: Wayne State University Press, 2000).

— 'Just another girl outside of the neo-indie', in Christine Holmlund and Justin Wyatt (eds), *Contemporary American Independent Film: From the Margins to the Mainstream* (New York: Routledge, 2004), pp. 193–210.

Lapsley, Robert and Michael Westlake, 'From *Casablanca* to *Pretty Woman*: the politics of romance', *Screen*, 33: 1 (Spring 1992), 27–49.

Lauret, Maura, 'Hollywood romance in the AIDS era: *Ghost* and *When Harry Met Sally*', in Lynne Pearce and Gina Wisker (eds), *Fatal Attractions: Rescripting Romance in Contemporary Literature and Film* (London: Pluto Press, 1998), pp. 20–37.

Leonard, Suzanne, *Fatal Attraction* (Malden: Wiley Blackwell, 2009).

Levine, Elana, *Wallowing in Sex: the New Sexual Culture of 1970s American Television* (Durham, NC: Duke University Press, 2007).

Levy, Ariel, *Female Chauvinist Pigs: Women and the Rise of Raunch Culture* (New York: Free Press, 2005).

Lewis, Jon, *The End of Cinema as We Know It: American Film in the Nineties* (New York: New York University Press, 2001).

Lotz, Amanda D., *Redesigning Women: Television after the Network Era* (Urbana: University of Illinois Press, 2006).

— *Beyond Prime Time: Television Programming in the Post-Network Era* (New York: Routledge, 2009).

Malin, Brenton J., *American Masculinity under Clinton: Popular Media and the Nineties 'Crisis of Masculinity'* (New York: P. Lang, 2005).

Mann, Patricia S., *Micro-Politics: Agency in a Postfeminist Era* (Minneapolis: University of Minnesota Press, 1994).

Martin, Nina K., *Sexy Thrills: Undressing the Erotic Thriller* (Urbana: University of Illinois Press, 2007).

Mayne, Judith, *The Woman at the Keyhole: Feminism and Woman's Cinema* (Bloomington: Indiana University Press, 1990).

— *Cinema and Spectatorship* (London: Routledge, 1993).

— *Directed by Dorothy Arzner* (Bloomington: Indiana University Press, 1994).

McCabe, Janet and Kim Akass, *Quality TV: Contemporary American Television and Beyond* (New York: I.B. Tauris, 2007).

McDonald, Tamar Jeffers, *Romantic Comedy: Boy Meets Girl Meets Genre* (London: Wallflower, 2007).

McGilligan, Patrick, *Backstory 4: Interviews with Screenwriters of the 1970s and 1980s* (Berkeley: University of California Press, 2006).

McRobbie, Angela (ed.), *Back to Reality? Social Experience and Cultural Studies* (Manchester: Manchester University Press, 1997).

— *The Aftermath of Feminism: Gender, Culture and Social Change* (Los Angeles: SAGE, 2009).

McRobbie, Angela and Trisha McCabe (eds), *Feminism for Girls: an Adventure Story* (London: Routledge, 1981).

Mellencamp, Patricia, *A Fine Romance: Five Ages of Film Feminism* (Philadelphia: Temple University Press, 1995).

Mittell, Jason, *Genre and Television: From Cop Shows to Cartoons in American Culture* (New York: Routledge, 2004).

— *Television and American Culture* (New York: Oxford University Press, 2009).

Modleski, Tania, *Loving with a Vengeance: Mass Produced Fantasies for Women* (Hamden: Archon Books, 1982).

— 'Time and desire in the woman's film', in Christine Gledhill (ed.), *Home is Where the Heart is: Studies in Melodrama and the Woman's Film* (London: BFI Publishing, 1987), pp. 326–38.

— *Feminism Without Women* (New York: Routledge, 1991).

— *Old Wives Tales and Other Women's Stories* (New York: New York University Press, 1998).

Moine, Raphaëlle, *Cinema Genre* (Malden: Blackwell Publishing, 2008).

Morley, Christopher, *Kitty Foyle* (Philadelphia: J. P. Lippincott Company, 1939).

Mortensen, Ellen, *Sex, Breath, and Force: Sexual Difference in a Post-Feminist Era* (Lanham: Lexington Books, 2006).

Mortimer, Claire, *Romantic Comedy* (New York: Routledge, 2010).

Mulvey, Laura, 'Visual pleasure in narrative cinema', *Screen*, 16: 3 (1975), 6–18.

Neale, Steve, 'Melodrama and tears', *Screen*, 27: 6 (1986), 6–22.

— 'The big romance or something wild? Romantic comedy today', *Screen*, 33: 3 (Autumn 1992), 284–300.

— *Genre and Hollywood* (London: Routledge, 2000).

— (ed.), *Genre and Contemporary Hollywood* (London: British Film Institute, 2002).

Neale, Steve and Frank Krutnik, *Popular Film and Television Comedy* (London: Routledge, 1990).

Negra, Diane, 'Romance in/as tourism: heritage whiteness and the international imaginary in the new woman's film', in Matthew Tinkcom and Amy Villarejo (eds), *Key Frames: Popular Cinema and Culture Studies* (New York: Routledge, 2001), pp. 82–97.

— 'Quality postfeminism?: Sex and the single girl on HBO', *Genders Online Journal*, 39 (2004), www.genders.org.

— *What a Girl Wants?: Fantasizing the Reclamation of Self in Postfeminism* (London: Routledge, 2009).

Newman, Michael Z., *Indie: an American Film Culture* (New York: Columbia University Press, 2011).

Nicholson, Linda J. (ed.), *Feminism/Postmodernism* (New York: Routledge, 1990).

Orenstein, Peggy, *Flux: Women on Sex, Work, Kids, Love and Life in a Half-Changed World* (New York: Doubleday, 2000).

Otnes, Cele C. and Elizabeth H. Peck, *Cinderella Dreams: the Allure of the Lavish Wedding* (Berkeley: University of California Press, 2003).

Parrill, Sue, *Jane Austen on Film and Television: a Study of the Adaptations* (Jefferson: McFarland & Company, 2002).

Paul, William, *Laughing Screaming: Modern Hollywood Horror and Comedy* (New York: Columbia University Press, 1994).

Pearce, Lynne and Jackie Stacey, *Romance Revisited* (New York: New York University Press, 1995).

Pearce, Lynne and Gina Wisker (eds), *Fatal Attractions: Rescripting Romance in Contemporary Literature and Film* (London: Pluto Press, 1998).

Pearl, Monica B., 'Symptoms of AIDS in contemporary film: mortal anxiety in an age of sexual panic', in Michele Aaron (ed.), *The Body's Perilous Pleasures: Dangerous Desires and Contemporary Culture* (Edinburgh: Edinburgh University Press, 1999), pp. 210–25.

Perkins, Claire, *American Smart Cinema* (Edinburgh: Edinburgh University Press, 2012).

Person, E. S., *Dreams of Love and Fateful Encounters: the Power of Romantic Passion* (New York: W. W. Norton, 1988).

Petro, Patrice, 'Film feminism and nostalgia for the Seventies', *Canadian Journal of Film Studies*, 8: 2 (Fall 1999), 3–20.

Phoca, Sophia, Rebecca Wright and Richard Appignanesi, *Introducing Postfeminism* (New York: Totem Books, 1999).

Press, Andrea L., *Women Watching Television: Gender, Class and Generation in the American Television Experience* (Philadelphia: University of Pennsylvania Press, 1991).

Preston, Catherine, 'Hanging on a star: the resurrection of the romance film in the 1990s', in Wheeler Winston Dixon (ed.), *Film Genre 2000* (Albany: State University of New York Press, 2000).

Prince, Stephen, *A New Pot of Gold: Hollywood Under the Rainbow, 1980–1989* (Berkeley: University of California Press, 2002).

Projansky, Sarah, *Watching Rape: Film and Television in Postfeminist Culture* (New York: New York University Press, 2001).

Radford, J. (ed.), *The Progress of Romance* (London: Routledge and Kegan Paul, 1986).

Radner, Hilary Ann, *Shopping Around: Feminine Culture and the Pursuit of Pleasure* (New York: Routledge, 1995).

— *Neo-Feminist Cinema: Girly Films, Chick Flicks and Consumer Culture* (New York: Routledge, 2011).

Radner, Hilary Ann and Moya Luckett (eds), *Swinging Single: Representing Sexuality in the 1960s* (Minneapolis: University of Minnesota Press, 1999).

Radstone, Susannah, *The Sexual Politics of Time: Confession, Nostalgia, Memory* (London: Routledge, 2007).

Radway, Janice, *Reading the Romance: Women, Patriarchy and Popular Culture* (Chapel Hill: University of North Carolina Press, 1984).

Rapping, Elayne, *Media-tions: Forays into the Culture and Gender Wars* (Boston, MA: South End Press, 1994).

Rich, B. Ruby, *Chick Flicks* (Durham, NC: Duke University Press, 1998).

Riley, Denise, *Am I That Name? Feminism and the Category of 'Women' in History* (Minneapolis: University of Minnesota Press, 1988).

Roiphe, Katie, *The Morning After: Sex, Fear, and Feminism on Campus* (Boston, MA: Little, Brown and Company, 1993).

Rosen, Ruth, *The World Split Open: How the Woman's Movement Changed America* (New York: Viking, 2000).

Rosenfeld, Michael J. and Reuben J. Thomas, 'Searching for a mate: the rise of the Internet as a social intermediary', *American Sociological Review*, 77: 4 (2012), 523–47.

Rowe, Kathleen, *The Unruly Woman: Gender and the Genres of Laughter* (Austin: University of Texas Press, 1995).

Rubinfeld, Mark D., *Bound to Bond: Gender, Genre, and the Hollywood Romantic Comedy* (Westport: Praeger, 2001).

Sandberg, Sheryl, *Lean In: Women, Work, and the Will to Lead* (New York: Knopf, 2013).

Sandler, Kevin, *The Naked Truth: Why Hollywood Doesn't Make X-Rated Movies* (New Brunswick, NJ: Rutgers University Press, 2007).

Schatz, Thomas, *Hollywood Genres* (New York: Random House, 1981).

Seidman, Steven, *Romantic Longings: Love in America 1830–1980* (New York: Routledge, 1989).

— *Embattled Eros: Sexual Politics and Ethics in Contemporary America* (New York: Routledge, 1992).

Shalit, Wendy, *A Return to Modesty: Discovering the Lost Virtue* (New York: Simon and Schuster, 1999).

Shattuc, Jane, *The Talking Cure: TV Talk Shows and Women* (New York: Routledge, 1997).

Shumway, David R., 'Screwball comedies: constructing romance, mystifying marriage', in Keith Barry Grant (ed.), *Film Genre Reader II* (Austin: University of Texas Press, 1995), pp. 381–401.

— *Modern Love: Romance, Intimacy, and the Marriage Crisis* (New York: New York University Press, 2003).

Sikov, Ed, *Laughing Hysterically: American Screen Comedy of the 1950s* (New York: Columbia University Press, 1994).

Snitow, Ann Barr, 'Mass market romance: pornography for women is different', in Ann Snitow, Christine Stansell and Sharon Thompson (eds), *Powers of Desire: the Politics of Sexuality* (New York: Monthly Review Press, 1983), pp. 245–63.

Sommers, Christina Hoff, *Who Stole Feminism? How Women Have Betrayed Women* (New York: Simon and Schuster, 1995).

— *The War Against Boys: How Misguided Feminism is Harming Our Young Men* (New York: Simon and Schuster, 2000).

Spigel, Lynn, *Make Room for TV: Television and the Family Ideal in Postwar America* (Chicago: University of Chicago Press, 1992).

Spigel, Lynn and Denise Mann (eds), *Private Screenings: Television and the Female Consumer* (Minneapolis: University of Minnesota Press, 1992).

Stacey, Jackie, *Star Gazing: Hollywood Cinema and Female Spectatorship* (London: Routledge, 1994).

Talley, Margaret, 'Something's gotta give: Hollywood and the "older bird" chick flick', in Suzanne Ferriss and Mallory Young (eds), *Chick Flicks: Contemporary Women at the Movies* (New York: Routledge, 2008), pp. 119–31.

Tasker, Yvonne and Diane Negra (eds), 'In focus: postfeminism and contemporary media studies', *Cinema Journal*, 44: 2 (Winter 2005), 107–33.

— *Interrogating Postfeminism: Gender and the Politics of Popular Culture* (Durham, NC: Duke University Press, 2007).

Taylor, Anthea, *Single Women in Popular Culture: the Limits of Postfeminism* (London: Palgrave Macmillan, 2012).

Thornham, Sue, 'Starting to feel like a chick – re-visioning romance in in the cut', *Feminist Media Studies*, 7: 1 (2007), 33–46.

Wearing, Sadie, 'Subjects of rejuvenation: aging in postfeminist culture', in Yvonne Tasker and Diane Negra (eds), *Interrogating Postfeminism: Gender and the Politics of Popular Culture* (Durham, NC: Duke University Press, 2007), pp. 277–310.

Weber, Brenda R., *Makeover TV: Selfhood, Citizenship, and Celebrity* (Durham, NC: Duke University Press, 2009).

Wexman, Virginia Wright, *Creating the Couple: Love, Marriage and Hollywood Performance* (Princeton: Princeton University Press, 1993).

White, Patricia, *Uninvited: Classical Hollywood Cinema and Lesbian Representability* (Bloomington: Indiana University Press, 1999).

Williams, Linda, 'Film bodies: gender, genre and excess', in Keith Barry Grant (ed.), *Film Genre Reader II* (Austin: University of Texas Press, 1995), pp. 140–58.

— *Hard Core: Power, Pleasure, and the 'Frenzy of the Visible' Expanded Edition* (Berkeley: University of California Press, 1999).

— *Playing the Race Card: Melodramas of Black and White* (Berkeley: University of California Press, 2000).

— *Screening Sex* (Durham, NC: Duke University Press, 2008).

Williams, Linda Ruth, *The Erotic Thriller in Contemporary Cinema* (Bloomington: Indiana University Press, 2005).

Wolf, Naomi, *Promiscuities: the Secret Struggle for Womanhood* (New York: Random House, 1997).

INDEX

bold page number denotes illustration